Lift Up Your Hearts

A True Story of Loving Your Enemies

Tragically, Killing Your Friends

And the Life that Remains

By

Douglas W. Kmiec

Obama's Faith-filled Ambassador

𝕰𝖒𝖇𝖆𝖘𝖘𝖞 𝕴𝖓𝖙𝖊𝖗𝖓𝖆𝖙𝖎𝖔𝖓𝖆𝖑 𝕻𝖗𝖊𝖘𝖘

Valletta Malibu* Longford * Kiltimagh & the World*

Related texts, by the same author:

Can a Catholic Support Him? Asking the Big Question about Barack Obama (Overlook Press, 2008)

The Attorney General's Lawyer – inside the Meese Justice Department (Praeger/Greenwood imprint, 1992)

Commentary:

Throughout his career, Douglas Kmiec has had a powerful voice in the world of faith and politics. His story of the past few years, a struggle with both life and death, is both profound and deeply compelling. The reflections he shares and the stories give great insight into tragedy but still paint a picture of faith and hope.

**–Jim Wallis, President and CEO of Sojourners
and author of *Rediscovering Values***

Doug Kmiec's book reminds us of something too often forgotten in America and especially among those with power: We belong to a different Kingdom first. . . .This is not a book about politics really. It is about the strivings of the human soul and the consolations that await those who strive.

**– Michael Sean Winters
Columnist, National Catholic Reporter**

Over the last few years, Kmiec has emerged as one of this country's most important witnesses to the proposition that religious conviction and political civility need not be at odds; that reasonable people of determined good conscience, whatever their faith or lack thereof, can find ways to cooperate in the common good.

**– Mike Rutten
Syndicated Columnist, Los Angeles Times**

Representing the United States is a great honor, but it is an honor that comes with tremendous responsibility which Ambassador Kmiec fulfilled with thoughtful excellence. Our diplomats are the central figures in demonstrating friendship of the United States and explaining our policies. Ambassador Kmiec was especially well-qualified to undertake duties in Malta because of his Catholic scholarship refined for close to 20 years at the University of Notre Dame and by his cutting-edge dedication to promoting faith-based diplomacy."

– U.S. Senator Richard Lugar (R-IN)
Ranking Minority Member, Foreign Relations

. . . . No better spokesperson for progressive Catholicism-- deeply loving, genuinely holy, and solidly rooted in the Gospel and in the learning and literature of our own day— Monsignor John Sheridan's person and presence resonates for all of us through Kmiec's intensely personal and yet profoundly insightful memoir.

- **Fr. James Heft, S.M., Alton Brooks Professor of Religion, Institute for Advanced Catholic Studies, USC**

3

Then as the trumpet call, in after years,
"Lift up your hearts!" rings pealing in our ears,
Still shall those hearts respond, with full accord
"We lift them up, we lift them to the Lord."[1]

And what John Sheridan realized early on was that a simple and profound faith could be found in everyone he met. He realized that deep down inside, everyone - whether rich or poor, whether famous or infamous, whether sophisticated or simpleminded - had inside them the seed of faith. And, the seed of faith would crack open during times of suffering and would flourish and grow in an atmosphere of compassion. And, the great gift that he could give to them was not just his inquiring mind, but his heart, a compassionate heart. This was a heart that had grown large through his experience of suffering. And in giving his heart, he received, in return, the experience of the loving God, the tender God, and the God incarnate in person of the Risen Christ living in and through the little ones.

Father Bill Kerze

Pastor, Our Lady of Malibu

24 September 2010

---

[1] H. MONTAGU BUTLER, *Lift Up Your Hearts* (1926).

4

In memory of

Monsignor John V. Sheridan
Sister Mary Campbell, SSL

Whose kindness bridges all eternity

Figure 1: A final photograph of three friends joyfully together again after a year separation. Sister Mary Campbell, SSL, Monsignor John V. Sheridan, and Ambassador Kmiec attend Mass in celebration of the highly positive and affirming mission of the Sisters of Saint Louis in the United States. A little more than 90 minutes later, the accident would take the life of Sister Mary and critically injure the Monsignor and the Ambassador, both of whom were evacuated by medical helicopter to the Ronald Reagan/UCLA trauma center. The Monsignor, 94, died three weeks later. After major surgeries in the U.S. and Malta, the Ambassador, 59, would survive. (August 25, 2010)

5

Contents

Grasping the "Gift" of the Cup of Grief

Foreword by Martin Sheen[2]

I n the early afternoon of August 25, 2010 as my son Emilio and I were driving east through Malibu Canyon we learned that three dear and close friends had been involved in a terrible accident on nearby Mulholland Drive. We turned around immediately and arrived at the scene about an hour after the accident to discover that Sister Mary Campbell had been killed instantly and that Monsignor John Sheridan and Doug Kmiec, the driver, had been taken to U.C.L.A. Medical Center both in critical condition. John Sheridan died as a result of his injuries three weeks later. Thus began a long and steep spiral into the depths of personal grief, guilt and depression accompanied by unimaginable suffering for Doug and his wife Carol.

---

[2] A Catholic activist in the tradition of Dorothy Day, Mr. Sheen has numerous stage and film credits, including a portrayal of Bobby Kennedy. He is well known as President Bartlett in "The West Wing," and presently, he shares the screen with son, Emilio, and grandson, Taylor, in the inspiring movie, *The Way*.

Under the circumstances one could not be expected
to return to an active public life particularly
someone with such a high public profile and
impeccable reputation. Perhaps the best
expectations might be a safe return to family and
hearth to heal and reflect but such is not what
Doug Kmiec expected of himself.

On the contrary, within a month of his
convalescence, he returned to Malta to resume his
post as U.S. Ambassador and soon enough he
organized and directed the perilous evacuation of
all U.S. Embassy personal from Tripoli to Malta at
the height of fighting in Libya. Recounted here,
along with his own perilous journey since August
25, in this extraordinary work, "Lift Up Your
Hearts"!

2.

While the far reaching ramifications of the accident
which took the lives of two of his closest friends has
not diminished, far from it, Doug's personal
recovery on every conceivable level since then –
physical as well as spiritual -- is both remarkable

14

and inspiring. Even a general reader being introduced to the story's trio here for the first time will find the book packed with inspirational moments and insights transferrable to your own – hopefully – lesser challenges.

Still in his hospital bed, I encouraged Doug to write *his* story. After all, Doug has been a public man since his "old-line, Daley Democrat" Father took him as a young boy on his appointed rounds in the wards and precincts of Chicago. "It was at the kitchen table of these

> What Doug accomplishes in this book is powerful because it is honest.

humble bungalows where Dad was luminously persuasive securing the 'fractional landslide for JFK.'" Asked about the rumors Kennedy won the presidency with cemetery votes, Doug winks and with a son's impish pride laconically declares: "just further proof, I suppose, of Christ's victory over death – assuming you were a Democrat, of course."

But machine politics was not to be Doug's path; indeed, the independence of mind which has yielded his latter-day political party swapping would, one suspects, have distressed his late father. "Dad took it personally whenever a constituent failed to pull the lever for a straight ticket," Doug says with a far-away fondness for his father who died only weeks before the accident.

No, Doug's life journey has been anything but straight or ordinary, and for now, Doug has declined my suggestion of an autobiography in order to center this volume on his lost friends and the faith they sustained within him. Nevertheless, there is enough of the personal here to hope that this is a first, not a final, volume.

The book reveals the very special friendship Monsignor Sheridan and Doug maintained and confirmed what Doug described as his "moral obligation to write a book to illustrate with gratitude how so much of my public and private life has been and continues to be influenced by the brilliant mind and gentleness of Monsignor John Sheridan. He and Sister Mary enriched my life and those of so many others beyond measure." Yes they did, and Doug's account serves an additional purpose for anyone failing to understand what is sacrificed in the Church by the dark shadows of priestly abuse scandals and contemporary declines in vocation.

A bio-pic is being produced by a respected indie film producer on the life of Monsignor, and the homiletic and personal correspondence Doug incorporates from Monsignor make this volume an essential companion. Yet, the most valuable dividend he generously chooses to share with us from the tragedy is that of redemptive suffering which is his constant focus.

It is not Doug's intention to offer a scholarly explanation or even to claim a definitive personal

> Even a general reader being introduced to the story's trio here for the first time will find the book packed with inspirational moments and insights

understanding of the mystery of human suffering because such an effort would prove useless in either case. What Doug accomplishes in this book is powerful because it is honest. Unlike many well intentioned offerings aimed at running us through glib "express line" of "drive thru" exercises to overcome grief, Doug asks us not to expect a short-cut. While Doug illustrates how deep personal suffering may be capable of being masked for a while, it is better to embrace grief head-on within the complex mystery of faith. Only then does grief serve its intended Divine purpose: a clearer, more self-assured way forward in "the life that remains."

"In the absence of the gift of suffering I suspect that I would have indefinitely floated upon the surface of the moment."

This outrageous acceptance of suffering as a gift enlarges the mystery, even turns it on its head and creates endless possibilities. Gift implies gratitude. "Ah, there's the rub!" We are invited to "accept the cup" as offered not altered. And Doug assures us with confidence that through redemptive suffering, loss is gain and surrender is victory, and it is by these sure means that our hearts are lifted up!

3.

Finally, as a parting gift, Doug invites us to bear witness to his *mano a mano* challenge with the devil himself. Notre Dame enthusiasts will luxuriate in Doug's obvious, continued devotion to Our Lady's University where he taught for a third of his life. Doug's "Fighting Irish" dispatch the devil far easier than those pestiferous Trojans.[3] This clever and satirical chapter achieves the desired effect with wit and wisdom but above all it serves to remind us that while his personal losses have been numerous and grave, they do not include his remarkable sense of humor

The Feast of Saint Patrick, 2012

Martin Sheen

Malibu, California

---

[3] Like his politics that has been drawn from both Democratic and Republican wells, Doug – an SC law grad – melded his love for the Irish by sitting on the ND side (so as not to give scandal) while silently saying a prayer or two for the men of Troy. "Most of my 20 years there," says Doug, "they needed every novena."

As we remember --

DWK

Monsignor John
& Sister Mary

Author's Preface

A. A True Story of Intersecting Lives

This is a true story. Set in both Europe and the United States, a good portion of what will be retold here occurred while I was serving as President Obama's Ambassador to the Republic of Malta.

It is an autobiography of faith; of three lives (and deaths) intersecting.

An odd trinity of souls – an elderly, erudite priest, a light-hearted nun, and your author, a U.S. Ambassador (active then; retired now) and teacher of law, it was our shared Catholic perspective that as part of "the body of Christ," all people – regardless of faith -- are deeply inter-connected and must be welcomed into our lives.

While there is great sadness in the tale told here, there is also abundant and abiding optimism. While two will perish, none feared death or view it as the end of anything lastingly meaningful.

As a matter of social justice, the three of us understood the mission of the Catholic Church as

21

devoted to the needs of the poor, the family, and an understanding of men and women that is of far greater significance than any of the material objects or aspirations of this life.

The three of us found this Gospel message affirmed in the presidential candidacy, and then, presidency of Barack Obama, but none of us would see ourselves or would want the gift of faith to be seen as the exclusive province of one political party or another; wishing to observe the admonition to "love our enemies," in the contemporary American political context, our greater concern might be that the word "enemy," itself, is one that should not be casually applied to those who simply have different views on how to address the common problems of life.

We rejoiced in Barack Obama breaking the color barrier by not allowing the moral irrelevancy of race to even enter the national discussion. We applauded as the new President steered our international and domestic policy toward the needs of the working family and the poor. Tragically, the applause of three would become one, as two would perish before the new president would seek re-election.

Two becoming one is an apt Trinitarian way to reflect how I --the driver in the story's tragic accident – now understands the life that remains; if my life was ever mine alone, it is not now, for in the sign of the cross I am tasked with lifting up the lives of my companions in faith.

From the foot of that cross, I found my work as U.S. Ambassador to take on renewed importance. Having witnessed the loss of my friends, and stared my own death in the face, I now approach tasks with a different level of honesty and intrepidness. Every moment is to be accounted for; every action has meaning, and in every moment and action, there must be a discernible love for the other.

Love takes many forms: feeding those who cannot feed themselves, helping free the addicted, and even rescuing citizen and foreign national alike from the chaotic, bullet-thickened skies that attended Muammar Qaddafi's last stand. And it will be seen, love also demands fidelity even at the highest professional cost; for this reason, it was love that dictated my resignation from the Department of State when it mocked the importance of faith. To return home from foreign assignment in a country that knew how to keep the faith especially well was difficult, but it was necessary to clearly make objection to those who would presume to substitute politics for faith. Salvation does not depend upon my retaining high public position. Salvation does not come by legal enactment imposing my belief on someone else, or vice versa.

B. In Dying We Are Born

It is fair to say that the last two years were life-changing, or perhaps more accurately, death-changing.

Death knocked loudly at the door in spring 2010; first my father; then a dear, favorite aunt who without children of her own had always given my brother and myself her sweetest attention. Death also called for the eloquent and beloved Malta statesman, Guido DeMarco, who had befriended this young diplomat in ways that far exceeded mere professional courtesies. Little did I think these

24

profound losses could be exceeded in grief, but they were. In late August, driving along a canyon road after lunch, it took all of 4 seconds for my small rental car to slip from the road and take the life of Sister Mary Campbell, 75, and send Monsignor John Sheridan, 94 and myself via medical helicopter to the trauma unit of the UCLA hospital. John died three weeks later. In a manner of speaking, after several major surgeries, I survived.

The tragedy stands officially characterized under the law as an accident; yet, in this kind of thing you hold yourself fully accountable in heart and mind, even as it is not clear what I could have done differently short of not agreeing to drive my friends that morning. In addition, people of kind heart have tried to convince me that there are multiple, possible causes some of which have nothing to do with me.

For example, in researching a potential conflict among prescribed medications during my hospital stay, it was noted how obscure the risk of blackout during the operation of a vehicle had been presented by the pharmaceutical company. As it happened I had just begun taking a new time-released version of the drug as a Parkinson treatment. Separately, a family devastated by the loss of their 30 year old son at the same abrupt turn in the road some years earlier informed me of their unsuccessful efforts to engage the county government or CALTRANS or both. And then, there was the entertainment company that apparently had left a large amount of gravel upon the road and returned to the fatal accident scene the next day to remove the gravel and elaborately fence the area. As a consequence, those who would come to pray before the simple white crosses marking the lives lost that day would never see the scene as we the passengers of that ill-fated car had seen it. First at the scene of the accident, and hearing the rosary being recited, a mother with young children later told me she approached the car with a sense of dread as "other cars had slipped repeatedly," she said.

Some tell me to insist on these other causes coming forward. But there is nothing that can be done now, save living for my faith companions; putting their lives ahead of my own in as many ways as I can. Every storm must end, and it will as God's purpose is understood and honored. As reflected in the pages that follow, it is not God who places us in locations of jeopardy; there are more than enough powerful forces of evil waiting to trap us whether the road is straight or badly aligned or miss marked.

I am a believer with many others whom I respect that, God never allows a greater challenge than we can handle. And take my word, *I am* handling this one. Indeed, you are helping me handle or conquer this challenge – or, if you will, to literally turn the page -- by taking hold of this book. In return, there is a true gift in the book: it is, as I will call it, Monsignor John Sheridan's **Theology of Kindness**. This is not just "chicken soup for the soul," which is Jack Canfield's very fine first course; John's theology is a useful, ennobling buffet of true insight that when applied will transform your life, and all those you influence, for the better. I urge you as you read to pay close attention to anything in *italics*, since this is where John is speaking directly. The interest in my diplomatic adventures will surely

27

fade, but in the Theology of Kindness you have something of tangible, lasting value.

C. How Are We to Live?

Because of the distinct honor of serving as a U.S. Ambassador, the book will at times have the feel of a personal memoire – which might have been interesting enough given the tumultuous "Arab Spring" uprisings in the Mediterranean region that overlapped my service. But separate and apart from the displacement of Hosni Mubarak in Egypt or Muammar Qaddafi in Libya, and others, assignment to geographically tiny Malta was significant because it is a Republic that looms very large in the history of the Catholic faith. By its "uncommon kindness," noted Biblically in the Acts of the Apostles, Malta lives and practices to its great benefit what Monsignor John and Mary Campbell gave as witness. In any event, please do not think of me in a starring or lead role in these pages; I am not. Ambassadors get to take credit for the hard work of many, and to a large degree, that credit deserves to be rightly placed with the career foreign service officers, military and intelligence attaches, and locally employed staff. Moreover, there is a theological or philosophical point to be made as well. It is this: until we realize we are not the lead role in our own lives, we are not really living – or at least living fully.

I hesitate to describe this book as one of philosophy, since that might prompt nightmarish memories of poorly taught seminars populated by large, incomprehensible words in search of an idea. Don't worry; there is not a Hegelian dialectic or a Kantian categorical imperative anywhere in sight. Indeed, using my far simpler, real life experiences keeps what you will read down to earth. Although even with our feet anchored in the here and now, I – like you – want to know what lies ahead, and any thinking about our future is spiritual thinking.

What densely worded philosophy and theological tomes seldom reveal is that they seek to answer only one age-old question: "How are we to live?"

The book supplies an answer to that question by honestly wrestling with what, for most of us, is the feared hidden question: "How are we to die?"

That's right, we must first grasp an answer to the question of death to know how to live, or at least to live life to the full. The inseparability of life and death prompts this subsection's title: "Why we hate life and long to live." An insightful, plain spoken man of letters, a French man, who came to study America's criminal justice system in the 1840s, put it this way: **We have "a natural disgust for existence and an immense longing to exist." (Alexis de Tocqueville)**

Where have we heard something like this before?

Consider the venerable prayer of Saint Francis:

> *For it is in giving that we receive.*
> *It is in pardoning that we are pardoned,*
> *and it is in dying that we are born to Eternal*
> *Life.*

Or the beloved Jewish prayer for peace:

> *And we shall beat our swords into*
> *ploughshares,*
> *and our spears into pruning hooks.*

Or a Hindu verse yearning to give up the unreal of this life, recognizing that only through the door marked death is their immortality.

> *Oh God, lead us from the*
> *unreal to the Real.*
> *Oh God, lead us from darkness to light.*
> *Oh God, lead us from death to immortality.*

Or the Christian prayer of peace in the title of the book itself:

> *But I say to you that hear, love your enemies.*
> *do good to those who hate you,*
> *bless those who curse you*
> *pray for those who abuse you*

D. A Love Story

The book is also a love story – these days, a very unusual love story between a Catholic priest and his devoted acolytes. Had you articulated that description as you purchased the book, I dare say your reading habits, given the world-wide dimensions of the now uncovered abuses in the priesthood, may have shocked your neighbors.

31

Indeed, given the contemporary pedophilia problem in the Church and the regrettable, but understandable, need for strict boundaries in show of affection or praise, I count myself very fortunate to have enjoyed the type of love story that once commonly occurred between the parish priest and every member of a Catholic family. Today that type of relationship is rare, historical artifact.

Yes, of course, the Church through lack of knowledge – or worse, cowardice and lack of integrity leading to shame and cover-up – brought this on itself. It is nevertheless to be regretted that the present generation of children are now more distant from priests and sisters than ever. The type of chaste and pure friendship that gives rise to conversations that strengthen faith and its good works is simply not likely to come again. Even apart from the scandals, the virtual disappearance of female religious orders in the United States, coupled with the drop in numbers following a priestly vocation, makes the likelihood of children seeing a priest or nun as a role model quite small. Indeed, given the horrible abuse scandal in the Church, it is hardly exaggeration to say that active steps are taken to prevent the type of interaction with young people that were common place fifty years ago during my own boyhood, based on a quite natural assumption of trust. The parish priest enjoyed the stature and personal influence that inspired complete faith and, as we will see in John Sheridan's own personal history, new vocations.

Understandably, parents have great hesitancy today to support a friendship between their children and a parish priest built on keeping confidences or the camaraderie of coaching, first in sports, then in life. And in every stiffened limb withholding an innocent hug, someone is prevented from sharing experiences of happiness or joy or acceptance. The book, therefore, serves the valuable purpose of underscoring the "extraordinary lives"[4] of priests and religious sisters. Drawing on a love for the Church some people may have thought disappeared with Bing Crosby in *Going My Way,* the book reveals even in the teeth of tragedy and scandal

---

[4] Francis P. Friedl and Rex Reynolds, Extraordinary Lives (Ave Maria Press 1997), for an eloquent first person account of the lives of thirty four priests, including the reflections of Monsignor John Sheridan, 13 years before his death.

how faith survives, sustained by Christ's love passed through John and Mary and the Holy Spirit.

Another example of priestly influence lost is how the voice of the Church in America in the 1950s was less that of hierarchy than professional men (and where gender stereotype did not get in the way, a smaller but still significant number of professional women as well) regularly being guided by local clergy. Doctors, lawyers, corporate executives, shopkeepers; all were within the regular ambit of clerical guidance, welcoming it and abiding by it. This is often inconceivable today, and because that is so, I have taken the liberty to illustrate how my personal friendship with John and Mary positively affected my life – from my public and private decisions as ambassador in foreign diplomacy, to how I perceived my role as a dean and professor in a law school, to my raising issues of unfairness as an attorney in court.

Of course, the importance of recording these other, now historical, aspects of religious influence takes nothing away from the book's purpose of conveying material that, God willing, will be of benefit to the end time itself: namely, Monsignor John's clarity of instruction in what constitutes faith, how hope conquers fear, and how following his example in the way of kindness can re-make and renew our lives.

You will find John's words in these pages, I believe, to be refreshing, progressive, provocative – in brief, Christ-like. John's writing is also consistently heartfelt. The book is representative of the vast emotional reservoir of a man who understood that a hug of compassion and empathy was a more long-lasting influence than aloofly delivered moral abstractions from the pulpit. John's voice was also one of ecumenical understanding, pursuing interfaith dialogue among Catholic, Jew, Muslim, Protestant, and Buddhist long before the notion that "mutual understanding would advance mutual respect" would come to occupy a world yearning for a means to avoid the clash of civilization and culture war. Let's take a moment to examine the upbringing of Monsignor and Sister Mary, for the shape of the twig typically reveals much of the tree.

Part I

Making introductions

1.   Why, you must know these "saintly creatures"...

Writing this book, as you might imagine, has been difficult, but one of the greatest blessings is in the opportunity to introduce readers to John Sheridan and Mary Campbell just as they introduced us to each other throughout their lives. John in particular would match as friends whoever was within the range of his embrace in the vestibule of the Church following Mass. Permit me now to do a reverse hug and introduce you to the sainted John Sheridan and that saintly creature Mary Campbell, to use John's familiar introductory idiom, or as I see it, the two God welcomed, and the one He threw back.

John Virgilius Sheridan

The derivation of the name John from the Greek is often given as "God's gracious gift." John Sheridan was surely that to all who knew him. Yet, when

John spoke of his name, his humility prevented him from claiming the name's precise meaning. Instead, John would write:

The name John means "God is gracious." He made us, He loves us, He wants us to be joyful. The reality is that we are not always joyful, and we have a lot of reasons for not being joyful. But we do have an insistent invitation, a mandate to rejoice - to resonate joyfully to God's presence.

Note how, exhibiting without fanfare his total submission to the Lord, the Monsignor turns the meaning of his name around to reflect all of the glory onto God. Monsignor tells us it is God who is "gracious," and that is what needs emphasis.

The word "gracious," itself, is a derivative of grace. John had overflowing and abundant grace.

The word "gift" is from the Greek word for charisma. Abundance doesn't begin to describe the magnetic quality, the persuasive innocence, or the persistent love embedded in Monsignor's charismatic self.

Like John the Baptist, John Sheridan possessed truly extraordinary charisma calling us not to be his acolytes, but apostles for Jesus. John

38

occasionally would trace his gift for recruitment for Christ to the poetical and charm-filled ways of the Irish, and there is much added from those deep wells of that source of inspiration. However, John also knew that neither his name nor his ancestry accounted for the power of his vocational influence. Instead, the source was the Holy Spirit.

From a young age, John submitted his very being to the Holy Spirit, allowing it to enable and embrace him. Enlivened first and fundamentally by the Word of the Bible and the accumulated teaching of the fathers of the Catholic Church (the Magisterium), John's life – past, present and future – gives constant example of a living faith.

In Ephesians (3:7), John the Baptist observes that he "was made a minister, according to the gift of the grace of God given unto me by the effectual working of his power." John Sheridan was nourished in the same way and held out the strength of this spiritual nourishment to us by consciously working to manifest "an understanding heart." This, you recall, is the quality Solomon requested and received. God affirmed the wisdom of this gift since it would not enrich the King, himself, but permit him to be of service to the needs of others.

The same could be written of John Virgilius Sheridan, through the Holy Spirit, prayer, and conscious effort, John overcame what many highly intelligent people have faced, but only a few conquer – namely, a conceit in our own view and a temper capable of flaring when matters don't go precisely in step with this view. Those of us who knew John in his later years, when he had fully opened his heart and disciplined his demeanor to permit him to aid anyone in need, find it incredible to think of the Monsignor with any shortcoming. John would refuse such one-sided adulation. He was human, born with strengths and weaknesses. But his very life reveals the happy result of giving oneself fully to the Lord.

John had a great effect on all who knew him in life, but like the Word he propagated, his effect does not end at death. John Sheridan's influence lives! He lives in our hearts.

Sister Mary's patience, good heart, and self-effacing nature, nourished John's immediate work space with familiar voice and a modicum of discipline and order that not even the Holy Spirit attempted to build into the nature of John himself.

John was a source of constant spiritual counsel, discernment, humor, and un-common sense. His common man qualities were enriched by generations of intelligent and studied ancestors from that part of Ireland where the high Celtic cross stands affirmatively in witness and promise. He was a man with unique insights into the mind of Christ who lived not in hermitage or monastery, but in community. Because his Theology of Kindness is altogether "other regarding," it is best illustrated by looking at John's relationship with me and with others.

For John, spending time immersed in the details of another's life was the only way he could help our hearts remain open to the Spirit. This is how John taught us to know that at all times God is with us, and "all will be well." Being immersed in the love and care of others was very much part of the Sheridan ethos, and in fairness, an inheritance of a truly blessed family to which we now turn specifically to take a closer look at John's upbringing.

John Sheridan's life was one of the simplicity and honesty of the farm. Born in County Longford in the center of Ireland on December 19, 1915, John was

reared in the town of Carrickmaquirk. In the heart
of the Irish countryside, the town is bisected with
narrow roads that are still lined today with natural
hedgerows of blackthorn, ash tree, wild fushia and
monbretia. The second child of Brigid Kiernan and
Farrell Sheridan, John grew up with an
appreciation for the contributions made by his
ancestors. The Sheridans had long been part of this
ancient place in the basin of the River Shannon,
where the fields supported good crops as well as
cattle. By virtue of blessing and hard work
Carrickmaquirk had some immunity from the worst
of the Irish famine, though the memory of the
famine haunted John's quiet and disciplined father,
Farrell.

During the bad times, Farrell, like many Irish, went
to America to work so that he could send money
back home to his family. John's youngest sibling,
Tommy, reflects: "While in America, father worked
twelve hours a day, six days a week on the old
horse drawn street cars of The Brooklyn –
Manhattan Rail Road. But he made time to go to St
John's College on Fordham Road, now Fordham
University, in the then distant Bronx. There Farrell

42

was tutored by the Jesuits, for whom he had a lifelong respect and love." Monsignor John would carry this respect of the Jesuits as well, though he disguised his admiration with the appellation "wretched Jesuits," which may well be a reaction to paternal favouritism. Said John's older brother: "Father thought that you were not validly ordained unless you were a Jesuit."

John's father was nearly twice his mother's age (43 to her 22) when they married, and Monsignor would inherit his eloquence and gift for story. Monsignor would also carry humbly the tremendous depth of contribution of the Sheridans unless asked directly or friendship permitted elaboration. Tommy recalls his father's penchant for liberal politics and fondness for his time spent in America. Tommy also recalls his father's having witnessed hard times, being a bit of a worrier with the responsibility of a large family, especially given his age difference with Brigid. Farrell died on November 19, 1960, in the family home at Abbeylands, Edgeworthstown, County Longford. He was 93.

Monsignor's mother, Brigid, was of the Kiernan family and proud of her kin from a nearby town, but she appreciated the history of the Sheridans and held the Sheridan name as a fine treasure – indeed, as a name that was almost "magical." If John or one of his siblings disappointed in some way, Brigid would exclaim: "Glory be to God, what will the people say?" And then, after a long and noticeably deliberate pause, she would follow up with "These are Farrell Sheridan's children." Deferential and respectful to her husband in the nature of the times, Farrell placed full confidence in her management of the large brood, while he devoted himself to the challenges of the farm. This allowed Brigid the latitude to fill the Sheridan household with young people for song and conversation every day and at almost any hour. When she passed, her obituary put her conviviality succinctly: "The tea kettle never ceased to sing".

The Sheridan farm prospered with a number of crops and provided enough for Brigid to take food to those less well off. Life on the farm nevertheless was rustic with no running water and in need of the light of candle or oil lamp in the evening. Electricity would not be introduced until 1956 well after John had left for America.

Brigid also saw to the children's schooling, enrolling John at age 5 in the two teacher Clonback National School. Here John would sit upon a dirt floor, warmed by a fire and instructed by the schoolmaster. A few years later, John's parents moved him to the larger, 4 teacher, Moyne National School, where the boys and girls were taught separately. In the Latin School at Moyne, John began to take note of the influence and stature of Father John Kearney and Father John Meehan, who replaced Father Kearney as Superior in September 1932.

Until that time, John imagined himself more farmer than cleric. He enjoyed horses, taking care of the cattle and engaging with his father in the plowing and mowing of the fields. In the evening he would overhear or participate in conversation about breaking in new horses, cattle breeding, agricultural fairs, and the like. However, he became increasingly interested in the impact of Fathers Kearney and Meehan. They taught in his school, visited the homes of the sick, and baptized his brothers and sisters. Most intriguing of all to his ever questioning intellectual mind, the good fathers spoke of the great missionary work in China, Africa, and the Philippines. Gradually, the life of the farm was giving way to the call of the Spirit.

The nature of faith and prayer in the Sheridan household was also pervasive. John's sister-in-law Teresa Sheridan comments: "There have been priests in the Sheridan Family dating back to the 1700's – John's uncle, Father Joseph Sheridan; his grand uncle, Father Farrell Sheridan; and great grand uncle Canon Farrell Duffy, to name but a few. There is an exhaustive list of cousins too, dating back through the ages . . . . Suffice to say, the Sheridan Family have a very strong ecclesiastical history where it appears there was no generation in which there were no ordained priests in existence, right up to and including the present generation where James Sheridan, a nephew of John's is a seminarian in New York."

In John's immediate family alone, of five brothers and two sisters, there were three priests (John and his brothers, Farrell and Patrick, both missionaries in the Holy Ghost order) and a religious sister, Mai also known as Sister Aquinas. John's oldest brother, Joseph, would practically dominate the Irish parliament as an independent Senator and member of the Irish house, and he clearly made intelligent application of the Tip O'Neill principle that "all politics is local." Joe Sheridan's moniker: "Vote for Joe the man you know." John's sister Kathleen married Peter Galligan, a County Cavan farmer. After Peter's death, Kathleen moved to Dublin where she passed a year following John after a long term illness. John's brother Tommy is the clan's survivor still managing the family farm. Of course, not to be overlooked are 19 nieces and nephews and their children, all of whom John reveled regularly to describe in detail at the slightest prompting.

This is John's introduction, so I will resist the temptation to mention how truly wonderful, intelligent and impressive in every regard is the extended Sheridan clan. Judge Bridget Reilly (daughter of Joe) is an incisive, no-nonsense jurist who, with her love of sailing-minded husband,

Michael, have extraordinary children, including especially Louise and Jenny who I have gotten to know and have tried (repeatedly) to claim for my marriageable sons, unsuccessfully so far. Judge Reilly's sisters, Mary T. and Kathy and Tommy's children, Aine and Ferghal and his wife Teresa (Fox) Sheridan are all well-read and respected in their work and communities. Teresa generously helped me fill in details of John's early life. Many of John's kin visited him in California. Being in their company for even a short while, you'd immediately want them as close friends and neighbors. In America, the Sheridan voice reaches across to New York and to points international, as Tommy's Aine and her husband Adrian maintain a strong Irish presence in media and related associations.

To say that John was of fine family doesn't say nearly enough.

After John completed his studies at the Moyne School, John enrolled in the college seminary in September 1933, but by spring, he had developed a case of pleurisy. This inflammation of the walls surrounding the lung was quite painful.

Nonetheless, John returned to college the following September. By December John was hospitalized again this time with the far more serious diagnosis of tubercular peritonitis.

Some initial success was achieved in early surgery, but that was followed by a great many intestinal complications considered by his doctors to be fatal. John wrote: *"the sheer necessity of facing death, immediate death, with my senses sharpened if anything by the morphine that had begun to alleviate the terrible physical pain, was something I can never forget."*[5] One of the priests, likely Father Meehan, who had redirected his life's vocation from agriculture to the apostolate, suggested that John now offer the few remaining days of his life to God. John recounts how his father of quiet intelligence was distraught. He searched for words that could make some sense of the good that might yet be found. The Monsignor's father, holding back tears, said: "How blessed you are to escape so many of

---

[5] *John V. Sheridan, in* EXTRAORDINARY LIVES – THIRTY-FOUR PRIESTS TELL THEIR STORIES 236 (Francis P. Friedl & Rex Reynolds eds., 1998).

life's hardships, to join with the company of heaven and hell, family and friends, here below."[6] John's father was right in part, John's life would indeed be a blessed one, but the Monsignor would not join family and friend in the heavens for another 77 years.

Healing came slowly. During much of the time during 1933 to 1937, John would be in hospital. An unhealed intestinal lesion required multiple surgeries and refused to stop bleeding. One Sunday morning in 1937, John would use the lesion as his request for a sign. John asked the Lord whether or not he should continue to study for the priesthood. If the lesion would heal within a week, John prayed, he would renew his seminary studies in earnest and give himself fully to God's will.

The lesion healed within a week. John's recovery was nothing short of miraculous. Several weeks later when John wrote to be readmitted into the seminary and needed medical confirmation of his

---

[6] *Id.* at 237.

healing, his doctor wrote: "John, I am convinced it was someone greater than all of us who brought you this far. You really should not be here. Your intestines were literally jelly. If this is not an answer to your prayer, then prayer is meaningless. Be grateful, do God's work, man, and pray for us."[7]

Advised by his doctors to seek a drier climate to avoid the return of the tuberculosis, John came to California and set about God's work, being among the 1939 inaugural class at St. John's Seminary in Camarillo. Ordained April 27, 1943, John would serve as an associate pastor at several parishes, including Holy Cross, St. Elizabeth (Altadena), St. Basil, and St. Vibiana Cathedral, from which he was appointed director of Our Lady Chapel and Catholic Information Center on Flower Street in downtown Los Angeles, where he served for 14 years. During this period, John gained a national following for a popular Catholic radio program, a widely syndicated Catholic answers column, and several books. Designated by the Holy Father (Paul

---

[7] *Id.* at 238.

VI) as the "Very Rev. Monsignor," John Sheridan
was appointed pastor of Our Lady of Malibu in
1965; he "retired" as pastor emeritus in 1990, only
to take up the rest of the world as his calling.

Retired was a nonsense statement when associated
with the Monsignor. John loved the priesthood.
There could never be retirement when the
ordination vow was as full and complete as that
made by John Virgilius Sheridan. John wrote: *"of
course I have thought of other ways of life, but I
cannot imagine any other that would be more
attractive, more fulfilling, more soul satisfying than
that of life of the Catholic priest. I know no other way
of life in which I could have a clearer sense of being
needed or a deeper realization that I have been an
instrument of untold blessings and consolation for
countless thousands."*[8]

The Monsignor was a prolific writer and poet. His
published writing includes hundreds of syndicated
columns as well as a number of books based in
whole or in part upon them, including: *Questions*

---

[8] *Id.* at 240.

and Answers on the Catholic Faith, 1963; *Our Sunday Visitor,* 1963; *The People and the Priest,* 1967; *To Be Reconciled,* 1967; *The Church Yesterday and Today,* 1974; *Saints in Times of Turmoil,* 1977; *Tourist in his Footsteps,* 1979; *And When It is Dawn,* 1980; *A Lay Psalter,* 1985; *From Malibu with love,* 1993; *Living the Psalms,* 1996.

As prolific as he was, John never let writing preclude his pastoral work. His emeritus presence at Our Lady of Malibu

> *I cannot imagine any other career that would be more attractive, more fulfilling, more soul satisfying than that of life of the Catholic priest. I know no other way of life in which I could have a clearer sense of being needed.*
> *–John Sheridan*

commanded a great following. For those who didn't know better, it might seem a bit of a cult of personality, but it wasn't. The Monsignor was scrupulous in redirecting his popularity for the needs of the Church. The Monsignor's counsel was valued by his successor pastor, Father Bill Kerze as well as by Cardinal, celebrity and neighbor alike. To the Monsignor, they were all his parishioners.

John was greatly appreciated – no, loved – by anyone who came in contact with him. Monsignor Joseph Pollard, a successor pastor at Our Lady of Malibu, observed on the 50th anniversary of John's priesthood that John's "is a tremendous story, full of chapters and verses and lines that write his magnificent humanity. John is a larger-than-life creation of God; there are so many dimensions to him. His interests are as wide as the total human condition in all its philosophical and experiential manifestations."

With characteristic humility and poetic elegance, here is how John described, himself:

Studying theology here in the States where family members on my father's and mother's side had worked and gone to school before me, I came from the remote, rural background of the Irish midlands, a farmer's and poet lover's son, with a lingering relish for the quiet of the fields and lanes, the call of the birds, morning and dusk, the companionship of the cattle, the horses, the plough. It was in that milieu, I felt the call to priesthood. God's call comes in an endless variety of ways.

What is referenced throughout as John's "Theology of Kindness" stems from his own joyous heart which is never very far from what one Irish poet described as a "heart that knows God."

"I turn the leaf — green down/ Gaily now/ And paint the meadow brown/ With my plough. . . . I find a star lovely art/ In a dark sod/ Joy that is timeless! O heart That knows God!"[9]

---

[9] Patrick Kavanagh, "The Meadow Brown".

Mary Campbell, SSL

Sister Mary Campbell[10] was born on November 28, 1935, to Norah and John Campbell, Mary grew up in a family of 11 children in Kiltimagh, County Mayo, Ireland. Mary had worked for a good while with the Mayo County Council in Castlebar in office and secretarial settings before entering the Sisters of St. Louis in 1959.

After profession of her vows, Mary was sent to California where she taught elementary schools for 49 years. She loved working with her young students and is remembered fondly by many former students and their parents as a kind, faith-filled and compassionate teacher. Of the many people who wrote tributes following her death, a comment posted on *The Malibu Times* website captures her nature well: "Malibu has lost a gentle soul who guided generations of our children, Catholic and not, toward wholesome adulthood. . .

[10] Reprinted with permission from the archive of the Sisters of St. Louis.

. Her death leaves a hole in the community."[11] Mary taught us to walk lightly on the earth and saw beauty everywhere. She generously shared her artistic talents both in religious community and in the schools and parishes where she served. Like Monsignor, Mary never really retired, and she devoted the last seven years of her life to pastoral ministry in the parish and devotedly caring for Monsignor Sheridan.

She and Monsignor could be seen walking each evening around the church grounds, reciting the Rosary, and admiring the seasonal flowers and plants. No one would disagree in the least with the assessment of her religious community that Mary is "enjoying the eternal reward of life spent in the service of God's people and as on Earth, Mary and John now walk in the presence of their God and Saviour."

---

[11] Jonathan Friedman, *Longtime OLM Nun Killed, Monsignor Injured in Car Crash*, MALIBU TIMES, Sept. 1, 2010, *available at* http://www.malibutimes.com/articles/2010/09/02/news/news1.txt.

Martin Sheen remembers Sister Mary Campbell

On the day of her funeral, actor and parishioner Martin Sheen gave the following moving eulogy:

> "As we celebrate Sister Mary's life we give thanks for the blessing of having been a part of such an extraordinary life and henceforth each time we reenter this sacred place she will be newly remembered and her powerful spirit will be evoked for intercession with confidence and gratitude.

> Each one of us holds a deeply personal memory of her presence in our lives that will sustain us through our loss. For my own part I am sustained by the reality of her enviable joy!

> Last fall, Janet and I were having dinner at the parish house with Monsignor John and Sister Mary when the conversation turned to Ireland (what are the chances?) then Irish literature, to Irish poets and to WB Yeats in

particular when suddenly Sister Mary began to recite, totally from memory, Yeats "The Lake Isle of Innisfree."

It was a recitation of such profound simplicity, honest beauty and personal joy that it took our breath away!

'I learned it as a schoolgirl,' she said, in her shy self-effacing way. Yet she could not hide a full measure of deeply personal Irish pride and that moment became my fondest memory of her, which I shall return to cherish always.

> 'I will arise and go now, and go
> to Innisfree/[12]
> And a small cabin build there, of
> clay and wattles made/
> Nine bean rows will I have there,
> a hive for the honey bee/
> And live alone in the bee-loud
> glade/

[12] William Butler Yeats, *The Lake Isle of Innisfree*.

And I shall have some peace
there/ for peace comes dropping
slow,/
Dropping from the veils of the
morning to where the cricket
sings;/
There midnight's all a glimmer,
and noon a purple glow/
And evening full of the linnet's
wings.

I will arise and go now, for
always night and day/
I hear Lake water lapping with
low sound by the shore/
While I stand on the roadway, or
on the pavements gray/
I hear it in the deep heart's core.

John and Sister Mary were in many ways different –
notwithstanding their Irish origins and delightfully
melodic accents.

Sister Mary, like Monsignor John, was Irish by
birth and beloved for her patient running and
teaching in the local Catholic parish school. Mary

kept John's library in accessible fashion, but her larger interest was the Catholic formation of children. She enjoyed the simplicity of life and the flowers in the garden, and she brought a genuine appreciation for art and nature to child and parent. Mary Campbell also served as a bridge for Monsignor to her religious order, the Sisters of St. Louis. Among many other aspects of religious mission, this order runs a highly respected secondary school for women in Woodland Hills, California, inland through a canyon in the direction of the San Fernando Valley from Malibu.

It is an understatement to say that John and Mary were revered in the community. They shared a chaste and pious friendship that could well have been the model for Bing Crosby and Ingrid Bergman in the film "The Bells of St. Mary." Yet, John and Mary were not Irish twins, even as I sometimes teasingly called them that, and others too might think them so because of their common ancestry. Different they were, but also highly inter-dependent.

You might say John was the "brains" of the outfit and Mary the "heart," but then that would not account for Mary's quiet intelligence and keen eye for the needs of the school. Clearly, as well, dividing their qualities in that bright-line fashion would not capture the enormous "heart" or understanding John brought to every circle in which he interacted. And in the present age drowning in divisiveness, Monsignor John's loving handprints seeking to bind up would, after 94 years, be found almost everywhere.

About your Scrivener - *"Dooug"*[13]

John's words are the ones best used to describe myself – not only because they are abundantly kind, but also because they are an apt description of a friendship nourished by tea and toast and Monsignor John's welcoming ways. What follows is a note the Monsignor wrote to the parish upon my leaving for Foreign Service in Europe in 2009:

It was my great loss not being in Doug's class mainly because of my poor hearing. I heard him of course at Pepperdine, on Radio and TV, in a number of nationally covered Debates or "Conversations" as Doug liked to call them and in our own ongoing conversations which like the Psalms ran the entire gamut of human life and behavior. Above all I heard Doug in prayer. Indeed in the broader theological sense of prayer, I have met no one whose conversations are more

---

[13] There is something quite infectious about the Irish syntax and pronunciation and this approximates John's for me.

prayerful, or more conducive to prayer than Doug. This is the simple truth, the truth about a very sophisticated public, private Christian man and scholar.

I suppose I could say it was Doug's devotion to the Holy Mass combined with his ever fresh and deepening interest and insights into things Catholic that I found most attractive: the natural law, those Divine hints of right and wrong that our church's teachers and scholars have affirmed and puzzled over, the human person whose built in characteristics, crowned by Grace, Doug's great patron and teacher Pope John Paul II made the foundation of his own encyclopedic Summa; and the down to earth, day to day ethical implications of our precious Gift of Faith.

It was all of this with his endlessly good humor, his clarity of thinking and speaking — above all his charity, the kind of Christian charity that never, never allowed an unkind word to slip from his tongue. It was those qualities of soul and heart I

64

found in one of my good and great friends, dear Doug Kmiec. I am glad Doug is going to contribute his great gifts to other peoples. We will miss him, continue to converse with him and look forward to seeing him on his visits to his family, to Pepperdine and to us, his O.L.M. special family. Vade in Pace, Amicus! Mentor, et Dominus sit semper Tecum.

I am certain that John and Mary could, and often did, write in the same generous hyperbole for many others. Their kindness found the best in us; it was upon this ground they would stake our hope for salvation and help us reform our shortcomings. They would never think of leading with the negative or finding some basis upon which the Church might object to our lives. The Monsignor's implicit understanding with us "wretched sinners" (for him a term of endearment) was that any sinfulness in our lives would not long survive the inundation of pure love he and Mary extended to us. Perhaps that was overly optimistic, but nevertheless, John's expressions of praise were more than idle flattery; they were aspiration, expectation, and

65

encouragement. Do we do the same with our spouses? Children? Friends? Let us never fail in the way of John and Mary to build each other up – to lift up our hearts!

Beset with scandal and cover-up, the institutional Church also has less intellectual and spiritual influence. This is why the loss of John V. Sheridan is the loss of a giant in the Church. A proponent of overstatement in introduction himself, John would likely demur to this description. I beg to differ. The Catholic faith works from bottom-up, from interior to exterior, one person made in God's image in our sight at a time; and in light of this measure of subsidiarity, as the theologians call it, John's influence is difficult to deny.

John's influence on my life was as profound as it was subtle. The entry point was in our often daily discussions over "tea and toast." As I prayerfully reflect now, I see John's intelligent witness of kindness in my efforts to join with those seeking to find common ground that could transcend differences in faith, wealth, politics, race, gender and nationality.

My 2008 campaign efforts in behalf of then-Senator Obama with various Catholic communities in the United States have been already mentioned and told in detail elsewhere.[14] They need not detain us long here. As has already been given emphasis, the Monsignor himself, did his best to not let political affiliation block access to faith. It was for this reason, unrelated to whomever his candidate was, that he was appalled when I was denied communion for endorsing the then-Senator Obama. You could tell, however, that John was pleased to encourage me to take up the social justice side of the faith that for so long had been neglected by a public debate fixated on how best to respect the sacredness of human life. The protection of unborn life is indispensable to uniting democracy with truth, but if little progress can be made there, it is simply strategically foolish not to press for a family wage and improved health care for those who lack

---

[14] *See generally* Douglas W. Kmiec, Can a Catholic Support Him? Asking the Big Question about Barack Obama (2008).

67

it. Likewise, John was passionate in his opposition
to the Iraq war, and frequently made reference to
John Paul II's proposition that "war is always a
defeat for humanity."

As it would turn out, my effort at bridge-building
tended to bring out the worst in former friends and
wasn't always supported by my new ones.
Suspicions run deep in politics. Nonetheless, I am
accustomed to swimming upstream. The Kmiec
family has a history of staking out atypical,
independent spots on the political globe to inhabit.
My earliest political memory was campaigning for
John F. Kennedy with my Dad as a child. Dad was
highly involved in the Regular Democratic Party of
Cook County, which some historians record
delivered just enough votes (not all from living
voters, it is claimed) to secure the election of John
F. Kennedy in 1960. I would follow my father's
path and the walls of my college dorm room were
covered with campaign materials advocating the
election of Robert Kennedy. That, too, as history
reveals, ended badly. Except for a later stint as a
White House Fellow, which came my way more for

academic than partisan reasons, Robert Kennedy's death stole the political passion in me.

My father never lost his passion for matters political. Even as a WWII vet with a family to raise, he freely chose (if you can call explaining himself to my mother an action taken in freedom) to indulge his political interests indirectly through friendships with some of Chicago's old-line Democrats, such as the elder Richard J. Daley and Dan Rostenkowski or "Danny Rusty" as Dad called him. Even that fraternization was much to the consternation of my Republican-proclaimed and offsetting-vote mother, who dearly loved Dad but detested what she perceived as the intrinsic duplicity in politics.

John V. Sheridan may well have been one of the wisest, most beloved prelates of our time. It was no accident that he was chosen to deliver the nationally televised eulogy for President Kennedy. Some years later, watching Ethel Kennedy and her daughter Kathleen interact with Monsignor following a sparsely attended 8:00 a.m. Mass at Our Lady of Malibu (OLM) brought to mind the last joyous moments of Bobby Kennedy's life which had been spent in Malibu. Today among my treasured photographs is one of Bobby full of promise running with his pant legs rolled to his knee on the beach where the Monsignor would stroll along the bluffs.

Of course, on June 6, 1968 – when Robert Kennedy was assassinated exiting the ballroom of the Ambassador Hotel in Los Angeles, just after he declared victory in the California primary – I had not yet met the Monsignor. And while envelope stuffers and neighborhood and phone canvassers like me shook the hand of the candidate as he breezed by, you would be right to suppose that the popular Senator's victory in the April 30, 1968 Indiana primary did not turn on the efforts of this college-bound freshman.

Of course, if you rode the train from Chicago into northern Indiana with me and the other youthful volunteers from my high school, you likely couldn't tell us that at the time. Just a few weeks earlier at the Saint Patrick's Day parade in Chicago, I met the young woman who would consent to be my wife, Carolyn Keenan. Much prettier and more intelligent than the type of woman who my bookish

personality normally dated, I can recall being truly
exhilarated with life by Carol's acceptance of my
invitation to a formal dance and by my RFK
campaign volunteer work.

Bobby's bright victory in the Indiana primary hid
only temporarily a darkness that had foreshadowed
even darker moments to come. In early April,
Kennedy was in Muncie, en route to Indianapolis.
As he boarded his plane, a senior campaign worker
informed Senator Kennedy of the shooting of Martin
Luther King, Jr. Those who were close enough to
see say his smiling demeanor instantly froze into
horror. It's a short flight to Indy from there,
especially on a charter plane, and Dr. King expired
during the course of it. In the next hour or so, a
whole lot of people frenetically urged the Senator,
for his own safety, to cancel his Indianapolis speech
to a largely African-American audience. The news
of the death of the charismatic civil rights leader
was already the spark for urban rioting. Kennedy
disregarded that advice and gave one of the finest
improvisational speeches in American political
history on the importance of kindness, compassion,
and above all non-violence.

71

Sound familiar? I am not claiming the speech for Monsignor; but friends do influence friends. All I know is that the very same Monsignor who brought out the best in the famous as well as the obscure was fatally injured while in my care. It is a heavy cross to be accountable for the absence of a humble, parish priest whose witness of love and kindness was so Christ-like that it was changing the world for the better largely without its notice.

In the next part, the elements of the Theology of Kindness are examined more closely.

Part II

The Theology of Kindness

2. Gift of the Holy Spirit

The Theology of Kindness practiced by John Sheridan was not written down – at least, not in one place. The Theology of Kindness is dynamically and unceasingly a product of the Holy Spirit. Hence, it is best illustrated, taught, and imitated by recalling and setting down here why -- when we were in the presence of John or Mary -- our hearts were indeed lifted, and we felt warmed by the presence of sheer love and goodness.

The Theology itself is not meant to claim or discount the systematic brilliance of Aquinas or Augustine or the scholarly ruminations of the present Holy Father, Benedict XVI. It is just that as much as John endeavored to read and study these great minds, their syllogistic or didactic methods of instruction were not his path. Those of us in university settings have to admit that reading the *Summa* or the *City of God* can be enlightening, but such reading is also intellectual labor of the first order. John wanted faith to be more readily available, to be inseparable from a beating heart.

The Theology of Kindness does have some common ground with these storied Catholic apologists, but if analogy be useful, it has more in keeping with the charismatic and personalist influence of John Paul II, with two salient differences. First, John Paul II found the Light of Truth to more easily divide saints and sinners than John ever could or would attempt. This reflects less disagreement than difference between the responsibilities of papal office and parish pastoral ministry. At the very personal, local level, the Theology of Kindness is far slower to judge, lest the spiritually transformative power of kindness be defeated by moral pronouncements of that which is intrinsically right and wrong. Both instructions are needed; kindness is not a license to remake the good into evil or to ignore evil's natural consequence for the soul. But kindness does more easily forgive than admonish.

Second, John Paul II's theological insights are contained in a vast body of encyclical writing. By contrast, John approached his exposition and demonstration of a living faith primarily through the love manifested by him in meeting the needs of every individual whose lives he touched. Like John Paul II and the fathers of the Church, John Sheridan wrote abundantly, but it was as the Spirit would move him in homiletic instruction or private correspondence or conversation. The Spirit's purposes seldom – unfortunately – included an index or even file folders, but wherever John's wisdom can be found, it is pure gift. John himself, as we reflect in the next chapter, was most impressed by the effectiveness of 12-step and similar programs for meeting the needs of those who suffer from alcohol and drug addiction. John distilled his theology of kindness in like decanters especially one marked "active loving involvement in the lives of others."

3. An Engaged Theology Is More than Metaphor

How does one tangibly, practically, lift up one's heart? Without practical means, the expression remains just another religious metaphor – noble in sound, empty in result. More spiritual, than doctrinal, the Theology of Kindness as practiced by Monsignor John drew deeply, yet subtly, upon Scripture, the constant teaching of the Church, known to theologians as the Magisterium, and an appreciation for how Christ in taking on the human form makes possible our transformation and greater perfection in God's image.

To Lift Up Your Hearts, you must:

Love Recklessly

As John wrote: "On my efforts to be kind, do I hope for salvation." Acknowledging that his motives for kindness might not always stand the test of the Gospels, John nevertheless could be counted upon to extend love to all people out of a sense of his own"weakness." It was a kindness extended in imitation of God's own "deep, almost reckless, and unlimited" rejection of a legalistic or wholly logical faith. John's love – not just forgiveness -- was virtually unconditioned. In the Our Father, we ask for forgiveness, and we are impliedly given it on the basis of our having forgiven those who "trespassed against us." John's reckless love was greater: it was, in fact, love extended even without our fulfillment of the golden rule.

Be Unafraid of Death

The Monsignor faced physical death more than once. His extended reflections on death can be found in his elegant volume, *And When it is Dawn*. In his book, John writes prophetically: *"The circumstances of our death as Christians are no different from those of our brothers and sisters who are not aware of Christ. I may be killed in an automobile accident, . . . or I may pass on in the relative peace or obscurity of some hospital, home or hospice. But in the spirit and power of Christ I can accept my death even now, accept it in the joyful hope that with my death, my former life will have passed on and I will have joined the community where, as the Bible expresses it, "death will be no more, nor mourning, nor tears."[15]*

John does not mean to say that death is a casual matter. *"[O]ne of death's innumerable paradoxes is that, though commonplace, when it touches me, when it reaches me, really reaches me, it does so with unique poignancy; the intensity of it, the mystery of it, the sheer futility of it can benumb me. I know scores of elderly, physically weak, humiliatingly dependent women and men who are so tired, so unloved, so discouraged, so disenchanted with life that they daily call on God to take them from their miserable nursing home beds. And that does not neutralize the essentially mysterious character of death, nor does it make my own death the more casual experience."[16]*

He continues: *"[D]ying is the most essential stage in our living process. There is a temptation, however, to*

---

[15] John V Sheridan, And When it is Dawn – on living fully and freely our final moments 121 (Chervo Publications, 1980)
[16] John V. Sheridan, *And When It is Dawn*, 17-18 (Chervo 1980)

focus on the manner, the mechanics, the circumstances or dynamics of our dying; this is unfortunate; and lends itself to a misconception, and amputation, distortion of the total human condition; it robs life of its wholeness, its integrity; it gives us a false and radically incomplete picture of ourselves as persons in his community.... The physician who signs my death certificate will have finished his job; he will likely have done so without asking himself why I really am, why I should be, why he himself is; he may never question whether his death certificate represents my final and total cessation in any form, or whether the "I" he knew has entered a new phase of existence or a new level of life. If he should pose such questions he might feel called to make decisions that transcended trend traditional responsibilities of his location as healer. If you should decide to believe that death has spelled total Finis for me, he is making an act of faith that must seem, sometimes at least, to be out of harmony with the deepest moorings of his vocation as healer or life giver. Yet death should be, must be allowed, encouraged, to pose fundamental questions to all of us, regardless of our vocations."[17]

The fear of death, the Monsignor reasons is not its unknown so much what is intimately known by each of us and us alone with God: our sinfulness and the extent to which we have genuinely accepted Christ and the promised redemption or have only been going through the motions. I do worry of this, for I have fallen out of the weekly practice of reconciliation and examination of conscience. Indeed from the moment of First Confession, as it was then called in the 1950s, I can recall thinking more of getting the theatrical elements right, for Sister Frieda, the second grade Franciscan nun who did her best to touch the soul of a youngster of 7 or 8 years of age, but who was consumed with the memorization of an Act of Contrition or not stepping on the priest's words of absolution.

On the day of the accident, had there been an opportunity for an objective panel of say, guardian angel judges (who might have been a little more

---

[17] Sheridan, *Id.* at 29.

alert – but don't get me started), to speculate as to whom among the three of us was least prepared to meet his maker, those selected for onward movement would not have changed. In identifying which of us should fear death and which two could intrepidly present themselves, not as perfect, but as responsibly and maturely able to see God, no one – not even my sainted late mother – would have resolved the issue and selected me over John and Mary.

In this, the accident is a profound blessing, one of multiple blessings I, along with many others, have received from a loving and merciful God. The Old Testament reminds us that the beginning of wisdom is the fear of God, and we forget I suspect at our eternal peril that God's justice will not be a plea bargain. But the Monsignor in the best, most optimistic expression of the Theology of Kindness is also right to reduce the untoward fear of death, since John's counsel to a person dying or preparing for death, expressing distress about some sin, weakness or addiction that had lingered in her consciousness was to: *remind them quietly of who God, our God, the God of Jesus is. The God who comes to us in Jesus is the healing, forgiving loving God. The New Testament rings with the testament, its witness to God's unconditioned love incarnated in Christ Jesus.*

At no moment of our lives, no matter who we are, what our sins, at no moment should we ever doubt or despair. . . .God, like any really loving mother or father, caretaker, bewildered owner: God follows us, is with each one of us, but never more vigilantly than when we are lost, are in trouble with ourselves, with Satan, or with the world.

And this is not in conflict with the fear of God from the Old Testament, for, before the final judgment, the God of the Bible *forgives the infidelity, as John put it so well, of the Israelites worshipping the Golden Calf almost immediately after they promised to keep and live His Commandments. And if more reminder of God's lingering mercy were needed it is supplied in the embrace of the Prodigal [Son] by a loving, caring father who waited all the years for this so called "no good" son, to come back home and share the kind of affection none of the luxuries, eating, drinking, drugs, wild behavior or pretty*

83

women could ever give him. There is something about the story of the Prodigal Son, the loving, indulgent parent - mother or father — the jealous brother — or sister -- something about that story that can make it a companion piece for each one of us, every day as we go about our lives at home, at work or in the public square.

Be not afraid of death; be fearful of failing to turn toward life.
We are told that faith deprives death of its sting or victory, but seldom do we appreciate what that means. Some assume this to be merely an alternative way to console loss. "Dad is in a better place," we say out loud with others comforting us, as our inner voice says: "really? if it is better, why aren't you going?"

If our answer is because we fear the unknown, we have not come to grips with what death is and how faith achieves its victory over death. The victory comes only if we learn from death to reject all that diminishes us in life – hatred, pettiness, an over-concern with the material, and whatever is our sin du jour. It is the rejection of that which separates, excludes, judges by appearance and the embrace of that which binds us ever more closely to achieving the happiness of others, and through it, our own.

If by the death of those we love, we learn to love more strongly, we are ensuring death's defeat in our own lives by our rejection of that which brings death about. Once, we realize it is our choice – in the here and now -- whether we develop the habits of life that enrich us, or instead, succumb to the paths of death that lessen us, there is little to fear, except ourselves.

Be the Positive Light in a Skeptical World

To lift up one's heart is also being prepared to explain, in a positive and affirming way, the basis for faith belief. It is often at the moment of the death of someone who we know is irreplaceable that we are pressed by a close friend or family member – even a spouse or a child – to explain why we still believe? In this age when human authors demand that God show up at their book signings to prove the Divine to the human (and if that seems to have the allocation of the burden of proof in the wrong place, you're right), this question is around us more than we realize.

In modern life, religious persons are often challenged to give explanation of their faith. Some questions are put not in search of answer, but as a means to denigrate. Proponents of atheism tend to bias the scales of judgment in this way, labeling religious argument irrational, always assuming that God must bear the proof of His existence. Given the inability of much of natural science to explain the created universe, would it not be more fitting to expect the skeptic to assume the burden of going forward. Today religious skepticism – or worse, persecution – comes with more subtlety than the torture and detention faced by the early Church fathers and martyrs. The antagonists of the Divine hide beneath a cloak of secularism or indifference; or worse, bring faith forward only for comedic relief in mockery or ignorance.

To be effective, religious witness has to be refreshed and encouraged like everything else of value. Lifting up our hearts also means pursuing instruction that deepens our faith. Faith and reason do travel together but only if we open our minds and open a book.

Manifesting faith is not for connivers and sissies. Being a mentor of the light, rather than the darkness, may well mean a willingness to expose one's own dark limitations – and how faith has strengthened our ability to live a life free of the slavery of drugs, pornography, endless back-biting about our co-workers, or any one of a number of habits or vices of which we are anything but proud. There is much in this book of which I am not proud, including my tendency in recent years to put work over family – something I regularly witnessed against when the children were younger, but about which I lost sight as they reached adulthood. Not paying as much attention meant a failure on my part to be as attentive to the needs of spouse and adult children as I should be. True, as a Parkinson's sufferer, my system is sometimes slow and inconsistent – and, therefore, personally frustrating. But I cannot make up for that deficiency by taking every minute from my family at home (now most often solely my spouse) without there being an unhappy and unacceptable skewing of the needed work-family balance. At a minimum, to lift up our hearts means to be honest with oneself and one's family about challenges that may be getting out of hand. That admission alone will often yield empathy, if not a solution.

Husbands and wives allocate household budgeting differently, but whoever is keeping a close eye on the bottom line in these days of economic hardship has their handful. Lifting up one's heart means sharing this worry as well, so that financial anxiety is not mistaken for general irritability or lack of generosity.

My late father used to say that the benches of the church filled during the Depression. The benches or pews are curiously far emptier today. Perhaps it is because the Depression of 2008 and following is unlike the "great one" of the 1930s. Then, so many millions were cast adrift from the economic system all at once that the bread lines, despair, and suicide could not be missed. In the present times of economic stress, jobs are lost and families evicted from homes; and yet, for those seemingly unaffected, life goes on "normally."

Yet, when we lift up our hearts we will discover that there is little that is normal about today's level of poverty in our "affluent" America. The "occupy movement" that has spread across the land reveals a seething anger at the business-as-usual maldistribution of great wealth to the top one percent. U.S. Census figures reveal poverty among children to be at historic levels. Twenty-one million Americans are living in deep poverty — with their families having incomes less than half of the official poverty rate.

People of faith have a responsibility to serve the poor directly and also to speak out on their behalf, so that they are not forgotten as policies are set and resources allocated by our political leaders. Is this happening? Listen to the debates in the run up to the 2012 election, and what passes for empathy seems more like envy or one-upmanship.

Yet, it is not enough to regret the deceptions of those in public life who line the pockets of a few to enjoy political power over all. Many of us are caught up in a false life as well: we vainly look for lasting happiness in things; when we realize the material to be unsatisfying, we lack the Spirit to incorporate the positive opportunities around us to find ourselves in the service of others. We write checks, and donate a few cans of food or the out-of-style or ill-fitting sweater, but ultimately fail to connect with the hearts and minds of our neighbors in need. Charitable action "on the cheap" without personal involvement leaves us flat.

Unmask the Lie

The Theology of Kindness invites us to shed these mythologies. By what method? By showing us the beauty of extending genuine, one-on-one – kindness to others.   "Shed" is an apt word, since at its most basic level, John's theology helps us to have the courage to "unmask" our real selves. It helps us to put aside the lies that may have deceived a few, but that separate us from many, and that never fool God. Lying as a way of life is unhealthy; it corrupts and erodes, needing more and more deceptive effort to sustain. Worse, it prevents us from ever being at one or at peace with ourselves. The person who extends a hand without intending a true offer of friendship is only an actor, and the actor is too often us.

Attempting to live a double life is not fair to ourselves or those around us. Here again, the reflections on the lives of John Sheridan and Mary Campbell in this book point us toward the honest offering or "lifting up" of our authentic lives. In doing so, we are given some welcome relief from those special "all-knowing" others who seem to populate every aspect of our culture in academia, politics, business, and the media. Once the pillars of community, these sources today frequently offer marketing narratives in place of truth. Moreover, their messages come wrapped in toxic blogospherics and an all too contagious rude smugness, which neither inspire nor resolve public problem. We need scholars in universities, genuine statesmen in public life, men and women of integrity in business, and objective journalists. We don't need just re-invented narratives.

True, much of life is story, but libraries and bookstores have fiction and non-fiction sections. And if we, as a nation or individually, build more upon the former rather than the latter, we do little more than create distrust in others and anxiety within ourselves.

91

We search in vain for honest judgment upon the 2012 debating stage. Over and over we merely relearn that those political figures who hold themselves out as heroes seldom are.

Do we cheer for a one-time presidential candidate who extolled the values and responsibilities of the working class family while he insensitively ignored the needs of his own, including a spouse diagnosed with cancer? Or do we cheer for a presidential candidate from the other party who did the same, but topped it off by fathering a child with a young campaign aide?

Okay, you may think like my late mother: politics is a dirty business so just turn away from the presidential audition stage. Fair enough, but soon we discover the duplicity is more widespread. Even the high profile prosecutors who speak grandly of the rule of law in their prosecution of political or corporate misdeed seem to be driven more by notoriety than by principle.

Sports? Take your pick. Scandals built on dishonest and endangering steroid usage, illegal betting, or sexual assault abound. Should we cheer for the professional athlete who abuses his spouse, the coach sodomizing boys in the shower, or for the college player accepting improper gratuities (who never once thought about the losses of integrity he was imposing on his institution or teammates)?

And there are the mortgage lenders whose loans, constructed on false appraisals, misled hundreds of thousands of families into their own foreclosure. No, politicians are hardly the only prevaricators. Nor can we overlook retirement investments manipulated by corporate insiders who misleadingly allocate quarterly earnings to make a company "look" more profitable than it is.

And, of course, if honesty is to be restored, we must first remove the log from our own eye and see the family torn asunder by alcohol, drugs, pornographic addiction, or simple neglect.

And while we are at it, let's renounce the myth that women can only achieve social and economic success if they are guaranteed a right to sacrifice children to abortion.

And without hesitation, let us also resolve the hypocrisy and wrongfulness of a Church leaving the crimes of pedophile priests unreported and unpunished.

How would John Sheridan respond to these personal or cultural lies? Here comes the surprise: not by legalistic condemnations, but by unqualified welcome. Primarily by manifesting a level of kindness and acceptance that in itself illustrates lying to be wholly unnecessary. A woman who bought into the corporate cultural lie that her professional position depends on abortion would never be turned away from the community by John; nor would those in the grip of alcohol or drug abuse. The Theology of Kindness is a theology of inclusion; lifting our hearts to the Lord means standing with the wounded, misled, and gravely mistaken hearts. To be sure, neither John nor Mary would be accepting of abuse, failing or sin, but in rejecting these shortcomings, they would never turn away the person.

Do Not Mistake Law for Morality

Lifting up one's heart is not lobbying the legislature to pass a law. We need to assume personal responsibility to end the narrative lie. We are challenged to address the various forms of dishonesty present in our lives directly or in church community or workplace. Of course, a well-ordered nation will also have adequate laws to safeguard against violence, be it physical or economic (i.e., fraud). But laws are minimalist; faith calls us up higher to a better self. Sadly, some in the contemporary faith leadership prescribe legislative, rather than personal amendment. We avoid our own need for change by pressing the community to "do something." That "something" often amounts to passing a law.

Law is needed, but personal conversion is needed more.

Thomas Aquinas was right; one cannot prohibit every vice or enact every virtue. Nonetheless, over and over again we think we can solve one problem or another by "passing a law against it," even as doing so misses the point (the need for interior change).

Once upon a time, the Church sought to save our souls by forming our conscience to know how to evaluate the most complex ethical dilemma. Today, the antagonists of the Church, and the Church herself, seek to have the "last" word by having a law passed that imposes our favored perspective. John Paul II said it well in an address to clergy: "You are priests, not social or political leaders. Let us not be under the illusion that we are serving the Gospel through an exaggerated interest in the wide field of temporal problems."

Religious leaders who too quickly turn to the law to coerce change favorable to their particular perspective quickly discover that, as Dad used to say, "Two can play at that game." Meaning, of course, if you seek the coercive affirmation of the law for your religious perspective, others with contrary perspective will do the same. You may think that that is all well and good, just another form of competition in the "marketplace of ideas." However, unlike private products in an actual marketplace, where we are not forced to buy brand X over Y, using force to narrow the range of acceptable religious choices is a dangerous invasion upon religious freedom. Even using the law for the punishment of something as basic as lying – long the object of perjury and related laws against fraud – has prompted the opposing view to argue that lying should be an aspect of protected free speech. The notion is not likely – thankfully – to get Supreme Court approval. But do not be overly sanguine, since there is an awful lot of fabrication going on in them hills (e.g., "I only lost 10 dollars at poker"; "The doc says you're getting better"; "Gee, you've lost weight"; or the ubiquitous "The check is in the mail"). We shall see whether the Supreme Court gives lying constitutional protection, but even if it does that would hardly make it right.

Be Open to New Understanding

As John saw it, when the church entered the present ecumenical or interfaith age, *it was not diluting or neutralizing the basic realities of the Catholic faith – incarnation, redemption and sacramental expression,* but [recognizing] *that people just don't want to belong to [solely] an institutional church... Of course we must have an*

97

*institution – there is no way out of that – but I think
we are approaching more of a world church, one that
will embody different cultures. For example, the
incarnation can apply as easily to a culture that has
produced Hinduism and Buddhism as to a culture
that operates out of a legalistic framework, such as
Judaism. We have to develop an increasingly global,
inclusive vision of God's world [but] this doesn't
mean that we should repudiate our basic Western
axioms. It means we need to be open to the beliefs of
others.*[18]

In lifting up our hearts beyond our usual religious
habitats, the level of kindness to which we are
called is that which we would manifest toward
innocent children, whom Jesus admonished us
never to obstruct from Him. When Isaiah pleads for
trust in God he anchors that plea in the feeling a
mother has for her offspring.

Like sentiments can be found in all major faiths. In
Islam, the main characteristics of God are mercy

---

[18] Friedl, Francis, and Reynolds, Rex (1998). *Extraordinary Lives: thirty-four priests tell their stories.* Ave Maria Press. Pg 243-44

and compassion and the appellation "God the Compassionate" is used throughout the Quran in virtually every reference. An essential aspect of the month long fast of Ramadan is to build a shared understanding of suffering and hunger. The sacred Vacana in Buddhism provides that kindness or compassion is that which makes the heart of the good move to lessen the pain of others. It crushes and destroys the pain of others. It is called compassion because it shelters and embraces the distressed. Similarly, the three central virtues of Hinduism are charity, self-control and compassion ("daya"). In particular, Hindus are to adopt *ahimsa,* an attitude of spirituality that avoids harm or hurtfulness toward others.

Catholics have no monopoly on the Theology of Kindness.

God is "with us"; are we really with Him?

A key element underlying all of the steps to emulating John's Theology of Kindness is full acceptance or trust in God's continuing presence in our lives – not just at Church and not just in front of others we seek to impress, but in every quiet corner of our lives where we think we have indulged every precaution to draw tight the curtains so that no one, not even God, is with us.

There is no such place to hide from the Lord. Honesty here requires an examination of conscience; do we really want God in our company?

One sure sign of disbelief in God – or more charitably, incomplete faith under construction – is the idea that we must hide from God the most shameful aspect of our lives. When we think God is ignoring us, it is more likely that we have shunned Him – shunned His mercy and forgiveness. We know our shortcomings: drug or alcohol addictions, laziness, anger. When we try to conquer these alone, or worse pretend they aren't there, we deny God in favor of ourselves.

John explains:

We are told that "Emanuel" means that "God is 'with us.'"

How is He with us?

He is with us in the core of our being, in our history in the people among whom we live and work and laugh and love and mourn and suffer and die. . . . If God be with us, who can be against us?

Yet, we know that God seems so absent in so much of life, so many parts of the world, so many fields of thought, the universities, laboratories, governments, brokerage houses and banks. And here is where a little reflection rooted in our own depths, in our traditions -- Scriptures, church -- here is where spending one moment, getting one good critical look into the life, character and mission of John the Baptist will be most helpful. Understanding more of John's personality will allow God's forgiving, loving, redeeming presence to be more accessible to us.

We first meet John the Baptist coming out of nowhere — the wilderness. It is as if he is determined to conceal everything about himself, and in this he

101

first seems like us, but there is something unique, too. John the Baptist is carrying the critical message of forgiveness. As he speaks, his humility and his realism are transparent. When he speaks, what he says has extraordinary forcefulness.

Do we act and speak from humility?

When John the Baptist speaks, every word is relevant, every word related to the message he is carrying for each us. People are flocking to him, and as in so many cases, they are so mesmerized by his words that the people listening wonder if is he not much more than he is disclosing."

Who are you? They ask John the Baptist.

But this morning, let us turn it around and ask: Who are we? Do we choose our words carefully? Not who we appear to be in relation to others – but who we really are.

John the Baptist, being a man of few words, says merely: "Look, I am not the Christ.

John the Baptist was not the Christ. And in this sense, it may be proper to say that John's calling as great as it was before the powerful sacrifice on the cross, is less than what we are enabled to be by the heroic gift of Jesus. Let me be direct: after Christ's life, death and resurrection do we have any excuse not to be more Christ-like ourselves?

To, if you will, be even greater evangelists than John, himself.

The Theology of Kindness as outlined by the Monsignor leaves us with a ready road-map for conquering sin and death in our own lives. Convinced? I thought I was and I certainly would have nodded affirmation to all of the Monsignor's teaching. Yet, faith expressed is one thing and faith challenged quite another, and a challenge which deprives us of the very source of instruction – as the accident did -- is especially difficult. Peter in his denials knew this three times over, but as revealed in the next part, your author had his own terrifying moment of doubt.

Part III

Why is there suffering?

4. Heart's Stopped, Broken, and Shattered

The question of suffering in the world has perplexed the wisest of philosophers. The question of why God would ever permit evil in His created world is a quandary John and I would speak of from time to time in a very academic, almost pedantic, fashion.

Frankly, when we would later confront death in the face, it seemed to me we were both far too glib.

Taking account of the short distance involved, including the closeness of the ravine and my travelling speed of 45 mph, the time elapsed from leaving the highway to impact is estimated to be a little more than four seconds. It took me longer to type this sentence. The short slide at 1:37 p.m. on August 25, 2010 took Mary's life instantly and resulted in John and I being taken by helicopter to the trauma unit at the University of California-Los

Angeles (UCLA). After multiple surgeries, I survived. John did not.

John and I were both lodged by a collapsed dashboard and an inflated air-bag. Mercifully, John was unable to pivot and he looked straight ahead likely enduring pain far greater than mine which was excruciating. My penalty for relative youth (my 59 to John's 94) was just enough flexibility to turn slightly and grasp immediately that Mary was gone. Her eyes, which on earth were always as joy-filled as a child on Christmas morning, were now as empty and sad as those one sees oddly cultivated on fashion models in glossy magazines.

My heart was shattered.

Worse, I knew John's would be broken.

"John," I said, "Mary needs us to pray." As the heroic sheriff and firemen from the Lost Hills and Piuma Canyon stations came rushing to our aide, John and I held the hand-made white string rosaries given to the three of us just minutes earlier at the luncheon in the refectory of the Sisters of

Saint Louis. As I write this, I remember Mary picked a different color – pink as I recall – a color of joy and happiness used especially on the third Sunday in Advent to express our anticipation for Christ's birth.

It was not apparent how conscious John was at that point. I recited the prayers aloud and I could hear John speaking in a low, almost whispered voice. Distraught as I was, I took comfort that John and I were together. Side by side we felt the intense suffering of serious injury and a short time later felt the airborne vibrations of the evacuating helicopter. Perhaps we even watched each other undergo emergency surgery, though this gauzy memory is more the product of pain medication than reality. One of the superb UCLA doctors would later recount how the surgical teams went back and forth between John and myself in our treatment. The larger point is that, in the immediate aftermath of the accident John and I were together sharing everything about the experience from the awkwardness of bed pans to delightful visitors, friends and family from near and far who came to wish us well.

5. John, I do not understand

The personal and tremendous comfort of not being alone ended as John departed. Suddenly, the question of why God would permit suffering returned with an unrelenting vengeance. I turned to John's notes on suffering. He wrote:

Suffering in one form or another, or at one level or another, is or can be our most obsessive obstacle to inner peace. If our search for meaning is our most humanly distinctive attribute — and it certainly seems to be — the horror of even seeing other innocent humans suffer without any apparent meaning can stun to silence or leave one constantly questioning the providence or existence of God or of any rational origin or explanation for who or what we are about.

Our Christian Faith has not reached into every corner of the planet, nor been accessible to every

*human being, nor is it just an attempted
explanation of human suffering but it is the one
Faith whose symbol is the cross, and at whose
heart is an innocent human being dying on a
Cross. It is in the light of that unique human, the
God/man himself moving into the center of our sin
sodden world and taking on the burden of us all.
And it is in the light of our belief, our total
confidence that God escort us through it all. In the
light of that Faith we can live in hope, and love.
Awaiting our resurrection.*

I find this passage a bit mysterious. This is in
keeping with the nature of my conversations
with John. I admired John's voice with its hint of
Irish, its almost innately jovial quality. Yet,
there were times when I couldn't make hide nor
hair of what the heck he was saying. I know I
wasn't alone in this because I would look around
sometimes at the morning Mass and see
everyone with their hands cupped over their ears
or leaning in toward the ambo. Even during our
tea and toast sessions where we sat just inches
from each other, there were times when at best I

was getting every fourth or fifth word. I found that if I asked John to repeat himself it would interrupt what, by facial gestures and the twinkling in his eye, seemed too important to interrupt for the purpose of comprehension.

Perhaps the reader has experienced the circumstance of finding a constant request to repeat a bit of annoyance. Indeed, this is a rather frequent occurrence for teachers in the classroom who expound at some considerable length with their erudition or instructions for an examination only to have a student in the back of the class say after 15 minutes or so of precious guidance or insight, could you repeat that?

Rather than inconvenience the great man and have him lose his train of thought, I would pretend to hear everything in the hopes of catching the train when it slowed down at the station perhaps for some oatmeal or to take a sip of tea. If the train continued without stopping, I would attempt the verbal equivalent of jumping aboard and boldly proclaim to make an insight of my own.

Now our Monsignor was blessed with particularly gathersome ears, and even if his Hollywood-bowl-style natural equipment failed him there were expensive hearing aids up in his drawer which he detested wearing. Nevertheless, with or without mechanical assistance, John only found his declining hearing a problem in a group where it can be difficult to differentiate one voice from another. One on one John did not share in our difficulty understanding him and he could hear us just fine. Proof of his acuity would be his masterful way of connecting the uttered "jump aboard" statement into his own, or so it would seem, but I really didn't know for sure. Sometimes parishioners would complain of their inability to hear or grasp Monsignor in his totality. Empathetic, and confessing the same, I would lamely pronounce "only God with Sister Mary's help" gets everything he says.

Well, I could use Mary's gift now. In the above passage, John confirms how the presence of suffering, especially the suffering of the innocent leaves us perplexed. He then moves all too swiftly to the strength of our faith being the symbol of the cross where an innocent human being is suffering again. All of this innocent suffering is then transformed into the light of belief and a total confidence in God awaiting the resurrection. God will be our escort, we are told. Good, just don't take Mulholland Highway.

If the accident did provide the occasion for John's ultimate gift of self, and passage to eternity, why was his passage so painful and turbulent? Surely a just God, our loving escort as John refers to him, would have taken account of John's kindness and his powerful witness of faith and allowed the dear man to join his mother and father and his accomplished siblings who preceded him in death to simply cross over during a sweet afternoon nap. And what did it mean for me to be tossed back into what I now perceived to be a much harsher world? I felt horribly alone and without answer.

Late at night when our many hospital visitors went home or were taking a well-deserved respite, I would struggle with the IV pole as a walker to go the short distance to John's room where the nurses and residency doctors in training kept constant watch.

Death comes for us all, but – despite its inevitability and Christianity's core promise that, by the unmerited grace of our faith in Jesus' life, death and resurrection, death is deprived of its sting – the death of one's best friend hurts like hell.

Toward his final days, as many of John's and Mary's relatives, who had travelled great distances to be by his side and now had returned home, my wife and I or my children would walk the corridors at all hours, sometimes seeing the bright light of a new day through windows not far from John. For me, this renewed light would nourish hope for John's recovery. As it would be, this extended earthly light proved only to be enhancing John's already ample heavenly halo.

Figure 2. Monsignor John and the author in conversation after "tea and toast" in the garden of Our Lady of Malibu (2008). Time Magazine had just interviewed us to ascertain our thinking on the extent to which there seemed to be increasing subtle insinuation by Republican partisans with certain American bishops that was resulting in a troubling understatement of Catholic social teaching which calls upon society, including the institutional church and the government, to help us meet our obligations to families and the poor.

114

6. Prayers Answered?

We are taught that God answers the prayers of the persistent. Remember the widow of the Gospel who received her due from an unjust judge only because she nagged until he gave in.[19] Yet, it is not the pestering that brings answer, it is the worthiness of what we request. "Ask for what is worthy of God," says Saint Basil the Great, "not ceasing to ask until thou receivest."

My persistent prayer for John was that he not be in pain. This prayer seemed ably fulfilled by the talented doctors of UCLA. Beyond that, I truly left it wholly to God. Full recovery with the sadness of Mary's absence would have wounded John. Partial

---

[19] Luke 18:1-8 ("Parable of the Unjust Judge").

recovery without the ability to walk the hills he so dearly loved would have likewise been cruel.

I am old enough to know the two faces of time. In our youth, the hours cannot be exhausted. In some places in our youth, like the school house, they seemed absolutely inexhaustible. Even with all eyes fixed upon the clock, the dismissal bell made us wait. My nightlong shared hospital time with John passed in similar interminable minutes.

In our twilight years, we are often astounded by how very fast the time has gone. Our lives are now akin to the digital numbers on a stopwatch. It was this express clock that supervised the tender moments of friendship that were running at hurried pace toward empty. Oh I tried to stop them, of course. Out would come the beads or Yeats, hoping the Glorious mysteries not the sorrowful would come to mind, pleading that John's favored poet would reward friendship with more than sadness. Yet, the Irish are a melancholy lot, and Yeats proved little comfort. Rather, he serves as a grim reminder that my bearing was that of "a man whom Sorrow named his friend."[20] Like that "comrade of Sorrow," I was Yeats' "Sad Shepherd." There was no other role to be taken. In my heart, I "called loudly to the stars to bend," as that ancient shepherd did, but it was not in their poetical nature to give comfort. No, the stars, then and now, stayed among themselves "laughing and singing."

---

[20] *See* William Butler Yeats, *The Sad Shepherd.*

117

7. John's Stigmata

John's precious hands bled from almost any touch, given John's age and skin grown fragile and thin. From time to time, John would wear protective gloves to public events. "The Michael Jackson look," I teased him.

Once John had been asked to give a prayer at a celebrity's star placement on the walk of fame. Unfortunately John's personal "stigmata," Sister Mary impishly reported the following day, nearly ended the ceremony when the unofficial mayor of Hollywood shook the Monsignor's hand so vigorously at the event's beginning that paramedics were needed.

Several years earlier, John's bleeding would be the centerpiece of another story. After Mass we went to John's chambers in the rectory for tea and toast. Sister Mary was in Ireland visiting her family and John insisted on making the tea. He wanted me to read an article from "The Tablet," one of his favorite

Catholic periodicals. When I sat at the small table near the entry door to examine the essay John thought so fascinating, I happened to look up just in time to see the uneven launch into space of teacups and platters, jellies and jams, and butters and knives and goodness knows what else out of the tiny kitchen. This was astounding enough, but these unnaturally airborne objects were followed by a pirouetting John Sheridan, who, in short order, followed the gravitational pull to the floor. Rushing to John's side I was relieved to see that, while stunned and disheveled, he seemed less pained than annoyed. It was a miracle he missed the abundant hard edges that surrounded him in that tiny space. John's biggest injury was embarrassment. I called downstairs to see if there was anyone else in the rectory that could help me lift the Monsignor. No one answered, so I picked him up alone. While nothing fell off or dangled unbecomingly, I did notice that blood was spouting from various bruises. "John," I said, "have you Band-Aids? We need to patch up a bit." After putting on five or six of the bandages, John and I headed to the local emergency care clinic in Malibu.

Ever thoughtful of the least inconvenience to others, John worried that he was bleeding all over the seats in the car, which of course he was. "Not a problem," I said, "blood, unlike grease and blueberries, comes right off." John laughed asking the source of my great knowledge of the relative solvency of stains." "My dear late mother, Beatrice," I told him, "like all mothers she regularly opined how this or that stain would never come out, but blood was not on that list."

When we arrived at the emergency clinic, I was distressed that we were greeted by a young doctor at the front counter who didn't seem to know the Monsignor. Rather too casually in the face of a Monsignor now spouting blood from a half a dozen or more spots, I didn't think pointing to the waiting area and saying he would be with us "in a few" was the best course. Thankfully, a more senior woman doctor emerged from the back, immediately recognized John and took him to the table for examination.

There were no broken bones or internal injuries discernible, but the senior doctor recommended an x-ray and some other checks just to make sure. These would be done at St. John's Hospital in Santa Monica about 8 miles away.

Again, the young doctor seemed to go in an unhelpful direction by ordering up an ambulance, which I could see added to John's annoyance and embarrassment. "Look," I said, "that's unnecessary, isn't it? I can take John without delay." The young doctor replied, "You'll get better service arriving by ambulance." "Doctor," I responded, "if you tell the administrators at St. John's that Monsignor John Virgilius Sheridan has had a tumble and is on his way, I can assure you that everyone, save a doctor in surgery, will likely line up waving their stethoscopes in greeting on 20th Street as we arrive."

The young doctor frowned, but John was relieved, and off we went. In terms of the predicted honored reception, I wasn't far off. A platoon of religious sisters met the car gushing (do nuns gush?) over the patient, who was playing the scene for all it was worth. Imagine, if you will, a prize football player being raised high on the shoulders of admiring teammates. If the good sisters had had the strength to lift John like the Holy Father in the papal throne or if he had requested it, I am certain these devoted and admiring friends would have performed the feat.

Moving John swiftly through the admissions area, a young administrator just coming on duty and who had not picked up on the VIP nature of the admission proceeded with all the authority youthful blunder could muster to say "wait one minute there sisters this man must be properly admitted."   All I can say is that the resulting look from the sisters moving John into his room was akin to the many received in Catholic grammar school as I or my classmates related that our homework wasn't quite finished, or that we had bargained away our milk money again for baseball trading cards. Looks may not kill, but they do silence. The admissions clerk was not to be heard from further.

Ducking into a restroom for a minute, I returned to John's room only to find the good Monsignor now surrounded by a veritable mob of giddy hospital staff of every variety overwhelming him with their delight by his visit. It wasn't clear anyone had bothered to ask why John was there in their joy-filled midst and had actually treated him. John, of course, was much too busy to tell them, lest he interrupt a good story or any one of a dozen recountings of how he baptized them or gave them First Communion. Exasperated, I raised my voice above the melee to inquire. Sure enough, no one there seemed to focus on the fact that John had just attempted Swan Lake in the course of morning tea. Tests were further delayed as John proceeded to make one of his patented over-stated introductions. "Why, yes, this is the Doug who single handedly changed Supreme Court and legal history working for President Reagan." Suitable sighs followed and, eventually, the necessary tests.

Coming back from a CAT Scan, I noticed that John had acquired a rather large, somewhat lopsided turban on his head. His grey hair protruding through the center like a floral table display, John seemed curiously proud of his new head gear, even as the nurse told me it was just a precaution. I captured John's be-turbaned head on film in a photo which the good Monsignor relished but made

123

me covenant I would never release. Promise kept, John.

8. Suffering as Gift?

That somewhat whimsical story and others akin to it drifted unpredictably into my sleep-deprived consciousness as I shared what would be our final nights together at the Reagan Hospital at UCLA following the crash. The silliness of these recalled memories were true gifts, happier times that could never have contemplated the somber and dismal moment. These remembrances would yield momentary smiles to catch the tears welled up in my eyes. They still do.

I constantly asked the emergency room surgeons for John's prognosis. My persistent questioning could not yield a more desirable answer than the charts and sophisticated monitoring warranted. John's age was working against him, the surgeons would say, doing their best not to be entirely discouraging. Unlike the young doc at the emergency clinic care clinic in the morning tea ballet episode, these highly trained surgeons, even if they had never met John before, implicitly sensed

John's greatness. There was a glow about him that even heavy sedatives could not quell. In the fullness of his faith, John embodied the Gospel's promise of life to the full.

The doctors, as our fiduciary for John's continued physical presence amongst us, would tussle with the Lord as long as medically reasonable. But ancient or modern medicine ends when God decides – not a minute earlier or later. The big guy Himself stops a beating heart and assumes what is rightfully His as the Divine reversionary. In the early morning of September 17, 2010, God would return home with the strong knowing eyes, mind, will, and spirit of John V. Sheridan, who had just weeks before been given the "gift of suffering" by his close and dear friend. The time for "tea and toast" had ended.

The notion of suffering as "gift," as John describes it, remains a difficult one. Is the difficulty traceable to a continuing sense of guilt? Yes, but it is also something deeper. The uncertain and multiple possible causes of the accident is partial relief. The conclusion reached by friend and official alike, that whatever took place was outside a reasonable person's knowledge or ability to control cannot exempt me from being behind the wheel. "The reasonable person" is a useful legal concept, but the authors of legal treatises and the most well-meaning friends aren't disturbed by the grinding sound of metal embedded within my mind or the impact or the horrifying reality of the sudden, immediate death of a truly gentlewoman.

What put us in that ravine? Some say, it could have been an unfortunately timed request and response for a dashboard adjustment. John, dressed in collar, sweater and suit coat that were suitable for an outside morning Mass, found himself out of step with the mid-day August sun in the canyon. Earlier on our ride, John had asked for help opening an air vent on the passenger side.

While we were in the hospital, a family wrote to me to reveal that they had lost a son in his early 30s near the same point in a single-car accident. They believe their sad loss resulted from the abrupt leftward turn of the road. Nevertheless, they had been unsuccessful in efforts to have a guardrail installed.

Still others who were at the accident scene point to a gravel hazard left on the road the day before by a movie company.

Finally, in the middle of the night prayer and reflection, I began to have my own concern over a possible side effect called "spontaneous blackout" from a newly prescribed Parkinson's medication I had begun taking only a week or so before the accident. Since I have no memory of the four second drift from the road, the latter seems most likely to me (and for this reason, I have brought the accident to the attention of the United States Food and Drug Administration with the help of my UCLA neurologist).

With the cause of the accident unresolved in my mind, I have voluntarily stopped driving. The 10 miles round-trip to my university office is accomplished by bicycle supplemented generously with rides from Carol and our neighbors. Dressed in coat, tie, bike helmet, I must look pretty silly on my cycling days; it certainly is a change from the flag-flying, chauffeured embassy life of the one-time Ambassador. But, with the continuing physical and mental pain of the accident, all is offered as gift.

The gift, I confess, is uneasily extended. There is a constant faith-testing doubt in my mind that I pray each day to expel. Doubt? Yes, doubt not as to the essentials of the Nicene creed but doubt nonetheless, derived from the inexplicability of how three people so much in love with each other, having spent much of their lives and the morning hours of that very day completely dedicated to and in the service of Our Lord would not be entitled to the full protection of Our Lord to find their way back safely to their earthly home.

9. God's Troubling Wager

There, I have gone and done it, John. I am sorry, I cannot help but question our Lord, and I might as well confess the great sin of doubt here and now. Any priest reading these words should feel at liberty to email me the appropriate penance.

Let me be clear, while John and I shared virtually everything from tea and toast to respect for the social justice message of President Obama (but not his view of abortion) to the surgeons who tried to reassemble us both, John would never share in this doubt. Indeed, I am certain I am disappointing him in this, but I have found that in matters both earthly and eternal honesty really is the best policy.

I do not question that John's suffering was accepted by God as his ultimate and complete gift of self – the perfection, if you will, of faith. John never uttered a single Job-like grievance. I do.

Job, you'll remember, complained to God about being unfairly singled out as a just man in an unjust way. Turns out, Job was right about that. God made Job the object of a wager with the devil. Yes, said God, you were unjustly treated, but in what seems to this Job-like complainer, God gives far too cute a dodge for his connivance with Satan, the source of evil.

The wager is a real problem. How could it not be? Still within our memory and the memory of our parents and grandparents, and in the special knowledge of those who survived the camps, are horrific medical tests, experiments really, upon our Jewish brothers and sisters. Of course, scientific knowledge was advanced by Nazi work upon the unknowing and imprisoned who sought only the human entitlement to survival and respect. No responsible ethicist would find justification for the "wager" of Jewish health put at risk to obtain these greater insights into disease.

There is little in Job's story that calms my nervous heart about the bipartisan heaven-hell examination to which he was subjected. At most, God seems more concerned that Job's so-called friends turned out to be total louts in the friendship department. In one fashion or another, each friend told Job that he must have been bad otherwise bad things wouldn't happen to him. Nonsense, said God. And had Job not calmed the Creator down, God would have punished Job's friends for falsely accusing Job of being evil.

This, of course, makes me feel a little better, but I still have the uncomfortable feeling that God has changed the subject.

Indeed, talk about changing the subject, God, but what's all the carrying on about "Where were you when I laid the foundation of the earth? Tell me, if you know so much."[21] You know where Job was. He wasn't there. None of us were there – not Job, not John, not Mary, not me, no one. We owe everything – our life and everything in it – to you. So, my Lord and source of all love and goodness, Job wasn't there nor was I. And please do not ask me, as you asked Job, to "gird up my loins." The

---

[21] Job 38:4.

footnote in my Bible indicates that the verb "to gird" means to be ready to defend myself in debate. While I'm as good a girder (debater) as you're likely to find in the neighborhood, I'm no match for you, God. The little that I know would not amount to a thimble within a thimble of your Divine knowledge, and frankly, I have all I can do to keep up with the Supreme Court; a President who sends me to faraway places to talk of faith; and a few inspectors who say I am not doing my job when I do. God, in girding, I concede.

10. Our Lonely God

Yet, you made us in your image. You made us free, not because freedom is a good thing in and of itself; it is not – after all, it is in that very freedom that we rejected you – well, not me-- Adam and Eve, but don't get me going on vicarious liability or punishing children for goofy parents. The law now makes parents liable for goofy children in many places, so I guess what goes around comes around. But you made us rational beings. We yearn to know our purpose – to know why it is you gave us life. What was your good purpose for the creation of women and men?

Dusting off my Baltimore catechism, the answer to why God made me or anyone pops up easily. It is "to know, love and serve you in this world and the next."

Dear Lord, I think I understand your motivation for that purpose, and it is a darn good one, if you don't mind a compliment from the creature that would have already been hung for blasphemy in certain parts of colonial America for what has been written here. I know you don't need my compliments and I also believe I would simply disappear if you forgot about me for a single second. Nonetheless, and I do hope I am getting this correct, you – even in your almightiness – did *need* us.

Therein is disclosed the rationale for giving us life and all that populates it. *You were alone.* Being alone is no fun. Indeed the alienation of being alone, I suspect, is very much what hell amounts to. It is the antithesis of love, which requires in any meaningful sense another person. So I have always concluded, dear Lord, that you made us out of the desire to manifest your love toward another. Now, I know you have your own little Trinitarian community what with Jesus and the Holy Spirit, but we don't call the Trinity a mystery for nothing. Anyway, if you'll pardon the irreverence, I just can't see Jesus or the Spirit in a bowling shirt or even exhausting the kind of conversational needs I imagine the mind of God enjoys (though admittedly us "little brains" – as Rip Torn in *Defending Your Life* describes us – grasp very little of the vast scope

135

of your mind. (By the way, that's a good movie if you have the time).

If love is your central motivation for those six days of hard work in Genesis. And if again, we are made in your image, it was rational for you to suppose that your demonstration of love for us would be reciprocated. Of course, we let you down; we promptly messed up badly.

Nevertheless, your desire (dare I say again "need" as I italicized earlier) for love cannot be fulfilled or met without freedom. Coerced love is not love. Thus, our profound error in not returning your love freely and fully could not be punished by a denial of freedom in its totality. We have to retain sufficient cognition and ability to make the choice to love you, and by your example, to make the choice to love others.

Yet, dear Lord, when two so beautiful souls as John and Mary are taken in such a harsh and startling manner, your third soul (me) is left with a daily anxiety and burden far greater than his aging (and not overly well made – let's talk later about my Parkinson's disease if you have a moment) – human

136

frame can withstand, yielding to the temptation to ask: "Where were you when the car slipped from the road?" How can you still say, as the Biblical account does, that all those within your influence should follow you? Is it not rational to anticipate even a little skepticism? Now, please don't be angry. There's no point in going on again about you being the only one who could measure the earth and the seas and so forth.

Yes, Almighty Father, I see I'm genuinely close to sounding like Job's wife. While Job's response is nifty ("you have to take the good with the bad when you have no entitlement to anything at all")[22], it is not at all pretty. Indeed, I bet Job was eating very little home cooking for a good long time. And could we really expect Mrs. Job to work through everything when she would hear Job himself say to you, in a less stoic moment: "What is man, that you make much of him or pay him any heed? You observe him with each new day and try him at every moment! How long will it be before you look away

---

[22] *Job* 2:10 (New Living Translation 2007) ("But Job replied, 'You talk like a foolish woman. Should we accept only good things from the hand of God and never anything bad?'").

137

from me, and let me alone long enough to swallow my spittle? Though I have sinned, what can I do to you oh watcher of men? Why do you not pardon my offense or take away my guilt? For soon I shall lie down in the dust; should you seek me I shall then be gone."[23]

Again, Lord, I'm not girding with you, but Job and the Missus have got a point here. If the whole point of creation is to manifest love, is it not time to lighten up just a bit so that it will be true that your yoke is easy and our burden is light?

Let's level with each other here – you lose a lot of people from the ranks of Divine lovers by not having as light a yoke as you may think you do. Sure, we American types may be spoiled with iPods and toaster ovens, but check the recruitment efforts. Are things going real well in developing nations? Take China, which – despite some really top flight missionaries – has never lined up behind you? I'm not telling you anything you don't know of course.

---

[23] *Job* 7:17-21 (New Living Translation 2007).

You know it all. (I didn't mean that as it sounds, but please remember Job's wife's response to the calamity that befell them: "Are you still holding to your innocence? Curse God and die.")[24] With the devil seemingly able to knock off the entire family save Job himself, scrap the house, and plague the livestock, you really couldn't expect chatter about the audacity of hope or the power of positive thinking to carry the day.

Indeed, Job's wife confessed that she had nothing to hope for from you and therefore nothing to live for. I confess to you Lord that to reach that conclusion is to hit a wall much harder than that which took John and Mary and injured me. It is to hit the wall of atheism which today manifests itself in people I love and who are dispirited and depressed by what has befallen a really kind and lovable guy (me). And don't forget France and whatever *laïcité* thing is going on there, or inside the heads of people who think nothing of taking their own lives let alone those of others in Syria,

---

[24] *Job* 2:9. (New Living Translation 2007).

Yemen, Afghanistan and Iraq – and good Lord, Norway? Atheism as far as I see is today the number one killer; a greater malady than any illness in the world.

Figure 3 Ambassador Kmiec among the diplomats welcoming His Holiness Benedict XVI to Malta in April 2010; President Abela, Prime Minister Gonzi and Cardinal Bertone, the Vatican Secretary of State all look on with seeming approval of the Ambassador's observance of the tradition of kissing the ring of Peter.

By the way, nice work getting Benedict XVI the white hat. B-16, as the kids say, is a lot quieter than JPII (say hello Father Wojtyla if you think of it), but a real thinker and he has thoughtfully made secularism his number one concern – well, not counting the priest scandal and all, which is its own nihilism and source of powerful anger for the victims and their families. John, as you know, prayed and prayed that the scandal would pass from the Church, and of course, now the Vatican is not diplomatically talking to Ireland because Irish governmental leaders believe the Vatican has been allowing Irish prelates to overlook the zero-tolerance instruction to report clergy abuse. Ugh, we need help.

A small editorial point, Lord: the profoundly unfortunate turning of Mrs. Job against you, thereby leaving another opening for atheism and the devil, might've been made plainer in the Bible, or at least Job could have taken the Missus' hurt and bewilderment more seriously. Job's response to Mrs. Job's pleas that he might as well give up on you is – to say the least – less than empathetic. Remember what Job said to his questioning wife: "Are even you [now] going to speak as senseless women do?" You may be the girder of girders, Lord, but that line of argument won't make it in the 21st century, trust me. You have the advantage of transcending gender yourself, so there is no reason to light a fuse under gender politics. It will only lead us into divisions that won't help us or our Church. Of course, if you want to take it up, go ahead, but count on using one heck of a lot of gird-power to explain the absence of female priests.

11. Can God Best Satan?

Tell me, Lord, that you can calm this weary and questioning soul. Most of all, Lord, please just reassure us that the bottom line explanation is not going to be the one I fear most – and I really do fear this – that somehow Satan and the forces of evil in our world are greater even than you. This is very hard for a Catholic school child, the one who still lives in this declining old body, to accept, and I won't. From the good book, I know all about not pulling up weeds too early. Indeed, as a young boy with a devout and pious gardening Catholic mother, it was one of my most quoted parables.[25] But now, somehow waiting for the last judgment to smite the old Beelzebub seems like it will be too little too late for a whole lot of people I care about, me, included. Dear Lord, you've always been our cavalry to the rescue. You are our real superhero. You are the source of wisdom greater

---

[25] *Matthew* 13:24-29 (New Living Translation 2007).

than anyone. Please don't allow the old deceiver to out-Madoff, Bernie Madoff?

Now I admit love and protection are not necessarily conjoined. John Sheridan and Mary Campbell were two objects of great love, and yet, no one had any realistic expectation that either of them could defend us against very much of anyone or anything, whether it be from disagreeable fellow parishioners or any of the very colorful animals described in the Job story. (I especially like your interesting observations about the Behemoth, the hippo in the shade.) And, as much as they surely loved me, I wouldn't blame John or Mary if they were spreading a few cautionary words among any of your guardian angels needing an earthly lift to stay clear of ambassadors (or at least this one) driving a sub-compact rental car in a California canyon.

The bottom line, Lord, is that we do have an expectation that our faith actively defends us against evil. And not to beat you over the head with this, but we do not envision a loving God wagering against us. Your son taught us to pray that you would (and therefore, presumably, could), help us avoid temptation.   This is also why we make the prayer to St. Michael to "defend us in battle against the wickedness and snares of the devil who wanders through the earth for the ruin of souls." You are the creator of Saint Michael, right? And if you can delegate to the very formidable Michael our defense in battle against the snares of the devil, might it not be reasonable for us to conclude that you can keep a subcompact car from drifting into a ditch and do such profound harm as occurred on August 25, 2010?

Going back to Job's plight – I'm afraid the answer from that account as to who has the present edge in this world, you or the devil, gives it to the bad guy. The Biblical account recites after all that while Job initially was surrounded with your protection, you withdrew it. The Bible recites that you concede that Job is in Satan's power and that you request merely that the devil does not lay a hand upon his person, that is, take his life. Finding these qualifications in the account of Job are not confidence building. Is it little wonder we Catholics avoided reading the scriptures all these years?

The whole Job story is very messy, Lord. I already hit this point, but it really bothers me. Our government has from time to time hidden various medical experiments from military service personnel or those detained in prison or by state authority as mental patients, and I can tell you that the government never looks good in these cases. Let me be blunt: the wager with Satan over the behavior of Job, with or without reward, stinks. From a personal standpoint, the crash on August 25, 2010 stinks worse.

All of this amounts to the conclusion that there is evil in the world that is seemingly beyond your control. I'm sorry, but what else could we conclude? Of course, the conquering of evil in **this** world is not your father's business? Your son, in his preaching, was honest about that; Give unto Caesar, after all, what is Caesar's.

Of course it is your choice how strongly or modestly to protect us against the forces of evil and against our own weakness which is a manifestation of that evil. Nevertheless, as someone who really loves you, let me recommend that you up the protection so long as doing so does not blatantly deprive us of free will. Since genuine love must be free, give us weaklings, the freedom to love you. But take an extra step or two to see that the world is not so much in the control of Satan.

Before concluding, let me confess what is by now obvious to the reader: John Sheridan never once doubted your ultimate goodness and embrace even as his suffering was great. Moreover, in asking here for your greater help, I am not shirking my own responsibility. You and I have opportunities to love more abundantly and lessen the pain and suffering of others.

A final confession and expression of gratitude: My grasp of the selfless love of suffering is weak. I am today largely sustained in faith by even more unearned gifts: the prayers of Monsignor John's wonderful families and thousands in America and in Malta, my ambassadorially-adopted home. Their kind forgiveness and understanding in those prayers was truly redemptive and sustaining. Indeed, six months later when my immediate family was in the States for Christmas, I actually felt both grateful and eager to feel again the pain of hospital treatment – (very good treatment I might add, but unavoidably painful in some respects).

While the paradox of suffering still rattles unsettled in my head, and I have been a little critical here. I do take great heart in the manner in which you, dear Lord, treated Sister Mary. Sister Mary made the journey to eternity, as best as we can tell from this vantage point, without extended, and if the medical technicians are correct, any suffering at all. How this fits the overall understanding of suffering I haven't a clue. The Catholic school child in me hears the voices of more nuns than I can count, saying something to the effect, "Douglas, you really are slow! God knows better than to make His religious women endure any more redemptive suffering when they have served priest and parishioner alike, often thanklessly or at least with far less of the earthly attention paid to you men." Good answer? I think so. At least it will have to do, lest I look forward to an eternity of ruler slaps and red-knuckles for being too obtuse to accept the obvious.

I do appreciate that while you did not keep this terrible tragedy from my life, you did extend your protection against my falling prey to evil thereafter by sending to me so many, friend and stranger alike in the United States and in Europe (most notably Malta, Ireland, and Belgium) with the message that they were all praying for me. I can never be grateful enough to you and to those you sent, especially to those who opened their hearts and memories to disclose that they had gone through something similar and had hidden it from view. These prayerful friends would often reflect on how it might make me feel better to know I was not alone.

It does, Lord, feel better not to be alone, doesn't it? But you know that, and I hope you also know that I love you. Let's wind up this chapter, then, by at last turning to Monsignor John's own reflection on suffering:

As thinking human beings we must confront ourselves with the question of why a good God should permit so much suffering. What's the purpose of it all? Again, there is no answer to this question as there is no answer to the ultimate question of being or existence. We simply do not have the capacity for comprehending God's mind.

John reminded us that we don't understand suffering because our mind is not as great as God's. Our conception of goodness is limited. If we had a choice, John wrote, we *would spare those we love all suffering because we do not comprehend interior values like courage and devotion. Love can, in our search for superficial pleasure, fall too easily before the immediate prize of the ease, money or success in a very worldly sense. We want happiness without effort and struggle; yet effort and struggle is the price for ultimate happiness. And effort and struggle means suffering.*

We can understand suffering only in terms of genuine love, and true love is the gift of self. Gifts, exterior gifts, unless they symbolize the gift of our self, are mere deceptions. Every selfless effort we make is a gift of self and an expression of love. If we can conceive of life as a continuous giving of self we are on the way to understanding suffering as the moral adventure of love, and adventure culminating in God's accepting us and uniting us to himself after the final pangs of death in our final act of self-giving is passed.

Part IV

The Great Summation of Faith

12. Trust in God

*T*he word faith is derived from the Latin,
*fidere, to trust. In the intellectualist spirit
of the time, the medieval theologians used
the Latin Fides to mean our assenting to the
Creeds. This was of course correct, but did not
express comprehensively the act **of trusting
and of entrusting ourselves** with total
confidence like Abraham and Paul and Jesus **to
God**.*

The idea of trusting and entrusting ourselves is
one to which we proclaim to yearn, but except in
our most devout moments of prayer, if we are
honest -- really honest -- with ourselves, seldom
do we truly feel we are accomplishing a total
submission. Why is it so difficult? Why do we
resist the notion that God will provide? Could it
be because in what we perceive around us, God
isn't providing?

After all, in affluent America, hundreds of
thousands have been evicted from their homes

and millions are out of work. In Syria, tank battalions of Syrians are killing other Syrians petitioning for freedom. In Somalia, drought causes famine while terrorist organizations block the provision of food. And in our individual lives, we sit numb before these profound events week after week offering petitions to God just hoping that by His grace nothing similar – even remotely similar – comes into our lives.

Yes, we believe, but it is very often unchallenged or casual belief. "Blessed be those who are persecuted for righteousness sake," but except for a few out of place jokes, we do not suffer for our faith. Recently, President Obama let homosexual persons serve in the military, and some fundamentalists objected. Catholic organizations would like a wider exemption not to have to buy insurance for employees who might independently buy contraceptives, but this hardly amounts to a "war on religion," which seems contradicted by, well, just about everything. Now it can be ticklish to raise faith-based questions, and some people like saying "Happy Holidays," which prompts others to sneer back, "hey, don't you mean: "Merry Christmas, buddy." "Yeah, peace on earth to you too, pal."

Many people reduce faith to such trivialities of expression, and that is unfortunate. Similarly, others view faith as the equivalent of fate or providence. Parents, for example, tuck children into bed thanking God for a good day, but spend little time thinking about the role of a believer to actively work to make the day turn out well. Even closer to home – mine and a lot of other parents of the baby boom generation – every few days, we call our single young adult children in their late 20s and 30s and pick up a definite disinterest in marriage and family, or to put it off as long as possible. We may silently pray for them as well, but we say we can only love them; we cannot dictate their lives. Frankly, though there would be far less anxiety if we could just have a peek at the script, and discern some Catholic sensibility emerging in the near term.

We want the happy ending, and we think faith

must be part of it, but often we do not actually assign it one. In faith, we say, we are just hoping for the best. We do not know what lies ahead. Instead, we content ourselves in telling our children, our parents, our closest and dearest friends, that by our every action and thought, we earnestly wish them health and happiness – in family, friendship, and career, and if there is anything we can do to help, we will. And, to the best of our station, we do: we seek out Catholic schools or at least good neighborhoods that reinforce family in public instruction; we drill our "scholar" children who would rather be doing just about anything else but studying for the college boards; we petition friends to open a door for a summer job; we keep the children afloat economically when the undergraduate degree seems to require yet another or simply a boost. We share our monetary resources as prudently as we can to assist an elderly mother or father, pay for college, give some to a favored charity (in exchange for community praise or some item in a silent auction or both) and we hope as we near our end that there is a positive balance left to pay our final bills upon our passing. This level of faith suffices for most people on most days in most places.

But then, the unwanted happens – the loss of a job; a child addicted to drugs and in trouble with the police; the untimely death of a spouse or parent; a failure of a business venture; a fatal car accident – and suddenly we must ask faith to sustain us against an emotional pain we had not previously experienced or ever expected to endure. It is no longer possible just to listen empathetically about the injured or the starving populations a world away on the News Hour or simply to commiserate with our neighbor about her son's drug addiction. There is no change of subject before sitting down to dinner or turning back to work.

At a parish celebration of his 60 years of priestly service to the diocese of Los Angeles, John implied strongly that if we would examine with him what faith is, and is not, we would see how total submission to God is inescapable for a living faith.

And nothing but a faith truly alive can help us get beyond real persecution and tragic events.

Here, then, is John's great summation of the elements of faith:

Faith is not and cannot be a mere assent to statements about God, about the Church, about life.

Faith is my personal search and surrender to all that is.

It is my acceptance and affirmation of life.

It is my journeying inward, onward, and upward toward God, even when God seems silent.

Faith is, sometimes, dying to myself.
It is my going out in love.

When I am tempted, obsessively tempted, to center on myself or on persons and things that fascinate me,

The mystery of faith confronts and envelops me
in this very going beyond myself,
in reaching into the depths of myself.

In transcending myself I find myself,
and in the process I meet God.

13. Withstand the Challenge of Tragedy

On the beautiful late November morning in 2005, when John presented his great summation of faith in the previous chapter, the Monsignor was, as one observer wrote, "luminous." In no one's contemplation on that happy day was its antithesis: a day that would draw to a close so darkly five years later that were a script writer to propose it as a story line, it would be renounced as overly cruel. Perhaps for that reason, the dark tragedy of August 25, 2010 needed to hide itself behind a morning as beautiful as the festival for John in 2005; but this time it was a liturgical celebration for Sister Mary's religious order and their effective ministry in the U.S. There, too, Monsignor would be feted – more simply than at his 60th anniversary as a priest in 2005 – but equally genuinely as the representative of the best qualities of the priests of the diocese in their collaborations with the religious Sisters of Saint Louis and other orders. Soon after, the accident would claim Mary and result in physical injury that a few weeks later would take John's life.

The emotional impact and challenge to faith represented by the accident is ever present in my mind.

The accident has a relentless ability to insert itself into *everything.* On days when it does, it seems a punishment worse than death – particularly if one remains optimistic about eternity. If we are in a state of grace and prepared for the final judgment, death becomes us, or perhaps it is better said that a natural death in the fullness of grace allows us to become what it is impossible to become in earthly exile. In the words of the song "Going Home", our burdens are lifted. But if we survive, the burden is not lifted, but magnified and then imposed over and over again. Find yourself enjoying a movie like Emilio Estevez's "The Way," starring his dad, Martin Sheen; the heart thinks of John or Mary and pushes enjoyment aside. Glance out at the blue Pacific, and the memory of John's lengthy walks along the bluffs – no longer possible – drain the color out of the most unusual ocean pigment.

Within our family, these lingering emotions spill

over and can hurt spouse and children. In my case, the lingering emotions may even find their way to compound the hate of some partisans, who hide behind an ostensible fidelity to the Church in order to launch epithets and distortions in my direction and that of any Catholic voter who in the last election resolved to endorse Barack Obama. The same invective from the right seems to be starting anew in 2012. Don't see the connection to the accident? There isn't one, unless you want to claim that the accident was a Divine punishment for my endorsing then-Senator Obama.

This is not the place to re-run the 2008 campaign, forecast campaign behavior in the present or to lump many responsible conservative voices or the Church hierarchy with irrational blogs, but it was no surprise when the purveyors of hate left over from the campaign wrote across the internet: "Baby killer kills nun."

14. Be Untroubled by the Uncertain

The experience of having the written word provoke unexpected anger or disruption in our lives is one Monsignor and I shared. Indeed, both of us had Catholic syndicated columns revoked, as it were, for inquiring into whether there was more than one way to be faithful to the Magisterium teaching – in John's case, regarding contraceptive practice; and in mine, abortion.

In both cases, the kindest of our objectors would simply claim that even asking such questions was preempted. Neither the Monsignor nor myself ever argued in the teeth of infallible teaching; but by the same token, we were in agreement that a Catholic university of any tradition needed to explore the challenges to faith from the sciences, secular philosophy, and other disciplines.

It distressed the Monsignor when my popular and widely syndicated column – "Faith and Precedent" – for the Catholic News Service was "suspended."

163

Having been asked by then-Senator Obama to be part of his outreach to Catholic constituencies especially, it made some sense for me to put my pen down and to not write on the campaign. But then, what doesn't get spoken of in political campaign? It was prudent not to jeopardize a long-standing and valued relationship with the Catholic News Service (CNS), which I assumed would resume post-election when I returned to university teaching in California.

There was to be no resumption. The prudent action of stepping aside during the campaign merely gave an opening to a handful of partisan, anti-Obama blogs to put pressure on the bishops (who responsibly oversee the CNS) to not welcome me back into the pages of Catholic newspapers, even as until then the column was frequently one of the most popular. With the column suspended, I had more time to trek across the country during the presidential campaign as part of the then-Senator's "Faith and Values" tour, speaking extensively at college campuses, parishes, and meeting halls throughout four pivotal swing states with a significant Catholic presence: Ohio, Pennsylvania, Michigan and Indiana. Obama would win them all by margins significantly greater than Bush in the 2004 election.

What was the substance of my talks? The details can be found in the book *Can A Catholic Support Him? Asking the Big Question about Barack Obama.*[26] For the most part, I would highlight Senator Obama's work to moderate the previously very pro-abortion language of his party's platform, as well as emphasize his foresight in being the only candidate – Democrat or Republican – to vote against the intervention in Iraq. On this, Obama's reasoning was similar to that of the Holy Father, who had pleaded with George W. Bush, through the Papal Nuncio, for a response other than war. Beyond that, candidate Obama often gave emphasis to the need to responsibly address the economic needs of those in the middle and lower tiers of our society. These needs were great: millions were without health care; there was a

---

[26] Douglas W. Kmiec, *supra*

stubbornly high rate of unemployment; and there seemed a growing separation of the very rich and everybody else that cried out for regulatory and tax changes. The Senator also articulated a level of environmental stewardship – talking favorably of alternative fuels – and meeting the dangers of climatic change. Many, if not most, of these matters put Barack Obama on the same side as the Catholic bishops in America and in Europe.

On abortion, Obama and the Church were far apart, and this would naturally be of great concern to me and any other Catholic voter. It was never my view – or the Monsignor's – that abortion could be justified, but in practical reality, I suggested that adequate pre-natal health care would likely do more to reduce the incidence of abortion by meeting the glaring needs of women in poverty than would more lobbying for laws that the Supreme Court was certain to invalidate. (John, along with some of those "wretched Jesuit" friends of his at Loyola University in Los Angeles, helped me find the right words to express this.)

166

Years earlier, John had engaged a similarly hot topic in Catholic circles: contraception. In a column for *The Tidings,* John did not write contrary to the teaching of the Church – that teaching proscribes artificial contraception; but John did ask whether the Church fathers might take up the role, if any, of individual conscience. On a long summer walk through Paradise Cove, John described for me in detail how he was told that the answer was: "No."

That was not the answer reached by extraordinary intellects in the Church, like John Noonan, who had served in a consultative role on the topic for the Vatican and a number of prominent theologians around the globe. Nevertheless, John would be penalized; not for contradicting the constant teaching of the Church, but for asking how it fit together with other aspects or applications of the Magisterium. As reflected below, today (40-plus years later), the Holy Father has taken up John's question, asking (as John did then), what if any role condom usage might play in efforts to avoid the spread of disease.

In the earlier contretemps, John had both the courage in faith to inquire – to "stir the flame" – and (when his inquiry was thought by the hierarchy of the time to be too incendiary (or at least confusing), to obediently (albeit reluctantly) withdraw and to clarify. I tried, with John's guidance, to follow that respectful and obedient path as well. John loved the Church, and never once did he in my presence denigrate the judgment of the Churchmen, high or low, with whom he disagreed. Interestingly, it is now the highest churchman, the Holy Father himself, who is making John's inquiries.

Monsignor John would admire Pope Benedict's probing of the question of the extent to which permitting condom usage may be the only realistic way to protect life against the spread of disease. It is important that the thinking of the Pope be heard in his own words.

In the book, *Light of the World*, (written in a question and answer format at pages 117-119), Pope Benedict XVI includes this question (and his answer to it)*:* "In Africa you stated that the Church's traditional teaching has proven to be the only sure way to stop the spread of HIV. Critics, including critics from the Church's own ranks, object that it is madness to forbid a high-risk population to use condoms." To which Benedict XVI responded: "[The Church] of course does not regard [contraception] as a real or moral solution, but, in this or that case, there can be nonetheless, in the intention of reducing the risk of infection, a first step in a movement towards a different way, a more human way, of living sexuality."

Might Benedict XVI now be responding to a higher heavenly voice – one with a kindly Irish tone -- that in its variation seems to have the capacity to insert parenthetical footnotes? I am not prepared to say, but John left the following additional notes with me; and based on our conversation, I am confident he would want me to share them at this moment of thoughtful papal inquiry:

Throughout our lives in our Faith, our beliefs or morals are often tested, sometimes to the crisis point. It's then, Paul tells us, to stir into flames this priceless gift, our Faith. In the Summer of 1968, an article of mine in the Sunday Visitor circulated nationally, and was sensationalized — not near as badly as it would be now – in the Los Angeles Times. *It so upset the late Cardinal McIntyre that I was notified under threat of suspension from my priestly ministry to retract immediately and publicly what I had written. The Cardinal, my superior, was a holy and highly respected, very conservative man with whom I continued to enjoy a warm relationship. Now by his orders I [had to] retract something which the vast majority of theologians and I believed, and believed sincerely, to be eminently correct and within the authentic teaching of the church. It may still be.*

. . . . It was a period of great depression for me, but I obeyed, and wrote my final article in The Tidings quoting from Saint Paul and his admonition that we "Stir into flame this gift of God, your Faith."

The lectionary out of which the readings for the daily Mass are provided indicate that, a few days after John's burial in 2010, this favorite passage of the Monsignor's from Paul writing to Timothy came around again. Coincidence? Maybe, but as alluded to above, the Monsignor is likely now in a greater position to help "stir the flame" of faith – a flame that will outshine all the dull tarnish of Church scandal and the corrosive effects of sin and inertia, including addressing the use of contraceptives made by many to avoid disease or to minimize the conditions that give rise to abortion. The Monsignor inquired whether there was room for individual conscience. The Monsignor was ahead of the curve. At the time John was writing in the arc of *Humane Vitae* (1968), His Holiness Paul VI thought it his encyclical duty to reaffirm the teaching that still abides in the Church that contraceptive use generally cannot be a matter of individual conscience. Uncomfortably this view finds millions of married Catholic women around the globe at odds with their Church.

St. Thomas Aquinas taught that the law must not ask more than can be reasonably expected from an imperfect being, and (specifically as commented upon in the preface) that the law not presume to enact every virtue and prohibit every vice. The reading of the letter from Paul to Timothy as Monsignor instructed can be understood in the same fashion. It does not urge rebellion against the instruction of the Church, but instead asks, as Saint Thomas does, what the limits of the positive law are in light of natural law which cannot be contradicted in our lived experience?

With due respect, ending the Monsignor's regular column in Catholic newspapers imposed a greater penalty upon us than him. It would have been much to our benefit had John not been asked to discontinue his respectful inquiries – inquiries which the Holy Father has now forty years later found appropriate to ask as part of a living faith.

15. Be Not Forever Mournful

Recalling the intellectual vibrancy of my many tea and toast conversations with the Monsignor, there are still very dark moments when I find his absence too great to accept. It is a fair statement that anyone who sees me is also prompted to think of John and Mary, and while all express understanding, and with great kindness, make offers of prayer, I fear in the local community that I am now a constant reminder evoking sorrow.

Do I have my own prayer?

Yes.

It is that the profound sorrow of today not be forever; that a day might soon arrive when my appearance will simply remind those who loved John and Mary, as I did, of the faith their witness nourished in life, and hopefully, by means of this

173

volume, sustains into the future.

The continuing legacy of John Sheridan should be understood as one anchored in an optimistic faith. This optimism asks us to see the signs of God's presence in our lives. Indeed, it sensitizes us to the signs of blessing that we might otherwise miss. The Monsignor believed this to be especially important because so much that is reported to us daily is only in the negative: unemployment, the trends of the stock market, even tomorrow's weather forecast with overstated concerns of rain or inclemency.

Monsignor John would put it this way: *Despite all the bitterness, the killings, the madness, the wars; if we look around at what is happening in our own country, we will see the signs, powerful signs of God's positive ways extending to all peoples.*

With Mary's presence near the back of the Church at morning Mass, the Monsignor would refresh her radiant smile and awaken all of us with his characteristic: "Oh, blessed, blessed day." John reminds us that what strengthens our faith is not always a blessing directly received. We must rejoice in the good fortune of others and draw strength from prayers answered, even if they are not ours. In this way, if we look, we will see a myriad of signs of Our Lord working among us.

John continues:

I think of a young woman just released from the hospital, fighting the very common addiction of alcohol. A few days ago, she was literally dying, dying from the effects of a drug she was unable to handle. Now God is giving her a new life and a new grace to begin again. This is an individual story, but each individual story is the story of God, the story of His universe.

And each one of us has a story; we are a sign of faith for others as well as ourselves; something surprising, sad, joyous, even ordinary, but since God is ever present, there are abundant signs – if we only see them – to begin again. These are the signs of faith renewed.

It is in Sister Mary that the innocent little children found their first signs of faith.

16. Mary's Sign

In life, Mary Campbell walked upon the earth with gentleness as if on tiptoe. She enjoyed riding her bicycle through the green, hilly lanes of the countryside. In later years, she similarly loved walking to the Marian Shrine at Knock, County Mayo. It was there, on August 21, 1879, that

Our Lady, St. Joseph and St. John the Evangelist appeared at the south gable of the Knock Parish Church.

Over a dozen people, young and old, witnessed this miraculous apparition. Sister Mary took special pride in the fact that Pope John Paul II in 1979 commemorated the apparition, which in Ireland and elsewhere has been of great influence. Mother Teresa, for example, made special note of it, and over 1 1/2 million people visit the shrine every year. Sister Mary loved to tell her classes of the luminous and positive changes that came about in the lives of the children who witnessed Our Lady, and she would say, "Let Our Lady make your hearts especially beautiful. You must simply believe."

Sister Mary was constantly surrounded by
children. She delighted in their presence in her
classroom; in her school offices as principal; and
always, always in her shared creativity at the art
table. Mary would ask in prayer each day not for
special favor for herself, but for the blessing of her
deep faith to be reflected in the lives of the little
ones she was teaching. She earnestly sought to
have her teaching and pastoral ministry each day
reveal some small part of the light of faith that the
miraculous appearance of Our Lady in 1879
brought to the children in Knock, so close to her
own village.

One of the engaging, and most effective, ways in
which Mary succeeded in this effort was by helping
young minds to see the magnificence of God's
creation around them. And as these young,
impressionable eyes took in genuine beauty that
the modern, video-centered culture often obscured,
Mary guided their young hands to sketch the
beauty so evident around them, but without her
example of patience, they might have missed.

Mary was especially happy when the children filled her classroom with paper gardens of bright yellow sunflowers, African daisies, birds of paradise, and butterflies. As each day drew to a close, John and Mary delighted in the small, simple, but elegant gardens adjoining the parish church. Often they could be seen reciting their evening prayers among not just the paper gardens of her students, but the actual flowers which were so well-tended by the parish gardener, Mario. That which God brought from the ground was now in friendly competition with those tended by the crayon and cultured-penciled hands of Mary's children.

When Sister Mary's family brought her cremated remains back to Ireland, they placed the urn safely in an honored place in the family's ancestral home in Kiltimagh at the end of the summer 2010. It would be a day or so before the proper funeral Mass and blessing at the cemetery could take place. It was with some wonderment, therefore, when Mary's siblings watched as a golden butterfly entered the room and settled upon the top of the urn. Mary's sister, Angela, worried at first that the delicate creature would not survive separated from the fresh, ever moist Irish countryside, and so she gently released the butterfly into the outdoors and went to make tea. Before she could take the cup from the cabinet and bring the kettle to a boil, the butterfly returned. Another sister, Peg, escorted the fragile creature outside a second time, only to have the butterfly return to make one *final* circle over Mary's remains before taking wing and departing.

In truth, it is something of an error to use the word "final" in reference to Mary. Those of us fortunate enough to have walked with Mary in life feel her vital presence still. And if we ever needed a reminder of her joyfulness, there is little question that the Holy Spirit would choose the form of a butterfly to remind us of Mary.

On the day and at the appointed hour of Mary Campbell's funeral, a golden butterfly fluttered again; this time, above the grave site.

Skeptical? No one would blame you. This is a rational world, after all. But one must be careful not to deify mere rationality and leave no place for miracles, or for signs and symbols of a force that transcends this world. Skepticism can open as well as close the mind to the presently unexplainable. Faith has nothing to fear from an open mind or responsible inquiry. That is not the skepticism that leads to close off discussion with a smug attitude that seeks to put only God to His proofs. The fact is that we scarcely have an understanding of the present world, let alone any description of the next. In the day-to-day practice of science, every step is not a matter of empirical verification. It could not be or the process of discovery would be slowed interminably. Much of what we call science is taken on faith, though in the vocabulary of the particular discipline it may be called a hypothesis or premise or presumption.

We do not know the mind of God, but we believe we have been created in His *thinking* image. Thought is not the antagonist of faith; it is reason's collaborator. As suggested earlier in our discussion of the Monsignor's discipline for suggesting a larger role for individual conscience, the best understanding of the Catholic tradition expects reason and faith to be mutually reinforcing.

While we do not know the mind of God, we have been given insight through Revelation directly and in that which can be inferred from what God has written upon our hearts.

The Theology of Kindness offers tangible proof to a skeptical world. It is proof found in the blessings and signs of the miraculous effect of the expressions of love given sincerely by one person to another. Sister Mary Campbell was the embodiment of that love. Her love was given freely and generously to the parish and in assistance to the Monsignor.

Figure 4. Monsignor Sheridan and Sister Mary Campbell in prayer in the gardens of Our Lady of Malibu (Spring 2010). (Photo Credit: Glen Sunyich of the faculty of the OLM School.

Mary's life was also a sign; it reveals something very important for those of us who can never hope to rise to the most senior position in our firms, or government offices, or even given the greatest respect within our local communities, families and households. For many generations, it was commonplace to preclude women from positions of leadership. The traditions of female religious orders like the Sisters of Saint Louis resulted; and no surprise, the capability of women leaders became superabundant. Nevertheless, putting aside wrongful or irrational gender distinctions, part of the Lord's plan is manifested in difference.

In 1630, as John Winthrop was crossing the ocean to settle the Massachusetts Bay Company, he noted in his famous sermon aboard the *Arabella* that: "God Almighty in His most holy and wise providence has so disposed of the condition of mankind, as in all times some must be rich, some poor but it is, some high and eminent in power and dignity; others mean and in submission..."[27] Winthrop was illustrating how differences in talent lead to the formation of community and our interdependence. Winthrop continued that "every[one] might have need of others, and from hence they might be all knit more nearly together in the bonds of brotherly affection."[28] In brief, as

---

[27] That we have unequal talent or wealth, however, does not mean that we are unequal before God. We are not.

[28] JOHN WINTHROP, A MODELL OF CHRISTIAN CHARITY (1630), *available at* http://history.hanover.edu/texts/winthmod.html.

my late father used to say, it takes all kinds to make a community. If all of us were uniformly expert at the same things our communities, first of all, would be quite narrow, and second, we would have little need to rely upon others. As it is, we have been made greatly dependent, not just upon our mothers who nursed us; but upon all those with special capability or expertise, be it in the most intellectual subject like theology or epistemology, or in the applied, highly practical sciences that are embodied in systems of electricity, plumbing or IT networks.

We need each other. Out of that need we are given many opportunities to be loving and kind, to exercise understanding. Here's where Mary was such a truly humble and fine example: to be enormously happy simply to care for others, even when one of those in her care – the Monsignor – had a national, if not international, reputation as being a truly saintly and wise counselor. It would be only natural for those witnessing the Monsignor's super-star status to feel some lack of capacity, perhaps even jealousy. None of us, including Mary, could ever hope to be his equal.

Indeed, the extent of Mary's love for the Monsignor was on full display at the morning Mass in honor of the Sisters of St. Louis hours before the accident. At the Mass, the auxiliary Bishop made special mention of John's graciousness and felicity in dealing with the women religious orders of the diocese. The Bishop thanked John for the use of his special gifts as a representative of all of the priests in the diocese. Sister Mary was not jealous of this well-deserved praise, but took pride in it. In a wink and a smile that only Mary Campbell could convey with soft subtlety, she immediately displayed gratitude on John's behalf and the love in her heart.

To take pride and to find happiness in the success of others is an indispensable part of the Theology of Kindness. Yet, in order to do that we must understand who we are and who we are not. Sometimes parents pretend to be amused at the end of sports season when all of the boys and girls playing T-ball, for example, get trophies. This uniformity of treatment is perhaps more for the parent than for the child; but it should not be used to deny our natural differences, since this is the basis upon which we depend upon each other to meet different needs.

To say that someone is not the equal of another in matters of erudition or skill is far different from proclaiming someone to be unequal before God because of gender or race or other condition over which the person has no control. All are equal before God. Mary Campbell and John Sheridan were equal before God even as they had very different callings. They accepted them. They accepted their difference, and in this they were alert for a sign of how best to honor God. Conversely, they were likewise alert for a sign when they were seeking to become something that they were not – a form of pretension, or a lie.

"Our day-to-day lives are filled with signs," Mary would remind her children in the classroom as she read from the great books, or demonstrated the uses of color to help bring out onto the sketch pad (the aspects of hidden beauty within the young minds whose hands could scarcely keep up with the inspiration Mary supplied). And reflecting on her own calling, Mary would continue: "You must be alert for those signs that guide you well to where you are most needed."

There's no question that Mary Campbell brought many souls who had been misdirected by the allure and corrupting symbols of modern culture back onto the path of salvation. In this, it is proper to say that Mary's most lasting sign is the sign of the cross. The little ones will be giving witness to their faith and the memory of Mary so long as school children are taught to begin the day "In the name of the Father, and the Son, and the Holy Spirit."

These pleasant memories of Mary deserve a short story. Call it (and you will see why in a minute) a side salad.

On very special days, my morning tea and toast sessions extended into lunch. This had its hazards. Once John invited me to lunch, saying

with great confidence that he could provide us with
a very fine salad; and sure enough, there were two
tossed salads on his small table in his rooms or
chambers. John always wore a full dress apron to
keep the food from dressing his shirt, and he
extended one to me. If I didn't take it, I almost
always regretted it as I took my tie to the cleaners
later. As we sat down and took healthy portions of
lettuce and fresh tomato, the door swung open,
and the bright and cheery Mary Campbell sat down
at the table a bit curious as to why an interloper
named Doug was eating her freshly tossed salad.
John, realizing his error, but not wanting his tea
and toast buddy (who if he stayed any longer would
have been there for a sleepover) feel in the least
uncomfortable. Ever so discreetly but also ever so
noticeably, John tried to slip Mary portions of his
own salad on his teacup dish. First, the tomato;
then the carrot, cucumber, and even a few pieces
of lettuce on the side. I pretended not to notice
until I caught Mary's eye and the three of us broke
out laughing. "Mary," I said, "don't worry. When
John next invites me over to lunch, I'll make
certain he is not inviting me to yours."

17. Carrying forth Mary's Signs of Faith

Even in a hurried and too anonymous world, we are richly blessed by the positive encouragement of others who come along side us at the most difficult times in our lives and hold us up. Monsignor John had some insightful words about the importance to the sustenance of faith to be derived from the support of a spouse and friends:

I have walked with Doctors, Priests, Friends in hospitals and lonely nursing homes, where poor old neglected mothers were wandering aimlessly in the corridors, alone, dreadfully alone, too broken hearted to allow the sights and sounds of better days to visit their memories. Wanting, wanting to die, to be away from the drudgery and ingratitude of it all.

In contrast, I have witnessed miracles at the words of a friend, man and woman, daughter, mother, priest, doctor, engineer, garbage collector - I saw the surge of life radiate the faces, eyes, bodies of those lonely abandoned people at words spoken by a companion. This miracle of caring I have seen more than once.

Very importantly I have seen these signs strengthening faith; I have seen it in the love of a spouse caring for a marriage partner who has been prematurely disabled or in the visit to a shut-in from a cherished friend. These moments have come to my notice when I was discouraged or dumbfounded and I didn't have the faith, the courage, the grace to speak, to listen, to hear God's word and to carry that word into that place, at that moment.

Thank God, the other times, when I did listen, did speak the word, touch the brother or sister crying out for just that simple touch, and suddenly there was new life; new life was theirs.

Our faith can make all the difference in the faith life of another – the unbelieving heart is a lonely one. Let us not fail to sustain each other.

Pray for peace, yes; but better yet, work for it – feed the hungry; clothe the naked; provide drink for those who thirst. That, as Monsignor and Sister

Mary would aver, is the *living* faith. A living faith is dynamically getting past the grief and the "what ifs" by taking advantage of the promise of God's infinite mercy in the present. In sustaining the faith of another, we reaffirm Our Lord's willingness to forgive and embrace us no matter how heinous or tragic our actions if we are sincerely contrite.

Part V

Skyping Kindness

18. John, I can see you, but not hear you

Whenever I accepted an assignment away from California, John and I promised to stay in regular contact. The ambassadorship in Malta presented the greatest challenge. Malta being 20 some hours away by air and in a time zone 9 hours ahead of California, it would take some forward planning. Bless him, neither John nor myself kept orderly calendars. Sister Mary was John's constant and constantly cheerful reminder of time and place, and so Sister arranged for a minimum Skype contact on Fridays (9:00 a.m. Pacific; 6:00 p.m. Malta). Lenese Walls, my office manager at the Embassy, put the conversation appointment with John as a virtually immovable object on my calendar. And so our "tea and toast" sessions continued, minus the tea and also minus the toast.

To watch John and I Skype made good theatre for Mary, and other parishioners and friends who wandered through my Office or John's chambers.

At first, John would get sound when I would have video. This was a bad exchange. Not that I didn't delight in seeing John even in silent mode on the screen, but more often than not, John's PC camera was pointing at his shoes or the fireplace rather than himself. And surely, I would gain far more by hearing him than vice versa. Earlier, remember, John wrote of missing my discussion class at the parish, claiming "to be unable to hear." On mornings when the 8:00 a.m. Mass began at 8:15, we would tease him: "Not hearing the alarm now, is it, John?"

Gradually over the months, we mastered the technology and we were quite proud of ourselves – as Mary would tell you. We got so good at the device that we would introduce guest speakers into the conversation. One Friday, for example, I introduced Suha Arafat, the widow of Yasser, to John. He thoroughly enjoyed Suha's exuberant personality and her reports of personal efforts to bring sanity to the long conflict between Israel and Palestine. Of course, interesting visiting Skypers were not always available; so on most occasions, we would just have to entertain each other. I wasn't all that interesting. Once when I was droning on and on in my State Department bureaucratese about something or other, I heard rather loud snoring from the Malibu end of the connection. I couldn't see John on camera, but of course, as related above, that was not at all unusual. "Mary," I said "what is that noise?" "Oh Doug," the sweetheart Mary says matter-of-factly, "the Monsignor is fast asleep on the couch, but he told me to insist you keep things going on your end as long as you like."

As the weeks of my foreign service became months and the months a year, you could tell John was growing weary of my job reports and our separation. With respect to the former, John could sense across the thousands of miles that there was something I was holding back. As will be discussed shortly, it was true; John was reading my heart. I had been sent by President Obama with some important inter-faith diplomatic efforts in mind, and much to my frustration, there was unexpected and unhelpful resistance within the State Department in Washington, DC. I very much wanted to speak with John about it and get his advice, but I refrained not wanting the Monsignor to be disappointed in the President.

"Not wanting him to be disappointed in the President"? Weird, huh? Maybe not. John went out on the religious limb to advise and help Obama through my writing and campaigning, so I felt a bit of the guarantor. The President just barely achieved wider health care availability – less than either John or I would have liked and too heavily dependent on the existing insurance structure. Moreover, the most conservative Catholic bishops were again arguing that the expanded insurance would ultimately mean remote taxpayer support for abortion. I don't think that's entirely right, especially in view of a clarifying executive order from the President expressly precluding funding, or at least indicating the executive intent to preclude it. Nevertheless, without being able to sit down with John for a tea and toast through lunch session for a thorough study of the complex health legislation – where we might even get Mary her own plate – we put that discussion off as well. No doubt about it, we needed to see each other – and not just whatever we saw on Skype. Even Skype loses its magic when friends have been deprived of literally walking upon common ground.

Without a common experience to laugh over and dissect, this hum-drum "how's the weather" Skyping for a number of weeks convinced John that some of the explicit reasons for President Obama to appoint me to Malta had been resolved or completed. When I broke down and related the internal difficulties with the inter-faith project, John shared my frustration, and we agreed to devote a good trail walk to working it out when next we met. "All will be well," the Monsignor would say, quoting Julian of Norwich. I mentioned that it looked like I would be able to be back in the States at least for a break sometime in summer 2010, probably mid-to-late August. "Oh, that's so good, Doug," the Monsignor would say. "All your friends here miss you and Pepperdine just announced that it needs a new dean for the law school." The previous and highly effective dean, Ken Starr, decided unexpectedly to take the presidency of Baylor University in his native Texas. "That should be your position now, Doug," the Monsignor would pronounce with all the authority a Catholic can have over a dean-ship that the Protestant Church of Christ-affiliated school had – appropriately in my judgment – reserved for those sharing in its history directly. "We'll see, John," I said lamely. Nevertheless, from that point onward John would seem to open and close our weekly Skype sessions with the query: "When are you coming home? I won't be lasting forever you know." The words today make me smile and tear up at the same time.

19. John, I can hear you now, but not see you

No one who wants to practice the Catholic faith has an excuse for not doing so in Malta. Indeed, Malta has over 365 Catholic churches.

In our weekly Skype sessions, John would inquire of the commitment I made upon my appointment as U.S. Ambassador to this ancient and deeply faith-filled Republic. "365 churches, why, that's one for every day." "Make sure you go," was the presidential response.

I strove to visit all of Malta's churches at least once for daily Mass. I didn't make it. After attending morning Mass at perhaps a third or so of the churches (those nearest to home), it became increasingly difficult both to make it to a distant church and also to arrive at the embassy in time for morning meetings. The night before usually returning from diplomatic events at a late hour, Jimmy Vella, my friend and embassy driver, would estimate the time it would take to make it to a new or distant church. While sometimes I pretended to be able to accomplish such task, I would find myself working late into the night, and then be unable to rouse myself for an overly early morning ride. As a result, we had a favored list of nearby chapels and churches that said Mass between 8 and 8:30 a.m. One of them was the Chapel of San Anton in the magnificent gardens and the Palace of the same name in which the president of Malta resides.

My Skype report would often mention attending Mass at San Anton. From my description of his homiletic outreach and instruction, even without a full grasp of Maltese, John and Mary thought how wonderful it would be to meet Father George who regularly said the San Anton Mass. It was not inconceivable to imagine Mary making a stop in Malta during one of her visits with her family in Ireland. Ryan Air has a good number of Dublin to Valletta round-trips at quite reasonable fares so long as one travels without luggage. We even had John contemplating a visit at one point, though the idea of the great man trapped even in expensive trans-Atlantic business class dampened his initial enthusiasm. But then, it is a small world, and Father George with a brother near Detroit had made the reverse trip in the past. California could be added to the itinerary in the future. Indeed, a prelate from the Maltese island of Gozo, who said Mass at the Cathedral of Ta Pinu, reported meeting John during his summer service in Thousand Oaks, California, where John inquired of his roving friend the Ambassador.

Like the regulars at the daily OLM Mass, the San Anton worshippers were uniformly welcoming. They included the president and his wife (His

Excellency George and Margaret Abela) and his
mother, all of whom very thoughtfully reserved a
spot for me in the pew and regularly invited me for
a light breakfast thereafter. Not tea and toast in the
Sheridan sense, perhaps, but close enough.
Indeed, John thought I was getting spoiled by all
the attention and worried whether he might have to
match these presidential sessions with extra toast;
"or goodness knows," he said, "you'll be requesting
fresh fruit like the president gathers in his garden.

As John and I discussed, I returned to the States
for a vacation break in mid-August 2010. John
asked if I could drive Mary and himself over to
Woodland Hills for a special celebration for the
Sisters of Saint Louis on August 25. "Delighted,
John, that would be perfect. It's my late mother's
birthday, and I wanted to attend Mass that day in
any event. It will be a wonderful occasion to visit."
"Come early if you can, Doug," John said. "Well,
we are staying in Glendale which is a bit of a hike
as you know, but count on me to be there in plenty
of time."

20. Mom's Birthday

The morning of the 25th of August was exceptional – clear skies and bright morning stars yielding to an even more magnificent sun. We were the guests of Rick Caruso at his residence in a stunningly beautiful development called "Americana at Brand." Rick has a gift for creating public/private spaces that enliven towns and cities, inspiring a genuine feeling of community. This was one of his best, with fine shops and residences above a lawn and ever performing fountain.

As I watched the morning sun come up beyond the towers of downtown Los Angeles, I felt the presence of my late mother. Beatrice Evelyn Neumann, born August 25, 1923, daughter of William Neumann of Kankakee, Illinois, and Mary Wood of Milwaukee, Wisconsin, remained ever present in my memory five years after her passing.

A diagnosis of stage IV pancreatic cancer would be enough to defeat most of us. Mom wasn't the least fearful even when the word "inoperable" fell from the professional, but hardly poker face of her youthful and somewhat infelicitous physician. Chemo? Radiation? "That's all right, doctor, you did your best." That was Mom, always thinking of the other's feelings.

In her final week, she made sure Dad's monthly bills were paid and insisted that, instead of frittering away my time at her bedside, I go out and verify that the cemetery would accord my father his proper military honors when his time arrived. "You know how proud your father is of his distinguished air medals and his 'Flying Fortress' service over Normandy in the Army Air Corps," Mom smiled as I nodded affirmatively. "I could never rest easy not providing for his parting moment," not thinking a thing about her own far more imminent exit. "Now, Douglas, be off with you."

Using "Douglas," my formal name, was the signal that she meant business. "And," as her hand chased me from the room, "don't forget to bring me a Chicago hot dog and tamale from the new shop

across from the hospital." As Chicagoans
transplanted for over 30 years to the West Coast of
Florida, Mom and Dad delighted whenever they ran
across a touch of the Windy City – whose news
they dutifully watched on WGN each evening. Here
in little Tarpon Springs, a "nice young man," in
Mom's terms, had brought Chicago's finest Vienna
Red-Hots to her own neighborhood and she was
not going to miss out. Of course, there is no way in
the annals of medical history that she could digest
any of it; but the mere aroma she would say later
"filled her to the very brim."

Others had predeceased my mother in our family,
but Mom's back-of-the-hand, see-if-you-can-throw-
me-off-my-stride attitude toward death – looking
after others, at home and totally at ease, passing
shortly before the break of day on the Ides of
March 2005 – defined the Catholic concept of "a
good death" for me. Most particularly, the
conversation we had leading to Mom's final "I love
you, Douglas," was and is an incomparable
treasure, especially since the events of August 25,
2010 would steal the sweetness of my mother's

birthday forever.

21. Malibu with time to spare

The 45-mile route to Malibu from Glendale was mostly freeway and took about an hour and a quarter, but since it was also the morning commute, I left early. There's a variety of routes to get to the Westside, but the Golden State to the Harbor to the Santa Monica to Pacific Coast Highway North to Malibu seemed best. Traffic, as predicted, was heavy, but PCH was reasonably clear. As I pulled into the Our Lady of Malibu lot, there was John and Mary in conversation with Mario, the superb gardener from Guatemala whose flowers delighted Mary, especially in the church garden. All three warmly greeted me with hugs and smiles.

It was a little early to leave for Woodland Hills, about 15 miles away through the canyon, but Mary was anxious. So we got underway after a few more hugs from friends I had dearly missed, like Peggy Thomas in the OLM rectory office and others who were lingering after morning prayers. Our conversation was animated, covering Mary's recent visit to Ireland and some background on those participating in the anniversary we were about to attend.

The Mass was truly poignant; the history of the order impressive; the conviviality and good feeling lasting right through a light lunch of greens and fish, a stroll of the grounds, and a glance at some vintage snapshots of days when the sisters wore black woolen habits and head gear that you wouldn't want to sit behind in a theatre. These were wonderful people. At 1:25 p.m. we left. Now the animated conversation, especially from Sister Mary, was of the glorious morning. Twelve minutes later, Mary stood before the glory of the Lord and paramedics rushed to aid John and myself.

The accident turned the Skype black. Well, not exactly. No one, it seems, comes to collect your name from Skype contacts after your death. On New Year's Day 2011, alone and miserable in ways that holidays can be when you are alone and miserable, I sat down and Skyped John and Mary a message. I had just returned to the ambassador's residence after 10 days in St. James Hospital, Malta.

22. The Ambassador's Operations

The trauma surgeons at UCLA saved my physical life, but to do so, certain changes in the way the body operates were necessary for a period of healing. Specifically, it was time for the follow-on surgical procedure that would reconnect the colon and other necessary internal repairs. The UCLA doctors had asked me to return to the United States for the surgery, but they readily admitted that the Republic of Malta had excellent medical care, and that it would be possible for the surgery to be done there. I was inclined against returning to UCLA given the travel, the need to find supplementary housing, and the imposition of interfering upon the busy lives of others for medical changes of dressing, office visits and the like. In Malta, these could all more easily be embedded in the work day.

This decision to stay in Malta for the surgery was confirmed when I received notice that the Office of Inspector General (OIG or IG) would be reviewing the work of the embassy from top to bottom for the

first time in about a decade. There's nothing
unusual in this. The Inspector General reviews all
embassies every five years or so, and ours was
overdue, because the previous ambassador had
convinced the Inspector General to await
completion of a new embassy building, which was
scheduled to be online in spring 2009. With the
election of President Obama, the predecessor
ambassador resigned, as appropriate, upon the
inauguration of a new president. While the
President signaled my nomination almost
immediately upon assuming office in February
2009, it would be August before the Senate
confirmation process could be scheduled and
completed. In the hiatus, the new embassy did not
complete itself, and labor shortages, procedural
irregularity giving rise to disputes with the project
manager, and permitting issues put the new
building substantially off its timetable (a 12-18
month delay) before my arrival. I made it a top
priority to refocus the building efforts.

Scheduling a visit by 10 to 15 inspectors from
Washington, D.C., for January or early February

2011 necessitated that I allow the shortest possible recovery time away from post, and also that I be available in either the embassy or residence office rather than being half a world away with a 9-hour time difference. As an academic, it was my habit not to keep the kind of extensive calendar that lawyers keep in private practice for billing purposes. I saw no reason to change this practice in the Foreign Service, since I had only one client: the United States. Unfortunately, the IG must have assumed the sparse calendar notes meant I was disengaged. They should have asked – *anyone.*

Much later, one of the Maltese citizens working in the Embassy dealing with procurement expressed concern that the IG team in her area spent very little time asking questions of those with knowledge of her division. Under direction of my highly qualified Deputy Chief of Mission,[29] Rick Mills, and myself, our embassy personnel had prepared

---

[29] I brought Rick to Malta from Baghdad, and he previously served in London and Washington. Today, he is Deputy in Beirut.

thoroughly for this inspection; they were as ready to supply information as an honors student on examination day. But like the honors student who gets an "A" in a course without being challenged by a serious final examination, they felt a bit let down. As to their functions, they let it go, since the boiler-plate narrative turned out to do no harm. They worried, but kept to themselves, that the team had some erroneous presuppositions in other areas, however. Shortly before I departed the embassy, these Maltese personnel told me that they were "kicking themselves" for not telling Rick or myself of their discomfort.

Anyone who has ever been interviewed for a news story knows that there are at least two types of reporters: those who want to report the actual news, and those who have a version of the world into which they fit whatever they encounter as news. From what my staff ultimately shared with me, it seems like the IG team was closer to the second "reporter." When they didn't find time sheets to their liking, they didn't bother to inquire how embassy operations were, in fact, conducted.

Had they, they would have discovered a far different picture than the one they brought with them.

Indeed, one of the things I most enjoyed is that embassy work had almost no down-time. I love teaching, but like the Broadway actor in a long-running play, the script doesn't change much. University teachers adjust for this repetitive boredom in a variety of ways: from research in the library to research in the field on sabbatical. With embassy work, seldom was there an hour during the day that wasn't filled with diplomatic activity testing a new, somewhat different skill set. I loved it. I was honored to represent my country in a foreign land, and I was, frankly, fully conversant with all the work being done under my embassy roof.

Often the morning was consumed with internal meetings or security reviews at the embassy. Late morning would find me speaking somewhere to promote American investment, or addressing some comparative aspect of constitutional law or foreign affairs at the university or the fine Mediterranean School of Diplomacy (MEDAC). And I would try to make it a habit to be home to share a mid-day meal with Carol and/or embassy guests with whom we had some specific business. Washington, D.C., on its 6 hour earlier clock tended to awaken toward the end of our work day, producing its own flood of new cables and calls that could march right into the night in Malta. Evening hours were reserved for diplomatic meetings and dinners with my foreign counterparts, or in Malta, because of its rich Catholic history and tradition, an event celebrating some aspect of that history in accordance with the Church calendar.

On many week-ends before, and every week-end since, the accident, I have made it a point to volunteer in social service work, be it an assisted living center or home for those with addiction or those severely handicapped. I have no clue whether this was official or unofficial time; I considered it God's special time, and I found, as so many volunteers do, that trying to help conquer the suffering or alienation or physical needs of others is a genuine tonic for a soul in similar need. In any event, the "mobile," as the Europeans call cell phones and blackberry devices, was never off.

In retrospect, there may have been some hints that the inspection team had made up its mind about me in advance. For example, on the team's second day in Malta, a Saturday, I greeted them before 8 am on the steps of the St. John's Co-Cathedral which they had requested to see. That is not an unusual request of those visiting the country for the first time; the Cathedral is a fine structure dating to the 16th century. It has magnificent carvings and a special display of Caravaggio paintings as well as tapestries as fine as any in Europe. It was naturally a source of pride for Malta, and the embassy was always given the favor of personalized tours for our special guests. Since showing appreciation for whatever a host nation considers to be one of its most important aspects of culture is a rather basic form of diplomacy, if not common courtesy, I was only too delighted to respond positively when our visitors requested to see something as objectively beautiful as St.

John's.

While I am uncertain what IG practice dictates about this tourist-like field-trip on a week-end during an inspection abroad, I would be reluctant to begrudge a team the opportunity to see the context of the location they were inspecting, for a number of substantive matters are determined by that context – everything from the security atmosphere to the relative isolation (or not) of the locale to determine the applicable compensation tables for Americans deployed there.

In any event, the chair seemed startled when she was about 15 minutes late for the tour I had arranged for her and her team; and to some minor embarrassment, I suspect, I was the one waiting on the steps for her so I could reunite her with those who had gone ahead at the appointed hour. "Why are *you* here?" the surprised chair inquired. "I don't mind getting up to greet visitors on a fine day like the sunny one that it is," I replied. In any event, I make it a point of making certain services or events for those visiting with us are in fact all in order," I said rather matter-of-factly. "Really?" came more disbelief. "Yes," I said, "and especially today we not only have you and your team on this special tour, but when you go inside you will meet a group of American citizens affiliated with religious higher and parish education who are here on their way home from Israel to meet and share ideas with the local archbishop and a venerable teaching order of religious sisters, the Silesians, on the island of Gozo."

When the educators finished the tour and separated from the IG team, I will always remember one of the gentlemen in the educators group, a bank examiner now doing accounting work for the Catholic Church, who pulled me aside and asked: "Who are those people? Especially, who was the lady who joined us mid-way?" he inquired. "Oh, I said, it's our embassy's time to go through a routine inspection, and the woman you met is the chair of the team." The gentleman looked at me with a sort of knowing twinkle in his eye and said simply: "Good luck. She's a tough one." I laughed, not at all concerned about my

personnel living up to very highest expectations.
And candidly, in light of the family sacrifice I had
made to get back on the job faster than the doctors
were comfortable with after the life-saving surgery
at home, I was anticipating – naively perhaps – this
personal promptness to be acknowledged as well.
As the next chapter discusses, however,
Ambassadors (or at least this Ambassador) had a
version of the rule families – back in the 1950s
when I was growing up -- applied to their children:
they were to be seen, but not heard.

23. Who's Running this Outfit?

arly 2011 proved to be especially busy for our embassy, as the so-called "Arab Spring" uprisings in nearby North Africa necessitated constant monitoring. About the only consistently quiet time was early Sunday morning, and I would make it a practice to rise early – usually well before dawn – to write about the week or some other public issue, typically tripped off by a news story or an essay that Secretary of State Hillary Clinton may have written and then invited us to elaborate.

During the week itself, I felt it important to be generally available with an open door without the necessity of my colleagues scheduling a calendar appointment. Some preferred appointments, and my excellent Office Manager, Lenese, would make those arrangements. Otherwise, it seemed like good practice to rely upon the prudent judgment of my career foreign service deputies or of our public diplomacy specialist, Elijah Waterman, to alert me to when there was someone in the Maltese government or visiting the country with whom I should meet. Elijah was very good at his job and kept me as busy as the hours in the day allowed. It is hard to know why the inspectors didn't comprehend the fuller picture of our activities just by talking with him alone.

At times, I knew it was awkward for Elijah having been saddled with me as ambassador. In many embassies, the public diplomacy chief prepares a script for the ambassador, and he reads it. In Europe, they call these "scenarios," and many ambassadors are only too delighted to read the bullet points, take no questions, and have a white wine. That was not me. I like to wrestle with ideas on paper, and while I welcome first draft help on topics unfamiliar, and Elijah was a fine writer, it was my nature to edit continuously until delivery. Moreover, if possible, I would set aside my own draft and deliver remarks conversationally without a word for word reading of the text, except, of course, where there was technical language

involved or I was quoting someone at length. Like
other speech activity, diplomacy that is spoken in
an accessible fashion compatible with the audience
is more effective, both because the particularized
effort shows greater respect, and because it can
take into consideration the up to the moment
perceptions in that place as well as last minute
developments elsewhere.

It is quite understandable that "main State" or "C
Street" or "Foggy Bottom" as our headquarters are
called would want some reasonable oversight over
messaging. There is only one U.S. diplomacy, and
that is the one responsive to the President and the
Secretary within the boundaries set by the
Constitution, international obligations, and
principally the Senate, since the House has no
formal ratification role for treaties.[30]

General presidential direction supplemented by on
the scene, in the moment, judgment is typical of

[30] The House of Representatives may have a say if the treaty or executive agreement
necessitates new public money, since all appropriation measures originate in the House.

many cabinet agencies. For example, main Justice has general supervision of the U.S. Attorneys who head the Justice Department's field offices, which are the equivalent field stations for law enforcement as the embassies are field offices of the United States in a foreign land. However, it would be viewed as an improper and questionable interference were even the Attorney General to micro-manage local prosecutions. These are to be conducted within very broad guidelines and within the sound discretion and judgment of the U.S. Attorney on the local scene. Occasionally, the field office would be more constrained because of sensitivities associated with a public officer being investigated or prosecuted or where there was a parallel prosecution in a different jurisdiction, but trust and confidence and discretion are conferred from the center to the field offices.

The U.S. Attorney-Attorney General relationship ought to be a model for the State Department, but it isn't. Now it is not clear whether the entire headquarters follows the one-way, singular voice practice, or whether it was only in the EU bureau or maybe only for me in particular; but for the most part, embassies write reports or cables back to their bureaus, and the bureaus then dictate the conversation the ambassador can have with members of the host government and what the ambassador can think and say in public discussion.

It was clear that the Department of State was unprepared for an ambassador from the academy. The internal structure for speech approval was more cumbersome and censorious than one imagines associated with a nation far less free than our own. There was virtually no allowance for the infusion of new ideas and approaches in this way. Yet, there was nothing in the regulations – the FAM or Foreign Affairs Manual – that prevented ambassadors from writing, speaking, etc. The EU bureau brought in a nice chap from the legal shop and he did his best to stretch way beyond their text and intent, regulations designed to protect internal deliberation or classified information to the work I was doing on inter-faith surveys and even rather mundane commentary about local issues in country or world events.

Occasionally, I would ask Elijah if he could clarify the rules for what had to be cleared and by whom; but try as he might, he couldn't because it was just too much of a moving target. One day it was any writing in a U.S. publication that needed pre-clearance, but not publications abroad. As a rule that made little sense since Ambassadors have more weight out of their home country, not in it, so ensuring consistency in international fora, one might think, is more important than what an ambassador says for U.S. domestic consumption.

In any event, Washington did not abide by that distinction either, once it realized that most international publications post their materials on the web which can be downloaded domestically. The internet exploded the distinction between the two audiences.

Whatever the rules for seeking clearance were for other generally non-writing ambassadors, the rule in my case became clear: *everything.* It was often Elijah's unhappy duty to tell me of the refusals to

225

clear a good deal of what I wrote because it referenced faith. I did my best not to unleash any frustration upon this good- hearted messenger. Indeed, I grew very fond of Elijah and his wife, Marilyn, who gave birth during my tenure to a beautiful girl named Marlaina. Elijah does, at times in speaking, have a hang-dog kind of manner. It's just his nature and those who value him as a friend, as I do, know his exasperations are often for effect, if not humor. Unfortunately, with an IG looking for something – anything – to criticize, I fear even the slightest statement that he spent extra time trying to navigate his ambassador's creative efforts may have been misinterpreted.

Similarly, the list of people who came during my service without meaningful compensation (often none at all) to lend their expertise to advance embassy objectives is too long to detail, but because of my deanship at Catholic and long tenure at Notre Dame as well as my previous life heading a division in the Justice Department, I was able to bring to faraway Malta experts useful to meeting U.S. concerns, such as judicial delay, transparency in financial regulation, and human trafficking to mention just three topics. In this regard, the local judiciary was very grateful to hear from one of the Nation's top law professors, as well as a highly respected Federal Appellate Judge and Supreme Court litigator.

The insights provided by another guest when combined with the diligent work of Tom Yeager, a retired Naval officer I was fortunate to recruit as my political/cultural officer in the embassy, led to a breakthrough with the Chief of Police on the procedures needed to address human trafficking. In like manner, a highly successful financier addressed the new securities legislation (the highly complex Dodd-Frank Act passed in the wake of the financial melt-down). He, with special relevance to the next chapter, established a foundation building schools and medical facilities in Kenya. Elijah, no doubt trying to give a good impression of his boss to the inspectors, may have bragged a bit that many of the embassy guests were personal friends who made time to visit to address these nagging

problems at my invitation. As I recall, this got
written up in the report as the Ambassador
entertained personal friends. Go figure.[31]

---

[31] I am writing in a somewhat light-hearted manner about the one-sided nature of the report as
it was altered to personally embarrass me in spring 2011; but for the record, the out-of-control
nature of an investigatory law enforcement agency is not to be taken lightly. Indeed, it is less
important that the OIG caused me difficulty (that the President chose not to address) than that
the President's international initiative to promote inter-faith diplomacy was, for all practical
purposes, scuttled by the OIG's labeling of the President's policy direction as work outside the
scope of the official interests of the United States. This type of substantive second-guessing by
the IG had long ago been resolved against them by the Office of Legal Counsel in the U.S.
Justice Department. *See* Inspector General Authority to Conduct Regulatory Investigations, 13
U.S. Op. O.L.C. 54, *available at* 1989 WL 595865. The IG is an essential and
important auditing office when it is focused at its best and most appropriate responsibility of
rooting out waste, fraud and abuse. Its responsibility is not regarding whether or not inter-faith
diplomacy is or is not a good idea, which is for the President and the Congress to determine.
This conclusion, by the way, has been sustained in judicial and legislative review; and frankly,
it was a surprise and disappointment that the respected and dedicated individuals heading the
OIG, whom I found most helpful in my ambassadorial briefing and preparation, allowed an
inspection team to encroach upon presidential authority in this manner.

24. Meeting the Needs of the Least Advantaged

O ccasionally I couldn't resist at least pointing out to my editorial friends in Washington that if one is trying to make a case for assisting the less fortunate, faith-based materials were often relevant and knowledge of local need and what religious or charitable sources in country are capable of contributing. For example, referencing a faith-based duty to meet the needs of the immigrant stranger was an important aspect of raising sensitivity to the needs of the mostly African (Eritrean, Somali, Sudanese) families who arrive by the boat load in Malta. These often extremely poor individuals seek relief from famine, violence, and general lack of opportunity that exists in far too many places on the African continent. A faith-based appeal made particular sense in a country like Malta where faith abounds. When the Holy Father came to Malta in the spring of 2010, he framed his remarks in exactly this way.

These African individuals and families are termed "irregular migrants," and Malta, not without reason as the smallest EU country, often feels that it is getting far less assistance from fellow EU countries to accommodate these men, women and children than a proportionate sharing of responsibility would commend. The "Arab Spring" worsened the problem as many more very frightened migrant families now sought to escape the uncertainty and dangers associated with life in Tunisia, Egypt, and especially with respect to Malta, Libya. In Libya, African migrants faced a no-win situation: as one Eritrean told me, "I can't go out in Libya because the forces associated with the transitional reform government will shoot me on sight of my skin color because there is a tendency to think everyone with dark skin is a mercenary hired by Qaddafi. Of course, Qaddafi's special forces just shoot us for sport."

The United States before my arrival had decided to build some good will with and for Malta by accepting a number of the irregular migrants into the U.S. This, it was hoped, would inspire like humanitarian action on the part of the other 26 EU nations. On my watch, the U.S. embassy increased the numbers of migrants to be resettled in the United States while at the same time regularizing efforts to be certain that no terror suspect or sympathizer with those who have no respect for the sacredness of human life would be admitted. By the time of my departure, close to 800 asylees[32]were re-settled in America. Great care was taken to disburse these new residents across the country so no one community would feel overwhelmed.[33] And in as many cases as possible, employment and/or social services – often supplied by the Jesuits – would be secured as well.

---

[32] "Asylee" is an immigration term of art for someone who would face violence and persecution were he or she returned home.

[33] The right to travel is one of our basic freedoms; so like the Poles, the Irish, the Germans, and the Italians before them, there are some pockets of concentration. Minneapolis, for example, is a favorite destination for Somali families – even as I did my best to tell them they would all need warm coats.

231

Figure 5. New "Cub fans"; some of the so-called "irregular migrant" families during a visit to the Ambassador's residence where our families could visit before these heroic adventurers embarked for the United States. Pictured in the back right is Father Joseph Cassar SJ who was always a compassionate resource for the embassy in these efforts that gave humanitarian witness for what needed to be replicated across Europe – although the true resolution is for the U.S. and other nations to invest 21st century enterprise and technology in the home countries of these men and women so that the economic motivation for migration is lessened as our export markets are widened.

Even our extended African re-settlement efforts were modest in terms of the dimensions of the problem; but as you might imagine, the Tea Party would subject the effort to tremendous criticism for burdening America with "these people." Some of this was racial hatred or disdain for the foreigner, but some was legitimate frustration over long-term unemployment, mortgage foreclosure, and the other effects of economic down turn that seemed only mildly ameliorated by President Obama's well intentioned steps taken to address the depth of the economic mess he inherited.

In actuality, however, there are good reasons – in addition to lightening Malta's burden for which we are thanked regularly – for assisting the irregular migrant family. First of all, it disabuses a great deal of false narratives spun by al Qaeda and similar Islamic fundamentalists, and instead allows the United States to be seen by severely deprived populations as a source of hope. This is a truly blessed gift. Second, making friends in segments of the world's population that harbor our most violent adversary is an excellent source of human intelligence. A family given new opportunities by the U.S. is often very likely to repay that friendship in kind letting us know of planned terror attack or other manifestations of hate being bandied about at the local mosque. Let me be clear: the U.S. does not condition its asylum determinations on someone becoming an information source. Rather, this is the natural consequence of friendship genuinely extended. It is no more complicated than the citizen watch efforts that exist among neighbors across the country.

To solidify friendship with our newest neighbors, it was Kmiec family practice to invite migrant families to our home in Malta for a light lunch or dinner, or (when the groups got larger) an extended reception. The benefit of getting to meet these heroic people individually cannot be understated.

Gathered around us at home, I would often see in the faces what I imagined was the look of anticipation and apprehension of my own great grandfather and grandfather making the difficult decision to separate from the familiar comforts of family and friend to come to the new world. Like the migrant families, our migrating ancestors from Poland, Ireland and Germany frequently lacked proficiency in English, but they were hungry to learn.

One difference between these migrant families and our ancestors, however, was likely the risk to body and soul that had to be endured by the African migrant to come first to Europe and then to America. I don't know about the reader's families, but I can tell you the Kmiec family from outside Krakow, and the Keenan family from Mayo and Cork, certainly did not arrive in the equivalent of business class; but they seldom reported having the female members of the family raped by marauders in the countries they passed through to make it to the water crossing. Nor were the young women brutally enslaved into prostitution as the present day practice of human trafficking results in; nor were their goods and lifetime savings stolen to finance a sea crossing by the hundreds on a make-shift raft that has a better than even chance of capsizing and drowning the lot of them. Hundreds, if not thousands, each year simply perish at sea.

The U.S. would not have been able to reach out to these migrant populations without the help of the Jesuits, who are frequently the principal source of contact upon arrival in the U.S. They do Jesus' work with the migrants by enhancing their English and job skills. The Jesuit motto is "men for others," and they truly are that. A few months after I left the island I heard from Father Joseph Cassar, whose quiet manner and soft voice expressed in word and deed an empathy and genuine love for these families that kept the pain of their unhappy circumstances in detention from becoming what would be an understandable source of rage at the injustice he witnessed each day. Religious, unlike independently minded ambassadors, take vows of obedience and go where their superiors think best. Father Cassar has been transferred back to the Jesuit college as its chaplain. I am certain Father Cassar is fulfilling that role very well, and that he is a joyful and wise resource for the students. It is equivalent to the loss of 10 men, however, for the migrant communities who he still ministers to in his week-end hours. You can palpably feel his desire to continue to work for the needs of these men and women who ask only a fair opportunity to provide for themselves and their loved ones without the constant threat of violence that pervades sub-Saharan Africa. In a recent letter. Father writes in great kindness: "Over the past two Sundays, as some of the detainees leafed through the pages of *The Sunday Times* – of which I buy copies to take with me [to the detention centers] – we stopped on the page(s) bearing your articles and later during Mass prayed for the good American Ambassador who made a difference in the lives of hundreds of African 'brothers' and 'sisters' by opening his house and his country to them. It would seem that there are moments when we experience God's presence quite differently from how we may imagine or prefer, such as in some of the sad events you describe in today's article and in the previous one or in the twists and turns of North African history and of personal history. On the other hand, the open sharing of your thoughts with Maltese readers from a deeply Christian perspective continues – I am sure – to be of inspiration to many even if it cost you your diplomatic post. The many contacts you made here, your interest in and commitment to social issues – and to suffering people, including refugees and migrants – as well as your recognition of all that is wholesome on this small rock in the middle of the sea has endeared you to many who never even met you and continues to make of you a most worthy Ambassador of the US even after your term was declared ended." Thank you, Father, for this kind note; all are in my prayers as well."

Figure 6. **The internet allows these migrants an opportunity to catch up on their home country. Here Father Mintoff shows Martin Sheen and the Ambassador how the PC can also be an effective language learning tool. (Photo credit: Times of Malta).**

Another priest of great dedication to the needs of
the migrant and the poor is Father Mintoff, a
Franciscan who ran the John XXIII Peace Lab on
the island. Father Mintoff is the brother of a large,
but controversial figure in Malta politics, Prime
Minister Dom Mintoff. Prime Minister Mintoff is
credited with many things of assistance to the
average family, including raising wages and the
standard of living as well as universal health care
and education through college. By personality,
however, he was seen as intransigent at times, and
from the U.S. perspective overly friendly during the
cold war with the former Soviet Union, Communist
China, and North Korea. The Prime Minister also
angered the Catholic Church by at first seeking
integration, rather than independence, from
Britain. The Church, of course, worried about
curtailed liberty by integration where the Anglican
Church was the established religion. There is no
one who doesn't see Prime Minister Mintoff as a
significant part of Malta history. He is especially
revered among the Labor Party, which as I write
this is out of power by one vote. It appears that the
present Nationalist Party Prime Minister, Lawrence

Gonzi, who is respected as a steady hand that has
seen Malta through the present world-wide
financial crisis, may by the usual parliamentary
maneuver be challenged to call for an election. The
Maltese care deeply about politics, take elections
very seriously, and vote at the level of 98% plus.
How fortunate we are to have this vibrant, stable
role model of a democracy near to the nascent
democracies emerging in North Africa.

Figure 7. Meeting with Father Mintoff at the John XXIII Peace Lab. Father is in his 80s, but has the energy of someone ½ his age.

241

The Center run by former Prime Minister Mintoff's Franciscan brother provides wholesome quarters far better than the detention areas, recreation, and educational opportunities for the migrants. Martin Sheen, whose "West Wing" acting is well known throughout Europe, very thoughtfully visited me in Malta with his grandson Taylor to premier the highly acclaimed movie "The Way" as a fundraiser for Father Mintoff and the refugees. It is a thoughtful film set along the way of Saint James in Spain, and the message of the film, like Martin's entire career, helps us appreciate the things that really matter.

The Maltese were enamored with the film's genuine and heartfelt religious theme, and with the spirituality of Martin who generously lingered with anyone who sought him out. A significant sum came to Father Mintoff by reason of Martin's talent, and his son, Emilio Estevez, who acted and directed the project with his Dad. The money came just in time to assist the influx of migrants coming because of the outbreak in violence in Libya. One of my greatest regrets in feeling that I had to offer

my resignation to President Obama after the
mistaken and unfortunate IG report was leaving so
much undone that could have been of support to
the migrant families, who for me, represent those
who value human freedom most.

Father Mintoff, who is 80+ years old, is as spry as
a man half his age. With a smile that could run
from Gozo to the Dingli cliffs, he escorted me
through one of the many religious processions I
was able to take part in during my stay in Malta.
(Indeed, occurring on the feast of Our Lady of
Mount Carmel, the procession was just days before
I returned to the States anticipating a short break,
but facing the tragedy instead.) These great
processions bring out thousands of men, women
and children of all ages, singing, praying and
greeting one another with smile and pride of place.
Each parish competes in these events on the
Church holy days which seem to occur almost
weekly in Malta. Much of the competition centers
on the band clubs, which do have very fine brass
bands, but which are also typically the place of
community activity of every type. Many of these

club facilities were built or hand-crafted by grandfathers of the present members and the present generation is usually trying to think of some way in which the club can be expanded or improved. Not infrequently, the improvements include incredibly beautiful religious art work, including new statues for the collection that is already exhibited with pride and carried – despite great weight – in the processions. Of course in Malta feast days are celebrated with one further element; fireworks – massive amounts of joyously colored, ever surprising and very loud fireworks. It is as if the firework displays affirm that the population survived the truly relentless Nazi bombing (lasting 154 consecutive days) during World War II. The Maltese effectively ended Rommel's campaign for north Africa and well deserve the Saint George Cross for Valour awarded to the entire nation which today adorns their national standard. As Franklin Roosevelt said at the time, "There is tiny Malta, alone and unafraid in a darkened sea."

Yes, it is sometimes said that the migrants really

try to avoid Malta, preferring instead if they can get cooperative seas to land in southern Italy where it is easier to reach the rest of the European continent. The Providence that brings men and women to Malta, however, is landing these hope-filled wayfarers in a land of ancient, Neolithic root; an intriguing Arabic- based but decidedly unique language and a people who are hardworking, intelligent, and who throughout history have been of service to their fellow man in the name of Jesus Christ, Our Lord. If Malta was good enough for God to have Saint Paul shipwreck on the island in the year 60, it will sustain those who come by the same sea route today.

The real question is whether the wealthier nations of the world will extend a helping hand to Malta in this responsibility as President Obama has permitted me to do on behalf of the United States. I couldn't help feeling at times that there was some trans-generational injustice that I was helping to work out in standing up for the needs of these men and women. I did see in the eyes of the migrant in Malta, the eyes of our grandfathers, Jan Kmiec and

245

William Keenan, looking back. There is always hurt and uncertainty in those eyes mixed with the two-edged happiness of going to America that was hoped to be "a shining city on a hill" for all, but we forget to our discredit if we fail to recall that some who came were not permitted to climb, and in truth, some were tossed over it.

In brief remarks, I would tell our new American neighbors that I understood the pain of being uprooted from home. Impoverished and as beset by violence as the places they left behind might be, they were still familiar, and they will always be their first home. What would they find in America? They all anticipated new opportunity, of course, but there is also the troubling realism that they now face also being scorned in the new world,. In some states where unbridled federal authority has defied the allocation of powers in the Constitution to give local police the power to judge and detain by appearance, a new, more subtle violence under law does equal damage to our national soul. But then, this too was witnessed by the immigrant eyes in our families. After all, our own ancestors met: no Irish need apply; No Catholics welcome here. We shouldn't forget that those who gave us their surname were often scorned or denied the right to vote or participate in education or election systems.

Like our ancestors, these families do not come empty handed to America; each of them come endowed by abilities that have already proven capable of withstanding adversity we could not imagine, nor would want to. And while it cannot be said to be always true, there is evidence from study of the Somali populations in Minnesota, for example,[34] that they have generated a significant uptick in small business opportunities. These new entrepreneurs have the tenacity to take on the economic risks necessary to be among the one out of five small businesses that make it after three years. And, as already noted, there is a natural level of gratitude that translates into loyal citizenship – the kind of citizenship that is not

---

[34] *See* Shannon Golden et al., *Experiences of Somali Entrepreneurs: New Evidence from the Twin Cities*, 10 INT'L J. SOMALI STUD. 89 (2010), *available at* http://digitalcommons.macalester.edu/bildhaan/vol10/iss1/9.

about to tolerate the propagation of hatred toward the nation that opened itself to the "wretched souls yearning to breathe free," to loosely reference the Emma Lazarus poem at the base of the Statue of Liberty in New York that welcomed in their respective times: the Catholic Kmiec's; the Jewish Waterman's; the Protestant Mills.

Speaking of Elijah, I could always sense his enjoyment in the migrant send-off receptions we would have at the house. The time was ennobling for us all, even the embassy's household staff, who served the food to our migrant guests with the same care and dignity as they would accord a visiting head of state. The thin migratory souls who came to our table made it through two or more years of detention in tents or cargo containers or overcrowded single-wide trailers incapable of keeping out the winds of winter or the stifling summer heat. They came with manners and clothing not refined by privilege, but those kind and gentle people who worked in our home for only the modest wage that this ambassador teacher could pay them appreciated that the beauty of

248

these guests was interior, not a matter of superficial tailoring. Joseph, Robert, Nathalie, and Joanna worked very hard for their salaries and they seldom complained in any respect. They did not begrudge the migrants' hope. Instead, with our refreshment, these good household friends served an extra share of happiness of a long-time neighbor pleased for a friends' good fortune.

By the way, I never was sold completely on our making reference to the Emma Lazarus poem. The general public in America likely would remember this statue of Liberty favorite, at least insofar as the words: "Give me your tired, your poor, Your huddled masses yearning to breathe free . . . ." Yet, seldom is the following line given attention: "The wretched refuse of your teeming shore." Even as those in attendance did not speak perfect English, and in fact, might well have been depending upon an available translator of one of dozens of African dialects, to make anything of the Ambassador's presentation, which they always dutifully pretend to be taking in. It is simply then wrong emphasis to call those assembled "refuse" or "trash." They are not. Their journey to freedom is along the trail of American heroes. By any rational measure, we should hold up their journey of freedom as that of a journey of heroes.

The Lazarus poem does end with a welcoming line: "Send these, the homeless, tempest-tossed to me, I lift my lamp beside the golden door!" I echoed these sentiments by urging my very diverse migrant friends to not forget their culture, but rather to hold it out as a gift to their new American neighbors. Of course, I told them, I understood their natural desire to fit right into the communities in which they were being relocated.

Here I had some fun. I told the assembled that they would shortly be introduced to America's past-time: the game of baseball. While many agents of misdirection from the overpaid Yankees or movable Dodgers might try to win their affections for a local team, they should resist, unless the locality was Chicago. With a twinkle in my eye, and the nostalgia that all natives of the "City of Big Shoulders"[35] have for the Cubs, I would distribute

---

[35] Per Carl Sandburg, not second-baseman, Ryan.

Cub caps indicating how much this would facilitate innumerable conversations about the boys in blue, known affectionately as "America's team." Probably there was no greater prevarication ever attempted in U.S. diplomatic history; but who can say, someday soon the Cubs will win their first series in over a century, and there will be a few loyal fans hailing from Africa who will cheer, remembering where they first savored not just freedom, but the joy of "Cubs Win! Cubs Win!"

25. Maltese Christmas Hospital-ity

I spent Christmas 2010 in the company of a Maltese comedian named Eric who moonlights as a nurse (or was it the reverse?); a fine, soft-spoken surgeon, Mr. Joseph DeBono; and his medical assistants at St. James Hospital (Malta). As the UCLA doctors predicted, I was treated extremely well and successfully at St. James. While it is depressing to some degree to spend a holiday like Christmas in the hospital, it turned out to be a good opportunity to carry forward Monsignor John's Theology of Kindness. Quite simply, the hospitalization was its own opportunity to spread the joy of the season in ways separate from the usual, expensive gifts and other commercialisms that block an understanding of the incarnational significance of Christ's birth. In any case, the Monsignor always made the best of any situation.[36]

---

[36] On Wednesday evenings, Peggy and Tom Thomas would often have drinks and dinner with the Monsignor and Sister Mary. On one of those

Of course, throughout my ten day stay, there were visits by government leaders, diplomats, Embassy colleagues, neighbors, clergy, and by the local guard who watches over the ambassador 24/7. The local guards cheerfully – and considering it was Christmas and I was interrupting their holiday, very generously – assisted the ambassador in learning how to walk upright with a reconstructed stomach. Besides a rendition of *Gesu Bambine*, a beautiful Maltese carol sung by Father Hilary and an accompanying nurse, most memorable during my stay were conversations with fellow diplomats – including some whose home countries were, to say the least, facing violence and change.

One of my favorite colleagues, Ambassador Taweel is the representative of Palestine. It's a curious

---

occasions, Tom who was in charge of making a dry martini for Monsignor noted that the dry Vermouth had run, well, dry. But Tom quickly added that there was some sweet red Vermouth in the cupboard. "That's fine, that's fine, Mr. Tom, make it with the sweet Vermouth," replied Monsignor. So after Tom proceeded to serve the martini, Monsignor took one swig of it and nearly choked on it. For a moment he could barely utter a word and then finally in a somewhat gasping voice he said "Ahhhh, Tom, it's perfect!"

thing to have one of your best friends from a country your own country doesn't recognize – at least not yet officially – – as I write this. The two-state solution, with appropriate land swaps to make sense of population patterns remains the obvious path to be followed. On one occasion, Senator Mitchell – at that time the envoy for these talks – requested that I stand in for him at a UN sponsored conference in Malta. The draft outline supplied by Mitchell's staff gave emphasis to President Obama's own sentiments that the U.S. should not be thought the agent for either side. I think that is how the average American would articulate it as well.

Difficulties arise given the bifurcated nature of the Palestinian side, and, of course, the continued complications of new Israeli settlements. President Obama has raised all these points, and most recently formally stated that "We believe the borders of Israel and Palestine should be based on the 1967 lines with mutually agreed swaps, so that secure and recognized borders are established for both states." He also stressed that the U.S. commitment to Israel's security is "unshakable," and said "every state has the right to self-defense, and Israel must be able to defend itself -- by itself – against any threat." These are words of some significance now in light of Iran's nuclear ambitions and recent missile-rattling. This is not news, and the increasing risk and complexity merits a referral. Here is mine:

> Dear Lord, now that Monsignor's there in your chambers, please listen to his earnest plea for fairness on both sides of a dispute that has taken far too much life, destabilizes an entire region of the world, and-draws us into violent conflict or has us look the other way at violent behavior in a manner that's inexcusable.

Another interesting hospital visitor who two months later would be a source of some bewilderment was the thoughtful Ambassador from Libya, Saadun Suayeh. Like me, he is a former academic (a master of languages and a translator of some rather magnificently sensitive and evocative poetry). Some months ago, the Libyan Ambassador's well-being was far from secure or even known. I prayed for his safety. To be Ambassador from a country you love;

but where your political leadership is anything but lovable, and where published reports and logic suggest your every move is being watched, to emerge on the side of the democratic reform is not the work of just any professor.

Many other visitors filled my long hours. They included Abdel Mawgoud El Habashy, the distinguished Ambassador of Egypt, who has a delightfully formal and informal nature that is seemingly in play simultaneously; and Jean-Francois Delahaut, the Ambassador of Belgium with a special knack for identifying common ground (and the Belgian root in, well, everything). There were many more visitors, including Britain's deservedly respected High Commissioner, Louise Stanton, and the dean of the diplomatic corps, the Papal Nuncio, Tommaso Caputo, who thoughtfully gave me his Christmas greetings from the Holy Father as a get well present that I shall always treasure.

Figure 8. A portion of the diplomatic corps during my two years in Malta; in the front row, from left to right, is: High Commissioner Quinane of Australia; High Commissioner Louise Stanton of U.K.; Prime Minister Gonzi; the author; Ambassador Gudenhaus of Austria. The ambassadors from Greece, Italy, Egypt, Turkey and Portugal populate the second row. Row 3 includes Professor Busitil, our scholarly convener, and the ambassadors of Ireland (obscured), Belgium and the Palestinian Authority (sunglasses). In back are the Ambassadors of the Netherlands, Russia and Germany.

257

I would have liked to talk with Monsignor John and Sister Mary about the so-called "Arab spring" revolutions. These Facebook abetted uprisings were given vague nods of approval by the President and Secretary of State Clinton at first and some cautious assistance thereafter. The caution was well-warranted. There is a troubling history of the rebel who you support with weapons today turning the weapon right back at your generosity tomorrow. In forming governments, it would seem insufficient to rely on the rationality of man because man's nature lapses from rationality. Inevitably there is a need to believe in something greater than ourselves – like, of course, "the self-evident truth of a Creator who endows us with unalienable rights."[37]

Malta's President George Abela visited on Christmas Eve, and brought a bushel of oranges from the trees in the San Anton garden. The oranges were delicious, but far too many for me to consume alone, which I suspect the president knew.

---

[37] THE DECLARATION OF INDEPENDENCE. 2 (U.S. 1776).

Malta may be the most stable nation in all the Mediterranean. It has only been an independent democracy since 1964, but its association with Catholicism, the established faith, dates much earlier, at least to 60 AD when Saint Paul shipwrecked on the island. The Acts of the Apostles record that Paul was greeted by the Maltese with "uncommon kindness," and that is still the way of Maltese people today. President Abela's citrus generosity was just one of many examples, which I should say did spawn its own when to my surprise and delight my brother, Warren, and cousin, Mary Gordon, returned early to Malta from a side trip to Rome. The three of us on Christmas night were able to distribute presidential oranges together with some small flowers to every patient in the hospital singing carols along the way. Some patients broke into tears when they saw us, but in fairness, I don't believe it was the singing.[38]

The joy of giving had thus become the centerpiece of Christmas 2010. Because of it, I was able, for a

---

[38] It was probably my brother. (Just kidding, Warren).

brief period in the hospital, to set aside the weight of the tragic accident. I somehow separated myself from the tragedy that put me there. It was a good feeling. It was as if the doctors at St. James had not just reconnected my internal organs, but had reconnected me to my life before. In the dark shadow of the tragedy, I can seldom make out the outlines of the Doug as he was before. That would seem foreclosed now, for that Doug no longer exists. I know Carol misses me. I miss me, too.

Nevertheless, to know that Carol finds some fragment of our life before in the protective glow of our grandson, Jackson, is a true gift as well. It allows me, in fact, to highlight something John, Mary and I had on more than one occasion discussed with university students – finding a career compatible with family and understanding work as loving service.

My life of teaching and writing could in some sense be described as service; but frankly as a senior member of the faculty, my compensation is significant and Pepperdine University provides every reasonable support. Carol was and is the real practicing theologian of kindness in our family. She established an English language volunteer teaching program for the University maintenance staff. It was Carol who volunteered time and again to teach fine arts at Our Lady of Malibu School, purchasing much of the artistic materials out of her own pocket and schlepping the materials around like a bag lady since the school at the time could not afford even an "art closet," let alone an office or permanently assigned classroom. It was Carol who would use her "extra" time to help young pregnant college women get jobs, shelter and prenatal care, and to encourage them to reaffirm life against the awful temptation of abortion. It was Carol who volunteered to help the Hispanic dorm staff at the university confront the anxiety of immigration matters, sneaking in a question or two to her lawyer husband or one of his many graduates specializing in the area from Notre Dame, Catholic University or Pepperdine. While I do not fully understand the psychology of it, the fact that the accident has strained Carol's ability to see me as a worthy object of her time and service is

261

one of its worst and more substantial after-effects.

26. Life "as is" and unborn death

H aving the surgery in Malta meant that my availability as Ambassador could continue largely uninterrupted, though occasionally re-directed through the residence office rather than the embassy. Often, this was the preferred venue by those seeking appointments since parking was easier, and the residence was in far better shape than the declining embassy structure (remember the supposition was that we would have moved well before my arrival). Moreover, receptions were less expensively arranged there with the help of a salaried staff who, by nature, made every person who walked through the door – be they visiting soldier from Iraq; leaders of the association of American school principals; or migrants who had been granted asylum from the violence in their home country - feel welcome.

Unfortunately, the surgery in Malta had one glaring downside: it meant continued distance from my family for Thanksgiving and Christmas. After the accident, my wife Carol accompanied me back

to Malta, but returned to the States in early
November.

Our being apart, frankly, was very hard. Yet, it
was comforting to know that Carol had a special
object of love at home. Yep, another man –
actually, little Robert Jackson Turner, our first
grandchild, then 16 months old. Jackson and
Carol today are inseparable, though as I write
these pages, there is now competition for her
attention: Oliver Douglas, 9.5 lbs, born August 6,
2011. Oliver is the second child born alive of my
very tiny 120 lb, daughter Katherine, the legal
counsel for a California county. Kate sadly lost an
earlier child well into the pregnancy a few months
after the accident.   As she is devoutly pro-life, the
medical similarity of the process for clinically
resolving a miscarriage redoubled Kate's
commitment to returning the fullest respect for life
in the culture she so ably counsels professionally.
In sharp contrast to the U.S. – where neither
Democrat nor Republican party is truly pro-life – in
Malta, both major political parties at opposite ends
of the ideological spectrum accept as a given the

deep immorality of abortion, and support its total illegality. Malta proves that abortion and promoting the greater participation of women throughout the economy is a non sequitur. Carol and I are very proud of Katherine for articulating, as well as living, this aspect of our faith. In any event there was good reason to rejoice in new life in 2011 after the dying times of 2010.

Carol would often have Oprah on television for background company while caring for Jackson. Jackson himself has not expressed a view on Oprah ending her highly rated afternoon program being somewhat more fascinated by tractors. (He lives in a small rural California town not far from our national border with Mexico). Carol, I suspect, misses Oprah greatly. As Carol regularly points out, Oprah has demonstrated the ability to practically and positively change lives of people who have come within her orbit of friendship. No plaster saints are needed; Carol prefers the inquisitive, positive and tenacious personality from the city of our birth, Chicago. She has created her own media empire and a following so large and impressive that the incumbent President is surely grateful – and maybe he is only President because she got behind his campaign early.

It was not surprising that Jackson would think that his favorite friend in his tiny but expanding world was named not Carol but Oprah – or as Jackson expresses it, "ah pu." As pronounced, it sounds a bit like a cute child's version of "apple," which may account for why he always seems to have one. Jackson is undeniably handsome and would attract a loving grandmother under any circumstance, but especially following an accident that reduced her husband from a respected scholar and public intellectual to what she fears today is little more than an object of pity. Taking up Monsignor John's definition of faith, Carol has built up a level of trust with Jackson that is unsurpassed and likely unsurpassable. In turn, insofar as Jackson represents a world without sorrowful baggage, Carol can entrust herself into his delightful little hands without risk of being evaluated, except upon the goodness of her own personality and Jackson's own innocence.

27. A Skype to Heaven

D
eath came far too frequently to the Kmiec family door often in 2010 (Monsignor, Mary, my father, my beloved aunt, and even as I lay recovering in St. James, my next door neighbor of many years in Malibu). Shortly before the accident, my late mother's only sister, who had always been the second mother for my brother and myself, died. Aunt Jean, like Monsignor Sheridan, was approaching her mid-90s; but for an inoperable weakness in her heart she would still be with us today sharp as ever. Because my duties at the embassy, including the upcoming inspection, required that I return to post, it was again Carol who held Jean's hand in hospice care as she made her final crossing home.

Knowing that Carol was much needed at home by many in our family did not make the alone times any easier. Turning on the computer on New Year's morning, I found John's Skype symbol to be bright green, seemingly indicating that he was signed-on to the Internet and ready for conversation. Even as I realized that all it meant was that someone else was using John's equipment, I sat down to Skype John and Mary one final time. Using the Malta-to-Heaven protocol, I wrote to them and my father and aunt who died just weeks before the accident:

Douglas W. Kmiec: John
[1/1/2011 9:54:55 AM] Douglas W. Kmiec: I miss you; the accident is blocking our embrace but I do so wish to embrace you
[1/1/2011 9:56:52 AM] Douglas W. Kmiec: and Mary, it is a new year and your eyes do surpass the accident and I am so grateful because they are smiling which tells me John is in the heavens
[1/1/2011 9:58:19 AM] Douglas W. Kmiec: may what we know as 2011 be good to you; you now have joined God in knowing how I have sinned and repented; and sinned and repented again; you now know how many prayers I have said and still need
[1/1/2011 10:00:23 AM] Douglas W. Kmiec: may the genuine and pure heart of so many in this our temporary Malta home help sustain our family and

all families

[1/1/2011 10:03:52 AM] Douglas W. Kmiec: so, dearest friends, I suspect no longer God's newest saints -- saints of seniority/ of last year -- already, I pour out my heart and prayer to you here as a reminder of the loss that I cannot ever hope to rectify or fill, and for which I ask God's mercy.

[1/1/2011 10:04:22 AM] Douglas W. Kmiec: I love you, John V. Sheridan

[1/1/2011 10:04:41 AM] Douglas W. Kmiec: I love you, Sister Mary Campbell

[1/1/2011 10:13:36 AM] Douglas W. Kmiec: I love you, Dad, whose imperfections I magnify, but upon whose fate my own is modeled; dearest Dad, forgive me, but it is much harder to find the sweet moments between us that I so readily recall with Mom. Perhaps it is the different way men and women express sentiment, but if so, the feminine is more real. Dad, you know what I mean. In her final moments, Mom worried more for you, Dad, than she ever did for herself. Nonetheless, it was Mom's love for you, Dad, that always permitted me, and perhaps Warren too, to see God in you and ourselves.

[1/1/2011 10:21:17 AM] Douglas W. Kmiec: And Jean, I hope the medical decisions made by all in your behalf were life-sustaining in the truest sense; I believe in my heart this was our intent, but when your voice and clarity fell silent, your needs to avoid pain became indecipherable, and we relied upon the hospice for the path. I know you were a strong, practical woman, well-prepared to fulfill your earthly account, and it is my prayer that in the gifts Warren and I make with your hard earned savings be one's that you would have made yourself.

[1/1/2011 10:31:27 AM] Douglas W. Kmiec: So dearest John, for whom Skype was as big a gift to keep us close even as we could not count on our joint ministrations to awaken and then aim your camera at something other than ceiling, here is my final new year's day confession for the year you went to the Lord; God has not permitted me to know what happened at the moment of His taking of Mary and preparation of you (what was He teaching us through your extended pain?). Here is where faith is needed to comfort this soul that even

in this new year is weighed down with not knowing
what it is that the crash brought to you and Mary.
Out of your faith example and that of Mary, we
assume it to be only good, indeed, the ultimate of
goodness. But I do not know. Here on earth none of
us know, and that has returned me, focused me,
on my own submission to God in faith, and I feel in
my heart it is not enough, never enough, so I try to
do good in your memory as a way of
inconveniencing the self, so that I may feel more of
God's assurance that you both are the happiest
that goodness allows for eternity, and that
someday here on earth -- though perhaps only
when God's door is opened to me in the same
unexpected fashion -- will I find the two of you
waiting to embrace me again, as we would have
embraced had we made it the intended and
expected half hour more to OLM.
[1/1/2011 10:55:02 AM] Douglas W. Kmiec: Love
always,
[1/1/2011 10:55:06 AM] Douglas W. Kmiec: Doug

Skyping your friends in heaven may seem silly, but
from the standpoint of emotional impact, there was

only one other moment of equal intensity in my life. On Friday, September 17, 2010, I was scheduled to see my surgeons at UCLA. Having only been out of the hospital a few days in home care, they were unsure whether I had progressed sufficiently to make the long 20 hour journey back to Malta from California. There were still open wounds in my abdomen and there would be for some time, necessitating that I dress these with the right materials to avoid infection for myself or with Carol's or a nurse's assistance.

The doctors proceeded to examine me, and reluctantly concluded that while there were risks of complication, I was determined to return to my post, and for that reason and with multiple promises to take care of myself, they gave me medical clearance to do so. Stoically, these two fine professionals said nothing during the entire examination about John, even though they knew it was my practice prior to my recent discharge to be with him during those long nights and early mornings.

As I stepped away from the examination table, I thank them and said that I now needed to go see the great man, himself, since I had brought a surprise of his favorite Irish music which I was convinced would inspire his further recovery. Dr. Elizabeth looked at Dr. Henry, the chief of trauma surgery, with grief and alarm. "Ambassador," they said, "The Monsignor died this morning at 4:30 AM. He was entirely peaceful."

Tears came; I had seen John just the day before and prayed into his ever kind, but then physically pained blue eyes; those wonderful eyes that welcomed all and with every twinkle said, "I understand; I am with you; nothing further is required; come walk in the beautiful hills at my side."

When I first arrived with my son, Kiley, the day before, John was looking better than ever. He was sitting up in bed surrounded by some of the senior surgical team. However, I speculated to myself that probably far more agreeable to John was the fact that he was also the attention of the bright-faced, white-coated surgical residents who had been so capably assisting in his care, and mine, from the time the helicopter set us both down on the roof of the UCLA Hospital on August 25.

As unwanted as it was to see my friend still confined by the after-effects of this awful accident, there was something distinctly proper and natural in the scene. Here was the Monsignor surrounded by the most splendid minds in medicine holding forth by the sheer beauty and spiritual strength of his presence. The metaphorical portrait of Christ teaching on the mountain-top filled the room with the Holy Spirit in every respect.

Waiting behind the observer's glass, I stood for a few minutes unnoticed. I was in a suit-coat masking the deep wound in my abdomen and other paraphernalia too awkward to mention. Suddenly, John's eyes met mine. I am sure of it, for at that very instant, one of our young surgical helpers turned to see where the Monsignor had suddenly fixed his gaze. Seeing me, and now recognizing me as the same recent hospital denizen who only a day or so before walked in an immodest hospital gown and an ever-present IV pole, they smiled and waved me in.

I came quickly to John's side and reached for his gentle hand of kindness. You'll remember that after making the 911 call and calling the parish, John's hand was in mine praying the Rosary. Now here I was again grasping that very same hand, a hand which had very nearly been worn thin – if not by the 94 years John bore so lightly, then by having been so joyously extended to me and every soul that came his way during his magnificent life of priestly fullness.

I cannot say whether John heard my voice at either moment, though it will always be my hope that he did. To the end, I lobbied to have John's favorite chiming mantel clock brought to his room to aid his comfort with a more familiar sound. When Drs. Henry and Elizabeth disclosed that the angels had beaten me to him, my satchel contained music by the brothers Clancy and John McCormick; the Irish tenors performing the "Fields of Athenry"; "Four Green Fields" and "Danny Boy"; a vast repertoire of songs known more to John than me (but that he

275

still permitted me to sing with him on the way to one of our long walks in the hills above Malibu).

The sight of the two of us in the convertible I owned before going into the Foreign Service must have brought a chuckle or two to Malibu regulars. But then, that was part of the fun, and John loved it, even once waving his cane aloft as we turned up the Pacific Coast Highway.

In the weeks in the hospital, John seemed to respond less by voice than look. His searching, almost quizzical look, I am convinced, was not asking the question: "Why me?" For to John Sheridan, even in the midst of suffering, that question would have been too self-indulgent to contemplate.

No, John was looking in our eyes searching for the light of faith – as if to say, "I don't get it, my friends – but it is not for us to presume to know God's mind. And you, Doug, don't think He doesn't know your heart. Tell me, my dear Doug, is yours still a believing heart?"

I gave the great Monsignor my ready affirmation, and as I did, it seemed as if his hand relaxed. John's wit and intelligence towered over just about all, including myself, and his power of discernment of the truth was unsurpassed. Thus, it was a happy moment of relief having seemingly reassured "the great man," as I had come to refer to him in the hospital while I inquired to almost every one of his condition.

Nevertheless, since John now knows far more than any of us remaining behind, I have confessed that I cannot say whether the affirmation I gave was without doubt. Forgive me, John; with so much of the present time occupied by horror and unbearable grief, I would be pretending if I said I grasped how this unneeded pain given to you is compatible with the idea of our being justified by a Savior whose own suffering is held forth in Holy Scripture as sufficient to redeem us all.

This, of course, is the crux of faith.

While I think matters could have been more charitably resolved, God, albeit somewhat grudgingly, has now given answer to John's longtime prayer for a "happy death." When John was my age (59), he wrote a book, *And When It is Dawn,* in which he recounts his first near-death experience at age 17 when the doctors in County Longford had given him up for dead. Of course, as we know, having dedicated his life to the Church, John was anything but finished.

Nevertheless, forty-some years later as John reflected upon death, he wrote that "death was a source of radical frustration and loneliness." Oh, were I capable of lifting the frustration and loneliness of every heart saddened by his farewell. I cannot, but this I pledge: If the way to see your welcoming and smiling face again, my dear Monsignor John, is to banish all doubt, then whatever time remains for me to walk the Malibu hills or the ancient pathways of St. Paul in Malta is time happily dedicated to keeping the faith alive.

I have always known the world to sometimes be a place of great horror and anguish. I now feel it personally. So let me be plain to the evil at the source of our grief in this exile: Whatever form you assume, you will be no match for the good of the Lord. For all of us who knew John Virgilius Sheridan have known and felt intimately the Lord's saving goodness, and we yearn for it still.

28. Keeping the Faith; Giving up the Dream Job

I kept my promise to Monsignor and spent the balance of my ambassadorship in Malta dedicated to keeping faith alive. To my surprise, in order to fulfill that promise, it would be necessary to submit my resignation. The President of the United States had sent me to Malta because, as was said at my swearing in, he viewed my appointment as having "a special presidential logic." The State Department bureaucracy apparently is no respecter of the logical.

From the oval office perspective, I would be moving from the position of campaign spokesman for faith and values in 2008 to serve as United States Ambassador in a land deeply respectful of the teaching of Christ in the Catholic tradition. Of course, at the time of appointment, the tragedy that would befall Monsignor, Sister and myself was lying in wait a year away.

From the moment I reported for duty in 2009, I sought to make our embassy in Malta a place of civil discussion that would enhance mutual understanding of the diverse faith traditions of the Mediterranean region. As the White House Special Assistant to the President for the Faith-Based Initiative explained at my swearing into office in the historic treaty room of the State Department, highly Catholic Malta was thought by White House strategists to be an ideal location to pursue inter-faith diplomacy. As mentioned earlier,

Figure 9. Ambassador Kmiec with President Obama after the Chiefs of Mission meeting in the White House (January 2011). This was the last time I spoke with the President. We talked briefly about faith issues and how well his inter-faith initiative toward mutual understanding and mutual respect in Cairo remained of great significance. I promised to help the President in every way possible to advance inter-faith diplomacy. President Obama is a good man, but he has not always been assisted in his Constitutional duty to "take Care that the laws are faithfully executed." In some cases, the views of career lawyers in the State Department's Legal Advisors office was still being shaped by Supreme Court opinion on church-state matters that had been superseded or disavowed by later case developments. (Official White House Photo)

Malta is perhaps the nation most overt and secure in its own faith belief of any nation on the face of the globe; and, therefore, sensitive religious discussions could occur without being perceived as a threat. "With my appointment," said one the president's top aides, "a person of sincere and shared Catholic commitment would be serving as Ambassador from the United States." Malta could now serve as discussion crossroads – as it always had demographically and geographically served in matters of trade – for the Islamic tradition in Africa to the South; the Hebraic tradition to the East; and Christianity to the North and West Europe, and more distantly, the American continent. The presidential assignment was ideal and I brought great enthusiasm to it. I began by surveying and comparing the educational practices in schools in Europe and the United States to see how well the comparative understanding of faith traditions was taught in either place. Such survey was not for the purposes of indoctrination or proselytization of belief, but of the advance of knowledge and correspondingly respect for difference. It was with great excitement that I spoke of these efforts with John and Mary in our Friday Skypes. I highlighted for them how our mission would be able to use the new Embassy compound to conduct convocations devoted to interfaith diplomacy, exploring in simulation and joint study of how different faith-based models of dispute resolution might be employed in such circumstances as the Middle East and the long-running dispute between Israel and Palestine. In brief, the program would coincide well with President Obama's optimistic humility recognizing that the U.S. has much to share, but also much to learn. As a hypothesis, it seemed logical to me and John (to whom I owe this good idea to him) that just as embassies around the world have cultural, economic, and political officers to smooth relationships in troubled times, it was worth contemplating having a similar officer who was steeped in an understanding of the nuances of diverse faith traditions and non-violent dispute resolution.

John and I spoke of Pope Benedict's efforts to address secularism in Europe and the sometimes stiff reception he received in his travels. Not in Malta! I said proudly, recalling the papal visit in late April and how Malta was enthralled by the Pope and his message. Nevertheless, the United States

was not immune from the secularism of Europe.
Indeed, rumor had it that the State Department
historically had been most resistant to faith-based
considerations in diplomacy. Therefore, expecting,
some resistance from the State Department prior to
my oath taking – even with the explicit presidential
mission – the White House convened a meeting with
the associate director of the European Bureau
(EUR) as well as the Malta desk officer and myself.
The purpose was to acquaint State Department
personnel with the objective of this additional and
important aspect of my assignment or mission.
That meeting seemed to go well, but it was only a
few weeks into my service when references to the
importance of faith that I included in speeches and
writing (which, apparently unlike most
Ambassadors, I greatly enjoyed drafting myself)
would start to disappear; later, they would be
subject to multiple pre-clearances. In the end, they
were outright disapproved.

From time to time, I sought John's guidance on how
I might open the minds of those closed to faith; but
in truth we both saw the problem in the
Department as longstanding, and a part of the

285

secularist mind-set being challenged by Pope Benedict XVI generally in Europe and the United States. The legal advisor of the Department removed faith references from everything I wrote including (outrageously) a magazine remembrance of my recently deceased father. Even a newspaper column I penned for the *Times of Malta* thanking the people of Malta for their many prayers and offers of support during my hospitalization was atheistically shredded. Soon one of the State Department's legal advisors would claim – fatuously – that even personal faith references when uttered by an ambassador established or coerced religious belief. The argument has so little support in the cases of the Supreme Court that it is not necessary to elaborate the error in its legal reasoning. Indeed, it was Obama's correct personal and constitutional understanding of this point – which is identical to my own understanding – in his 2006 Sojourner's speech that helped to convince me to separate from the Republican side of the ledger.

With every word of my ambassadorial life now being subject to censorship, I encountered new hostility from the public diplomacy staff, who seemingly took

umbrage with me for the extra burden of review –
even as they were the very source of the burden.
John and I had planned to spend a few tea and
toasts during my August vacation to see if we could
discern a way forward with less resistance –
drawing, John said with a twinkle in his eye, on
how well he had worked things out with the late
Cardinal McIntyre, who had taken issue with
John's theological exploration of individual
conscience in the use of contraceptives. For a
second time, John ended his Skype by saying, "Get
home, Doug. I won't be lasting forever." The
accident gave proof to that premonition, and of
course, it left me without John's guidance, as
humorous or tongue-in-cheek as that likely would
have been.

29. February 2011: Of Inspection, Rescue and Rebuke

The reader will remember that the Office of the Inspector General (OIG) had signaled a long overdue review of our embassy, which occurred in early February 2011. The inspection team was a large one; but in the end, it had fewer embassy recommendations than people, and principally it recommended easily accomplished administrative changes. I did think it troubling, however, that the OIG went out of its way to question the personal reliance I would place upon faith in meeting private and public obligation. Those raising objection to the "special presidential logic" of my appointment back in Washington apparently coached the chair of the team to use the inspection to have me disavow or abandon writing and speaking on this topic. And, as it turned out, the objective may have been to prevent me from writing or speaking on any topic not completely scripted by Main State (as the Department and the

288

Secretary's office are called). That was a short leash indeed. No other Ambassador would tolerate such, or so they proclaimed (instead of facing the problem personally).

As a citizen and constitutional lawyer, I worry when government power is used to suppress faith expression. Nevertheless, I wanted to be as cooperative as possible, especially since all of the U.S. and Maltese personnel with whom I worked in the embassy itself were a delight. We had an excellent relationship of openness in which no one needed to hesitate to suggest alternatives to my own view. Hence, I acknowledged to the OIG that, pursuant to an earlier instruction from EUR, I would not revive the convocation project on inter-faith diplomacy – at least until I could get better direction from the White House. John had respect for hierarchy when he thought it wrong on contraception; I thought attempted to exhibit like deference.

However, I never promised to give up making faith reference where appropriate, and I certainly did not foreswear all speaking and writing (which would have made no sense, given my ambassadorial function). I would also give renewed emphasis to matters of port security, expansion of economic markets, and the resettlement of migrants. This was not hard to do, as I inserted each of these items into our strategic plan. What the OIG failed to understand, however, was that these matters were not unrelated to faith-based considerations exactly as the White House and the President in his own speeches had made ready reference. Port security, after all, was often aimed at terrorism or human trafficking, both of which can require some level of faith understanding to address effectively. Anyway, as is standard practice, we were shown a draft of the report prior to the inspection team's return to D.C.; and as my career deputy, Rick Mills, characterized the report to the country team, it was "excellent overall." "We should be very pleased," said this career foreign service officer, "there are very few recommendations and virtually none we can't handle easily and promptly." We had most of them done before the inspectors boarded their plane home.

30. Between Hell and High Water

In late February 2011, our part of the globe suddenly became the focus of the world. Violence broke out in Green Square in the north African city of Tripoli in Libya. That violence threatened the safety of American nationals and innocents from other countries, including Malta.

We had, as noted in the last chapter, fulfilled the administratively straightforward recommendations of the IG almost before their departure. However, these events required me to put out of my mind the IG's unfortunate disregard of the President's inter-faith initiative, as well as its arguably improper interference with the expression of my personal faith.

The distance and travel time between Valletta and Tripoli is modest: it is a roughly 30-minute flight by standard commercial plane; and by sea, barring unexpected difficulty, it would take 10 hours at the speed of 20 knots to traverse the 200 nautical miles (a nautical mile being 1.15 that of a land mile).[39]

The conditions in Tripoli worsened quickly as Muammar Qaddafi met dissent with death, and began arming his special forces. Qaddafi proclaimed to occupy no position whatsoever in the political organization of the country. While nominally honoring an Islamic preference for impermanent decision making from the bottom up, this incredulous notion of a government without structure abetted Qaddafi's oppression. A nation without well understood boundaries or defined operations is far more manipulable than a country "planted thick with laws" as Thomas More is supposed to have said to an impatient son-in-law, Will Roper. (Roper said he would cut down every law in England to get the Devil; Thomas responded: "Oh? And when the last law was down, and the Devil turned round on you – where would you hide, Roper, the laws all being flat? . . . Yes, I'd give the

---

[39] A knot is short-hand for 10 nautical miles per hour.

Devil benefit of law, for my own safety's sake.")[40] As in the Swiss retaliation below, Qaddafi was not given to nuance and uncaring of persons caught in the crossfire whose abilities to exit were thwarted by the mindless shoot-on-sight rules that accompanied his reckless weapons distributions.

The American Ambassador in Tripoli had been called home well before there was any hint of the latest violence. In diplomatic practice, directing an ambassador to return to his home country for consultations is a method of showing both concern and displeasure with the host nation. In this case, part of the message was concern over the detainment and possible mistreatment by Qaddafi of foreign businessmen and investors in the weeks in advance of the uprising. Qaddafi tended to lash out in unpredictable ways. He tied up much of the travel and trade in the Eurozone some months earlier, when the Swiss government put his family on Switzerland's no-entry list in response to some ugly behavior by a son toward hotel staff. Qaddafi, in turn, denied visas for entry into Libya by all member nations of the Eurozone across the board.

---

[40] ROBERT BOLT, A MAN FOR ALL SEASONS, act I, at 66 (Vintage 1990)

Not surprisingly, then, Libya was one of the last countries to experience the so-called "Arab Spring" in the North African region below Malta. Tunisia and Egypt were first, responding at least at first constructively and with relative peacefulness to the demands for freedom often said to have been facilitated by the ease of organization on Facebook. But Qaddafi was hardly the type to yield to chants and placards inspired by computer networks. He pushed back swiftly and hard against those who might bring democracy to the shores of Tripoli. Forty embassy staff, including the Deputy Chief of Mission (DCM), and some 167 Americans were now stranded and at risk. The commercial opportunities for escape were limited and fast becoming nonexistent. The Tripoli airport was overrun, and it is unclear whether ground passage to the airport was safe.

If there was any doubt about the risk to civilians, it evaporated when two Libyan pilots defected. Navigating their French made Mirage fighters well below the normal flight path, the two planes literally appeared out of the blue at Malta's international airport in a relatively few minutes after take-off. The defecting pilots reported being ordered to fire on innocent, unarmed civilians in

Benghazi, which had been a long-time locus of Qaddafi opposition. The pilots were granted asylum and despite some fist waving by Qaddafi, the government of Malta – consistent with a posture of not giving aid to military hostilities of any kind – kept the planes out of commission. There were plausible accounts of Malta disrupting Qaddafi's efforts to export new Mirage flight crews to replevy the planes; that is, steal them back. He failed, but the threat to U.S. citizens and those of other nations closely associated with the North Atlantic Treaty Organization (NATO) appeared even starker. NATO moved to establish a "no-fly" zone, which later would persuade the United Nations to allow airstrikes to maintain it and protect civilians. In the final days of February 2011, time was of the essence to get people out to safety. What to do?

As it happened the evening before, I had dinner with James Satariano and his wife and former US Ambassador Kathryn Proffit, who had been in Malta visiting family. Satariano is a leader of AmCham, the American Chamber of Commerce in Europe, and he happened to mention that his son-in-law Frances Portelli had recently acquired a high-speed catamaran for his ferry service to Italy. The vessel was large and capable of transporting several hundred comfortably, and at high speed (approximately 45 knots). The ferry came immediately to mind when I learned of the foreclosed commercial options, and by my calculation – if the winter sea was behaving itself – we could do a round trip in nine or ten hours.

Having kicked around a number of possibilities with Washington, I called Satariano and asked him to explore the possibility of the U.S. leasing the vessel, even as I knew I was asking a great deal to put this significant investment in harm's way. It did not take long to get a call back. "He'll do it," Satariano said, with the kind of commanding influence or respect fathers-in-law assume they will receive (but in reality seldom do). Nevertheless, Satariano in short order had the boat in tow, as it were. I relayed the now concrete possibility to Secretary Clinton in Washington via her chief of staff, after crunching the numbers.[41] Presidential candidates who talk casually about "belt-tightening" and the like might want to keep the emergency needs of their citizens in mind.

---

[41] Even in a crisis, there's a budget. Indeed, because of delay associated with Libyan confusion and some resistance as well as bad weather, we broke the budget – which was another difficulty one would have preferred to spare the President who was in almost constant debate with Congress over raising the budget ceiling.

Little time was wasted pulling together a crew. The ferry had an experienced pilot, but we needed to have individuals from the embassy with proper clearances to access intelligence information on anything that might be seen as threatening the vessel en-route. This was a humanitarian, not a military, mission; but it couldn't hurt to have Lt. Commander Phil Webb and Greg Tozzi of the Navy aboard to bolster the determination of the commercial ferry pilot, and to give strategic advice should trouble break out. Because national borders were being crossed, there was a practical need for consular personnel to examine passports and arrange visas for onward destinations. Making it clear that I intended to go, I darted into my office for a duffle-bag. Rick Mills, my deputy, was fast on my heels. "You cannot go," said Mills. "Really," I said with a smile, "it sure looks like I'm going. Carol and the children are back in the States and I was planning on eating out in any case."

"Look," said Rick, "this is one of those times the general has to ride behind the lines to keep the overall focus of the operation." "Not very courageous, your hypothetical general," I said. "Maybe not," came Rick's lightning-fast reply, "but smart, because he knows the irrational and showy nature of his opponent – and targeting an American ambassador sailing into his port would play to his strength. And in that targeting, everyone's life would be put at greater risk." "Not to mention," I said, almost in unison now with his expressed wisdom, "creating a circumstance that could escalate a conflict involving multiple nations far too quickly."

At that moment, I knew I had hired one very wise deputy. While I hemmed and hawed a bit more, I knew he was right; and the crew embarked without either Rick or myself, but with several of our finest Navy and Coast Guard personnel, who were usually tasked with assisting the Armed Forces of Malta (AFM) with maritime training or assisting other humanitarian efforts related to the sizeable irregular migrant population in Malta. Also essential was our Consular Chief, Tracy Brown, to coordinate the immigration matters. Tracy was relatively new to Malta, and while highly capable, she certainly could use a hand. There was a need to process documentation promptly in order to get a large number of persons to their forward destinations in a hurry, without at the same time providing access to Malta and the rest of Europe to someone seeking to do harm.

And here came Rick's second surprise of the evening: he volunteered his wife, Leigh Carter. "Wait a minute, Rick," I said, "even putting to one side some sort of spousal immunity, surely there is some corollary of the rule in Doug's case that applies here." "Not really," he said. "She is not Ambassador." "Maybe not, but have you no interest in ever enjoying another home-cooked meal?" I said. The tension of the day was relieved by laughter. Once again, however, Rick was right. Leigh had a very distinguished Foreign Service career in her own right. While recently retired, she had been deputy chief of mission, and Charge, in Berne, Switzerland. Leigh stepped right up without hesitation, and as far as I can tell, Rick is eating all right.

Adding medical and other personnel, we pushed for a speedy embarkation both for the safety of those in the cross-fire in Libya, but also for the well-being of the catamaran, itself. There was a third reason. The U.S. has excellent weather forecasting resources, and even with the commonly described unpredictable winds of the Mediterranean, we could see a major storm approaching and its likely path. Since experienced voices confirmed that the trip should at most take nine hours, it was reasonable to anticipate a quick in and out well before gale force 5 (15 feet or greater) waves would threaten the vessel.

Getting access to the Libyan port threw all these calculations to the wind – literally. Qaddafi's forces may or may not have had the port closed; the information which the pilot, and relayed to us via satellite phone was sketchy, and often, inconsistent. This was a nation in turmoil, and at this early point in the conflict, one got the sense that the average Libyan was watching carefully – to see if this was a real opening to freedom, or just another of so many uprisings over the years, where Qaddafi would ultimately squelch dissent with the leaders of the present agitation (like those of earlier attempts at reform who disappeared in the night), never to be heard or seen again. Hours were spent out in the bay as the happenstance collection of Libyans loyal to Qaddafi – at the moment – debated what to do.

Precious hours passed, and we finally dropped anchor, but then there was more delay. Being in port did not mean that our crew and passengers could get off the ship. Those nominally in charge of the port made repeated calls asking for direction. Our temporary Libyan captors were seemingly still confused as to the treatment of noncombatant

citizens. While it was unlikely that the Geneva
Convention (which covers such matters) was being
researched on the other end of those cell phones,
those who seemed in charge maintained the status
quo, with the exception of the confiscation of some
camera equipment. (Qaddafi was notorious for
manipulating the media and that meant keeping
any unfavorable video out of the news.) Thankfully,
we had arranged for the ferry to have plenty of
water and light food. In the end, while no one was
threatened directly, neither the nearby gunfire nor
the bluster of some of those keeping watch of the
vessel were calculated to put one at ease.

That said, despite their years of oppression, the
Libyans are a very likeable people. While it may be
just as unreliable to take the measure of a nation
by the serendipitous kindness of a few as it is
unfair to condemn an entire people for the rudeness
of the same number, my experiences with Libyan
nationals was uniformly positive, and it came from
a cross-section of sources. First, my eldest son,
Keenan, following the hard work of a Supreme
Court clerkship with Chief Justice John Roberts,
took an extended "walking tour" of Africa. This
included some substantial time in Libya.
Ostensibly preparing an analysis of the fairness of
various African legal systems for a NGO that works

for justice on that continent, Keenan commendably took his time to experience life in countries in ways that cannot be appreciated from the top floor of a law firm in downtown Los Angeles. With Keenan's California blond hair giving away his origins, his journal reported feeling entirely welcome by the Libyans he encountered.

Likewise, members of the crew reported that the good hearts of those placed in charge of the port may well have protected those aboard from those less well intentioned. Finally, toward the end of the long day and evening of the vessel's return to Valletta, a corporate executive of a major hotel in Tripoli regaled me with story after story of Libyan hard work and just plain thoughtfulness. In the end, all of the Americans and foreign nationals were rescued safely, though because of the initial delay and the storm, it took far longer than anticipated – indeed, it took 36 hours, during which the satellite phone reports alternately raised and lowered our anxiety. During that period, Secretary Clinton interrupted her many responsibilities to speak directly to the crew and passengers to wish them well.

Meanwhile down at the quay, every member of Embassy-Valletta was working in full concert with a caring, effective, and cooperative Maltese government. Phone calls to the PM and his staff were immediately taken, and customs and immigration matters were smoothed. As a result, these weary and at-risk passengers, upon arrival in Malta, could get their first full night's sleep in two or three days, knowing that competent consular officers would await them in the morning to rush through a visa to permit travel to their onward destinations as quickly as possible. In addition, the Red Cross, Dr. Cassar's health department, and other paramedic or nursing volunteers were ready with emergency equipment and medical care. Thus, the few passengers who suffered injury in the travail could immediately receive care. It was my privilege to greet virtually every passenger as they disembarked in Malta; the first words to me, often preceding a hug from men, women, and children alike, were "God bless America" and a great many compliments to the Coast Guard, Navy and Consular personnel who were aboard.

As I have said many times, I accepted these gracious statements not for myself, but for the citizens of my country, whose scarce and hard-earned dollars supply the needs of our embassies around the world. It is the same taxpayer and the Senate and President of the United States who

303

permitted me to represent them in the Mediterranean region during this challenging time. America had been blessed that evening to get all of her people home safely, and to be able to assist nationals of numerous other countries in need of safe passage. I also have little doubt that what we accomplished was greatly advanced by the wisdom of the Maltese: to make no man their enemy. This American diplomat learned that the true meaning of neutrality is not indifference to the wars and skirmishes of mankind, but the sincere appreciation that the true enemy is the cause that gives rise to such violence. Also on display throughout was Malta's commitment to step up to heal the wounds that may result if man's efforts fail to avoid the injuries that flow from unwarranted suspicion and hatred.

31. Downed by Friendly Fire[42]

Rescuing those caught in the cross-hairs of Qaddafi's madness turned out to be child's play in comparison to an IG on a mission. It seems that back in D.C., it was noted that I had written a column on Monsignor John Sheridan and Sister Mary Campbell for the *Malibu Times*. The essay arose in conjunction with the paper's 2010 year-end wrap up of the news. Of course, in a town like Malibu where people care about and know each other by name, it was hardly surprising that John and Mary, who towered so largely in local (if not international) memories, would be given

---

[42] My gratitude to the late Joseph Feuerherd, the editor of the *National Catholic Reporter* (NCR), who in one of his last well prepared reports for the NCR prepared an almost line-by-line refutation of the IG criticism that I devoted insufficient effort to the work of the embassy, and assumed a mandate to advance the President's inter-faith diplomacy initiative. He Feuerherd concludes: "If outcomes are what matters, then Douglas Kmiec, US Ambassador to Malta, appears to be doing a fine job." Joe Feuerherd, *Kmiec Faces Friendly Fire*, Nat'l Cath. Rep., Apr. 8, 2011, *available at* http://ncronline.org/blogs/ncr-today/kmiec-faces-friendly-fire. I would hope that the reader might find the first proposition simply beyond belief in light of the work done in association with the rescue effort alone described in the previous chapter. As described in this chapter, the President's own "special logic," as it was recounted at my swearing in, contradicts the IG's mockingly sarcastic suggestion that there was no presidential inter-faith initiative.

proportionate attention. The editors of the *Times* are a husband and wife team who live just behind my house, and whose community spirit and sensitivity is much to be admired. They asked if I would write a reflection on John and Mary. I had not done this before for the *Times,* and as he pointed out, our neighbors in Malibu "needed" to hear from me. I agreed. It was a matter of simple respect for John and Mary that posed no risk or inconvenience to the United States.

Nevertheless, this column, and one other on the 100th anniversary of Ronald Reagan's birth, led to my being publicly rebuked for my continued faith-based writing and speaking of my own "promise" to forego such practice. (In defiance, it was now being trumpeted across the front pages of every Maltese paper.) With the permission of the *Malibu Times,* I reprint this column that so exhausted the patience of Washington here. Note, in particular, the disclaimer at the end.

A New Year of Kindness*
Remembering Monsignor John and Sister Mary

Welcome 2011, even as the somber imprint of 2010 shall be forever with me. In late spring, Dad died. In early summer, my late mother's only sister passed. Late summer claimed Guido de Marco, the revered former president of Malta and UN General Assembly, who had taken a special interest in his country's new American Ambassador. Christmas would call my Malibu neighbor, Bill(y) Miller, whose natural joviality brightened more than a few soggy coastal days along La Costa Beach. But it was a roughly 4-second slide off a canyon road that would leave the deepest scar.

There has not been a day, an hour, even a minute since I have not grieved for the loss of Monsignor John V. Sheridan and Sister Mary Campbell. Last week, waiting for a CT scan and ECG in a Maltese hospital before undergoing the follow-up major surgery to what John and I endured side-by-side in the UCLA trauma unit, I happened to encounter for the first time a blog commentary thoughtfully invited by the community spirit of *The Malibu Times*. These expressions of love readily tapped into my own memories of these clerical Irish twins, including our last joyful moments together (and they were joyful, since somehow God sheltered all of us from the apprehension of fear almost literally to the final moment). Sister Mary went immediately by angelic acclamation to God, whilst John and I held string rosaries given to us just minutes earlier at a Mass and lunch for the anniversary of the Sisters of Saint Louis. The highway patrol and

Calabasas rescuers were commendably quick with a transporting helicopter, but not even these local heroes could outpace Mary's early check-in to fashion John's heavenly study. Some say age determined survival. Maybe. But it is just as plausible that God saw two unblemished souls of extraordinary kindness, and their younger charge, with work yet to do.

The fact of suffering and death, observed C.S. Lewis and others, is undoubtedly the single greatest challenge to faith, since its distribution and occurrence seems so entirely random, and therefore, unfair. This was not John's way. Forty years ago, when almost exactly my age, John wrote: "Death [to a person of faith] is not the eyes' last episode following a long or short illness, old age, dotage, [or] auto accident . . . It is release from the bonds of mortality . . . [of] sin, sickness, pain."

The Monsignor's words were not gratuitously extolling death, but rather urging us not to fear it, and, in that intrepid confidence of faith, to seek the fullness of life. That is the way John walked ever confidently among the beautiful hills above Malibu. With Mary following closely, John can be felt there today, inviting us to his path of unconditional kindness, and calling our names even as he self-deprecatingly proclaims not to remember them.

And if you look to a very far horizon, you will find me, wounded physically, but redoubled in faith with a pounding heart proclaiming, "Death, where is your sting." And through that persistent tear that lingers in my eye, I will spot His shillelagh lifted high, so that I, and the vast numbers whom he loved, and who love him still, might follow.

Douglas W. Kmiec is professor of law (on leave for foreign service).

*MALIBU TIMES, Jan. 5, 2011, *available at*
http://www.malibutimes.com/articles/2011/01/06/opinion/opinion/opinio n1.txt. Reprinted with the kind permission of Arnold and Karen York, the publishers of the *Times.*

And the Reagan column? Having served as the late President's constitutional lawyer, this essay was requested in conjunction with a special centenary celebration of Ronald Reagan's birth – the 100th birthday being February 6, 2011. The request admittedly came late, or at least late for the State Department, which found that the easiest way to handle my requests for writing approval was simply to extend the pre-clearance time past the submission deadline. As a consequence, I submitted the essay to both the *Los Angeles Times* and the Department simultaneously, alerting the editor of the *Times* that I would need to withdraw the essay if it was disapproved of by the Department. The *L.A. Times* accepted the essay; the Department simply gave a categorical "No", without explanation. Faith wasn't mentioned, other than stating that President Reagan encouraged "good faith interpretation of the law." Hardly controversial. I sent the essay with my regret for its lack of publication to Mrs. Reagan. My university thoughtfully included it later in their alumni magazine. On re-reading the essay as I write, the most ironic of the paragraphs may be this one:

"Ronald Reagan deserves ample credit for making America stand tall in the face of the daunting challenges of runaway inflation and formidable Cold War threat. He was "transformative," as President Obama has reflected. My new boss is right about that, and lest you think it odd for this Reaganite to now be working for Obama, you need only to take a closer look to find the ingrained empathy and extension of open hand by which both men conduct their respective public responsibilities."

Shortly before the accident in a Skype conversation with Monsignor John and Sister Mary, they asked of my work in the embassy. Despite a quite busy week bringing the new embassy compound to completion, and having even secured some significant funding for solar energy, I laughed and turned their question around, saying something to the effect of "Well, what the heck are you two mischief-makers up to now that the whole country has health care, and prosperity for the average family – as opposed to massive profits for corporations – is right around the corner?" "That's right," said John, laughing. "All the more reason to get yourself back here; you know I am not going to last forever." This was the third time John spoke in anticipation of his death. Those last words spoken

311

in jest, of course, are haunting, and below I explain why it is my view they were mistaken.

When the Inspector General published its "rebuke" of my work for the President's faith-based initiative, a respected *L.A. Times* columnist investigated and found an effort to muffle inter-faith diplomacy, and perhaps some displeasure with my efforts to keep the U.S. an honest broker in the Israeli-Palestine dispute.[43] Maybe this is the definitive explanation, but I have learned in politics that there can be more than one "Machiavelli" operating at the same time. It would not be farfetched to think that some long-time Democrat partisans forged an alliance with some careerists out of some unfortunate jealousies between the career foreign service and presidential appointees. Still others might have been especially suspicious of the Catholic law professor whose most immediate party affiliation was Republican in support of Ronald Reagan. But then, all such plotters overlooked not only my father's campaign role for President Kennedy and my own college

---

[43] See the column by syndicated columnist Tim Rutten, infra.

politicking for RFK, but also my mother's personal calling to make the Kmiec household bipartisan by reflexively cancelling Dad's vote.

No person and no government can or should impose faith belief. Coerced faith, like coerced love, as our Creator and we His creatures know only too well, is an oxymoron. Yet, by the same token, no person, whether ambassador or not, should be rebuked for seeing the world through the eyes of faith. In any event, I knew I could not subtract faith from my make-up. For one thing, I had a moral obligation to write this very book, to illustrate with gratitude how so much of my public and private life has been, and continues to be, influenced by the brilliant mind and gentleness of Monsignor John Sheridan and his Theology of Kindness. Monsignor John and Sister Mary enriched my life and those of many others beyond measure. While in some ways it would have been easier to be far away from the personal and physical reminders of the accident, I am reasonably confident that John and Mary would have nodded approval to the decision now made.

I offered my resignation to the President.

When I put together the surprise OIG "rebuke" in conjunction with its surprise leak and with the inter-faith conference cancellation and months of ascending pre-clearance censorship in disregard of the "special presidential logic" of my appointment, it seemed reasonable to conclude that I was being asked to choose between faith and freedom and the privilege of continuing to serve in high position.

That said, no one asked for the resignation or even hinted at it. My career Deputy Chief of Mission tried to talk me out of it. I would have liked to have been persuaded. I wasn't.

Unless the President would affirm his inter-faith diplomatic initiative, the rebuke which had been leaked so prominently to all the papers in my host country –the IG more or less admits to being the source – seriously wounded my credible standing as the U.S. representative. An independent, democratic nation, Malta often sees global issues as we do. Yet, Malta has a unique Mediterranean perspective, a constitutionally-embedded obligation of neutrality, and free-port and trading interests that can also place us in disagreement. When some as-yet-unforeseen issue puts us on different paths, the President is entitled to have an ambassador with full credibility in order to have the highest chance of diplomatic agreement in favor of the view of the United States. Without so much as even a small nod of presidential confirmation of the President's own logic, the credibility of my service had been damaged. How could it be otherwise? As one senior EU diplomat put it, I had been "wiki-leaked" by my own Department.[44]

No, an offer of resignation was the only honorable step; even though I thoroughly enjoyed my work and assignment in Malta, and the Maltese people were to me, as they were to St. Paul, "uncommonly kind." The President of Malta has generously written: "A great applause was reserved for you

[44] "Wiki-leaks" refers to the alleged theft and then Internet disclosure of thousands of pages of classified and confidential diplomatic documents by a low-ranking Army officer, which prompted a government-wide effort to limit access to such documentation. (In Kafka-esque fashion, State Department personnel can neither admit nor deny the existence of such documents, let alone their theft, under the laws as they now exist.) As reported in the press these documents contain candid and sometimes unflattering portrayals of foreign leaders. The EU ambassador made a comment about my situation, asking (unfortunately almost rhetorically), "What is it with you Americans; don't you like diplomacy? First, you leak nonsense about us, and now you leak nonsense about yourselves."

when I mentioned your name in my speech[45] at the inauguration of the new embassy. Mingling later with the visitors, they kept mentioning your name in high regard even the embassy staff. Well deserved."

By comparison, President Obama never responded. For months, I audaciously held an Obama-sized hope that the silence signaled his intent to let the furor precipitated by the unjustified IG-leak abate; and then, without fuss, he would just utter a four word "carry on good friend," to resolutely keep me upon our shared course of inter-faith diplomacy. But there was only silence. When fall approached, and the university needed to know whether or not to include me in the teaching line-up, I asked my life-long friend, Senator Dick Lugar of Indiana (who is often regarded as the Senate's unofficial "Secretary of State), if he thought it worthwhile to

---

[45] In his prepared remarks for the dedication of our new embassy compound on July 15, 2011, President Abela stated: "I wish to salute Ambassador Kmiec and to thank him for the sterling work he carried out with such grace and dignity to see Maltese-American relations strengthen even further."

inquire further. In a typically thoughtful gesture of friendship and bipartisanship, Senator Lugar had attended my swearing in at the State Department – as he had done for my previous federal posts in the Reagan White House and the Reagan and senior Bush Justice Departments. In addition, a young Senator Obama had valued his close friendship with Senator Lugar, who burnished the younger man's knowledge of foreign policy. The Senator now wanted to know the answer himself, and he inquired of the President's thinking by formal letter. No response.

I suppose an answer might be inferred by the Department's discontinuance of my salary, but personnel decision by inference is certainly odd; and, frankly, given what foreign service entails in one's personal and family life, not consistent with the thoughtful father and spouse I perceive the President to be.

Even more perplexing than my own vaporous end as Ambassador is whether President Obama knows that his international inter-faith initiative – in the Mediterranean at least -- has been scuttled below

317

him. He may not. Joshua DuBois, his good friend and capable presidential assistant for faith-based issues has had a full agenda reaching out to domestic religious leaders, but the international side has been lethargic.

2011 drew to a close. Secretary Clinton dropped by Malta to announce the President was nominating Gina Abercrombie-Winstanley, a diplomat with excellent credentials presently in the Department's office on C Street in Washington, as my successor. Nothing was said as to whether she would pick up the President's inter-faith diplomacy initiative, but I hope that she – or someone – will do so.

To prepare the Secretary for her State visit to Malta, I did a comprehensive written briefing of the Mediterranean region and Malta's existing and potential role in lending stability to the democratic transitions in that vital region, and I have publicly and privately offered to help my nominated successor in any way possible and appropriate, though it was an offer met with more silence. As we approach the Lenten season, Ms. Abercrombie-Winstanley had not been confirmed. This likely has nothing to do with her and her fine credentials, but would rather seem to be part of a larger campaign of "no" indulged by the Senate opposition to President Obama.

Recently, the President made several "recess appointments," which permit service under a temporary arrangement when the Senate is out of session. These have been controversial for many presidents, but they signify an even further break of relations between President Obama and the opposition. Anyway, Ms. Ambercrombie-Winstanley is caught in the switches, and were it not for the superb judgment of my Deputy, Richard Mills, who has been serving as Charge d'Affaire, I am certain Malta's foreign minister, Tonio Borg, would be distressed by what a less knowledgeable foreign leader might perceive as a diplomatic slight. It most assuredly is not, but the United States is most fortunate to have relations with Nations accepting (or at least not misreading) the gamesmanship of American politics.

319

As I wrote in farewell to my embassy and the people and leadership of Malta, "Disappointed? Yes. Defeated? Never."

The challenges facing President Obama remain substantial. Unemployment remains just below 9 percent, though the American auto industry in Detroit, where many Maltese migrated, has lately performed very well. Less encouraging for millions of homeowners who have lost or are losing their homes is the distressing reality that foreclosure relief seems to be eluding those most in need. The stock market gyrates wildly both here and abroad. Congressional temporizing over debt ceilings and super committees to reduce deficits, triggered by mistaken military missions and corporate manipulation and dishonesty, puts downward pressure on the U.S. and Euro-zone economies. Greece adds confusion over whether it should tighten its belt in exchange for half its national debt being excused. Collaterally, the dour economic conditions have contributed to "occupations" and other public disturbance from London to Washington D.C. to Los Angeles, and so far have left the "Arab spring" without democratic blossom.

Were it possible to reconvene tea and toast, our conversation might well press the limits of the available slices. At a minimum, John and Mary would have had great empathy and concern over the plight of the average working family.

My Republican friends are urging my return, but perhaps "audacious hope" springs eternal; and, for now at least, I retain the belief that Barack Obama has the leadership capacity, the individual talent, and well-formed conscience to be a transformative president. However, presidents don't run the country alone; the people do – especially those people whom the President attracts to government to faithfully execute the laws as well as to carry forward his vision. Here the President has been let down, but it is his constitutional duty to address and correct – because, unlike the uncommunicative nature of his White House, the American people will be heard in 2012. Those who share the President's view that government exists to secure the common good will be even more entitled than myself to know: "What happened?"

Here is what the *L.A. Times* determined:

A voice for faith-based diplomacy is muffled[46]

Elements with the State Department are attempting to silence an American diplomat who believes he was personally charged by the White House with promoting President Obama's interfaith initiatives.

The diplomat is the U.S. ambassador to Malta, Douglas Kmiec, a professor of constitutional law at Pepperdine and former dean of the law school at Catholic University of America. He served in

Kmiec has emerged as one of this country's most important witnesses to the proposition that religious conviction and political civility need not be at odds

---

[46] Tim Rutten, *A Voice for Faith-Based Diplomacy Is Muffled*, LOS ANGELES TIMES, Apr. 13, 2011, *available at* http://articles.latimes.com/2011/apr/13/opinion/la-oe-0413-rutten-20110413.

the Office of Legal Counsel under Presidents Reagan and George W. Bush and, as a devout Catholic, for many years has been prominent in the antiabortion movement and among those arguing for a larger role for faith-based efforts in public life. Even though he and the president disagree on abortion, Kmiec said he found in Obama someone who had "a deep faith himself and was capable of understanding the difference among people and of having empathy for that difference."

After his election, Obama appointed Kmiec as U.S. ambassador to Malta, and, at his swearing-in ceremony, a White House spokesman talked of how the president was counting on the new envoy to further his interfaith initiatives abroad. The appointment was a good fit; Malta is a socially conservative, overwhelmingly Catholic country where abortion and divorce still are illegal. Kmiec is, by all accounts, popular with both the Maltese people and their government.

Last Thursday, however, the State Department's inspector general issued a report on our embassy there that castigated Kmiec for his "outside writings," demanding that he cease, while also reporting that his efforts in Malta had been effective and that his staff's morale is high. Kmiec, the inspector general wrote, "had achieved some policy successes. He is respected by

Maltese officials and most mission staff, but his unconventional approach to his role as ambassador has created friction with principal officials in Washington.... Based on a belief that he was given a special mandate to promote President Obama's interfaith initiatives, he has devoted considerable time to writing articles for publication in the United States as well as in Malta, and to presenting his views on subjects outside the bilateral portfolio.... He also looks well beyond the bilateral relationship when considering possible events for the mission to host in Malta."

If all this sounds familiar, it's because all bureaucrats share the spirit, if not the politics, of the commissar.

According to a source familiar with the situation who asked not to be named, Kmiec first found himself at odds with the State Department bureaucracy shortly after taking office, when Mideast peace envoy George Mitchell asked him to fill in at a U.N.-sponsored conference in Malta at which Mediterranean parliamentarians were to discuss the Israeli-Palestinian conflict. The Israeli delegation walked out over the Palestinians' characterization of the Gaza situation, and officials in Washington urged Kmiec to follow suit, or at least not to deliver a planned address. He reportedly replied that he would require instructions from

Secretary of State Hillary Rodham Clinton to do that, then delivered a forthright speech affirming Obama's commitment to a two-state solution and Israeli security.

Since then, Kmiec has been harassed by officials at State over his outside writing, even when it involves personal matters of faith. A memorial piece on his father's death for the Jesuit magazine America, for example, was so severely edited that it misrepresented the dead man's views. He was prevented from writing about Ronald Reagan for these pages, and he has been forbidden to speak or write the words "faith-based diplomacy." He also was forced to cancel a prestigious international conference on interfaith cooperation that he had organized.

It's a petty campaign being waged against ideas and values that desperately need a hearing.

After the release of the inspector general's report, Kmiec told the Associated Press that he was "troubled and saddened that a handful of individuals within my department in Washington seem to manifest a hostility to expressions of faith and efforts to promote better interfaith understanding. Our Constitution proudly protects the free exercise of religion — even for ambassadors."

325

Over the last few years, Kmiec has emerged as one of this country's most important witnesses to the proposition that religious conviction and political civility need not be at odds; that reasonable people of determined good conscience, whatever their faith or lack thereof, can find ways to cooperate in the common good. Though Kmiec has not sought their intervention, the president and the secretary of State ought to deal with the bureaucrats seeking to silence a voice whose only offense is to speak in the vocabulary of our own better angels.

*****

32. Transcending Politics; Respecting Difference; Finding the Way

I doubt whether John or Mary saw me as sitting at the right elbow of President Obama, and as Ambassador to a distant country, I certainly wasn't. Nonetheless, the three of us were attracted to the young Mr. Obama for his social vision of greater economic fairness for working families and his good sense to oppose the war in Iraq and the promiscuous introduction of American force – rather than an American sensitivity informed by inter-faith dialogue and diplomacy – to resolve dispute nonviolently. Like myself, John and Mary were never ideological partisans. That is not the way of the Church.

The Catholic way transcends politics, and even most of what passes for serious debate and discussion. John and Mary were always careful to keep their focus, like that of our Church, on respect for the human person made in the image and likeness of God. How we answer Matthew's questions – do we feed the hungry? Clothe the naked? etc. – far more than our politics determines our personal destiny, and I venture to say, our democratic republic as well.

Oh, and why was John's quip that "he wouldn't last forever" in error? The answer obviously rests in the fullness of their faith.

As described, I concluded that to stand up to the bureaucracy in a restrained, but firm voice of faith, that I was honoring the Theology of Kindness given to us in the life witness of Monsignor John and Sister Mary. Perhaps, however, you disagree. Part of the Theology of Kindness is to remember that people of different faiths, and even within the same faith, will see the world differently even on issues that to a believer may appear to be easily answered from the Magisterium or scripture. I have illustrated the impact of Monsignor John's Theology in the context of the faith challenges presented to me.

In the remaining parts of the book, our perspective will be looking forward in order that we can benefit from the Theology of Kindness that yields clarity for action. Pope Paul VI told us that "if we want peace, we must work for justice." Monsignor John's instruction to "Lift Up Our Hearts", and his suggested means for doing so with The Theology of Kindness, is now put to work. We will see that even in 2012, a presidential election year, when primary campaigns bring out extremes and the general campaign motivates vacuous bromides, Monsignor's Theology brings insight to the most contentious public issues.

The Theology of Kindness does not proceed by legalistic or moralistic prescription. That, again, was not John or Mary's way. Instead, the Theology of Kindness for John and Mary was dependent upon trust in the Holy Spirit. It is the Virgin Mary's resounding "Yes! Let it be done unto me."

Drawing upon John's optimism and Mary's gentleness, and in the Spirit of the Magnificat, let us turn to the quandaries and challenges we are now faced with addressing without John and Mary physically among us.

Part VI

The Life that Remains – bringing Kindness into the Public Square

33. Love Your Enemies

Monsignor knew we learn greatly from each other. We "glorify God when we do good works and form community." However, John would have asked, "What is it that we are doing when we engage in name calling or by our actions or influence divide one from the other?"

John was seldom discouraged, even as he knew we had a long way to go to build a civil order upon kindness, understanding and respect. Yet, even when criticizing, John had the gift of removing the sting of criticism, so the genuine love behind the correction could be seen. In the following passage, John gently, but firmly, illustrates how the well-known Catholic writer, George Weigel, by belittling those Catholics who see their political choices differently than Mr. Weigel, defeats his own message

Hear the gentle, but clarion instruction from John himself:

George Weigel, a lover of words, distinguished scholar, writer, the biographer of John Paul II and a recognized apologist for our church, just this last week, when commenting on Catholics who supported President Obama rather than voting for Senator McCain as he did in the recent 2008 election, used phrases and sentences like "tribal voting," "described by some bishops as immoral," and "certainly stupid."

Having complimented Mr. Weigel's erudition, John accepts Weigel's criticism that demands churchmen make more "effective use of the pulpit to unsettle settled patterns of mindlessness." In case, Mr. Weigel or John's readers missed the compliment to soften the heart and open the mind, Monsignor delivers it directly:

George's readers and admirers - of whom I am most often one - will by and large agree [regarding the need for fuller insight from the pulpit]. But, when we ask ourselves, what is happening here, happening in our church? Does Mr. Weigel expect his fellow Catholics who he has just belittled to feel good about him, much less to think through what he is trying to tell them? Is he really speaking to them? Or is he addressing himself just to the ones who see everything through his lenses?

Tragically, we Catholics have set ourselves up in two camps, with our dual media, print and electronic. And the end result of our heated language is not charitable conversation but a hardening of hearts. And here is where the Gospels are at their clearest.

"But I say unto you, love your enemies, and pray for them that persecute you." (Matthew 5:44)

How can we possibly love those who hate us; those who constantly lie or distort our views? Obviously, the instruction is not to endorse or sign onto the hatred or the distortion. The Theology of Kindness would easily find that to be rank contradiction. No, the instruction given in Matthew and by the Monsignor is not to approve the uncivil or bad conduct of another, or to engage in it ourselves, but to rise above the animus in a manner that conveys our best wishes for the personal well-being of even those who have turned their backs to us, or wrongly persecuted us.

It is from this aspect of the Scriptural teaching that we learn to distinguish the sin from the sinner. Sin, especially a sinful practice contrary to the very nature of the human person, needs no further condemnation; it is already contrary to the laws of God. What is needed from us is a kind word for the sinner. In that kindness is a seed of hope that good may yet come from evil. We casually wish those in our circle of friends "God's blessing." It is easy to think well of those who have flattered or befriended us. However, the admonition to love our enemy ensures that the circle is not that restricted. It challenges us to speak well of those who speak ill of us. This is often characterized as the most difficult of Christian duties. John and Mary made it look second nature.

Prior to the accident, it had been my privilege to lead a religious education or enrichment hour for adults before Mass on Sundays. There was some worry that with my absence in Europe on foreign assignment and in the aftermath of Monsignor John's death that these discussions might simply end.

They did not. These class sessions had taken hold and were now taught by a wide variety of parishioners.

Indeed, the first Sunday I returned from Europe, Sister Brigid was leading a discussion of the consequences of failing to forgive our enemies – the most obvious being our continued nourishing of grievances, bringing us only simmering anger, depression, and unhappiness.

Christ does not want our misery. He wants us to be happy. In this way, we come to understand the most difficult duty of loving our enemy to be the source of our greatest good. God is clever that way, and the times in which we live – characterized by ever nastier cable and Internet banter – supply ample opportunity to be the beneficiaries of that cleverness.

When an enemy holds hatred in his heart, our happiness and his possible transformation depends on our meeting that hatred with love. When blogs and other publications slander us, the best response is to find that which can be praised in the speaker or writer. Injurious and abusive actions require the assistance of others for our immediate protection, but they depend upon our prayers for correction.

The Monsignor would frequently end his instruction with a reference to a feast day or prayer. His plea for civil discourse, so beautifully given in concrete example was delivered on the Feast Day of Christ our King, who invites us to begin, the Monsignor noted, *living the language and the joy of Christian love.*

34. Better yet, have no enemies

As I write this book on my time as Obama's Ambassador, recording the memories (both happy and bittersweet) of John Sheridan and Mary Campbell, it occurs to me that people might begin to think of them as superhuman – the equivalent of those martyrs of the Holy Church who seem perfect and utterly selfless in their willingness to die for Christ.

It would be wrong to think of John or Mary as so sainted as not to be bothered or troubled by the temptations and weaknesses similar to our own. Unfortunately, sometimes even they too held onto animosity toward others.

Could it actually be that there was someone in the universe, let alone a parishioner, keeping hatred in their heart for John Sheridan or Mary Campbell? I was always incredulous, but John assured me it was true, sadly so.

On one or two occasions, John would recount how someone in the parish – and he was very discreet not to mention names or to disclose confidences – took issue with a sermon or essay and simply would not let go of the matter. As he would tell of the disagreement, it was plain that John himself bore no continuing grudge, let alone hatred. John sought peace categorically, in the world and in his relationships. He truly did strive for no enemies. Moreover, John would use evening vespers to pray for those who might hold anger toward him. By means of these devotions, John would free himself of the worry or the burden that he might be the occasion for the anger of someone else and a separation from the Church.

These moments would tend to be serious ones, but John would find a way to lighten the reminder of the dear cost we pay by not forgiving those with whom we may have once been in disagreement.

At a recent awards banquet where I gave the invocation, the youthful master of ceremonies, intrigued or intimated by my advanced years, told us about the previous Sunday's sermon given by his new pastor, in All Saints Episcopal Church, Pasadena. Its subject was "Living 'agape', or authentic love". At a high point in his eloquent probing the inner dynamics of human love, and hate, love in the reverse, the pastor paused dramatically and asked: "Is there anyone, anyone here in this vast congregation who can truthfully say that he or she has no enemies?"

One old man raised his hand, at which there was an enormous outbreak of clapping. When the rousing acclamation subsided, the preacher left his pulpit, walked down to the back of the church and handed the microphone to the old man. You have no enemies, Sir?" "Nope," the old man said. "What is your secret?" "All the S.O.Bs. are dead", the old man said, with an air of exhilaration.[47]

Whimsically, John would reflect on occasion how he outlived his golfing foursome. I doubt whether

---

[47] Gratitude to Brian and Kathy Oppenheimer for sharing this recollection of the Monsignor.

anyone truly saw John as an enemy. There were
certainly none among the hundreds who bid him
farewell on September 24, 2010.

Likewise, if we are ever to re-establish a civil
political discourse, we ought not ever characterize
a differing political view as that of an "enemy." In
his pithy 2008 campaign refrain that we are not
blue states or red states, but the United States,
Barack Obama was reminding us that the
objective of political discourse is "a more perfect
union." For this reason, President Obama has
been especially attentive to the voices like those of
Jim Wallis at Sojourners and the Reverend Joel
Hunter and Pastor T.D. Jakes, all of whom are
devoted to finding the common good premised
upon common ground.

35. Remembering 9-11

We are well-instructed by the Theology of Kindness to find happiness in the success of others. When Justice Samuel Alito was appointed to the Supreme Court, it was a very happy day for me. Sam and his wife Martha-Ann Alito are good friends from previous days in Washington D.C., where at one point Sam and I even shared an office in the Justice Department.

The fifth anniversary of the madness of September 11th presented an opportunity for me to bring the recently appointed Justice to the University for a lecture both on the significance of the day as well as the importance of the rule of law to withstand its brutality. Whenever I would bring dignitaries to Pepperdine, I was anxious for them to meet John, and I would make every effort to prevail upon John to open or close the event with a prayerful reflection. These reflections are often as good as the main presentations themselves and very witty.

Monsignor was respectful of high office, but he was in no way cowed or overwhelmed by it. Proof of that was affirmed a day or so before September 11th, when I brought Justice Alito to the rectory to see if we could engage the Monsignor. John sent word down that the two of us should come up to his rectory chambers, but that he could not immediately attend to us. John's delay was because he was in the middle of a fine story with one of the parishioners, a story that simply could not be deferred for even someone sitting on high bench.

Enjoying a well-told story, anecdote, or poetry was not infrequently part of John's repertoire. John's stories would steady a troubled soul and assist needful parishioners with at least a touch of happiness greater than they had when they first called.

The story completed, the Irish laughter abating,

343

and without question the parishioner now far more at ease, John gave his full attention to the good Justice.

Justice Alito, the following day at Pepperdine, gave us an insight about the rule of law arising out of the traditions surrounding nomination and appointment, including the poignancy of signing, as a new member of this select body, John Marshall's Bible. The Monsignor and Justice Alito were fast friends. An excerpt from the Monsignor's invocation from that day follows. Parishioners who regularly attended Monsignor's 8:00 a.m. Mass will recognize, and no doubt hear in their memory, the Monsignor's inspiring voice as they read his often spoken opening words: "Good morning, and a Blessed, Blessed day to all of you."

Good Morning, and a Blessed, Blessed Day to all of you. Whatever its place in history, or however it has affected us personally — and it has, all of us - the images of the September 11th New York of five years ago this day, will continue to haunt our

344

memories with a world where violence and vengeance have for a few terrifying moments replaced our world of law and love.

***

One thing is certain today: our biggest contribution and our best access to the human family at large is our Western prowess, not in technology or in the empirical sciences, great as it is, but in the rule of law. There is a real sense, I believe, in which all people can view the entire drama of human civilization as the creative tension, the interplay between law and history, between truth and freedom, between who we ought to be, [children of the same erring parents] and who we find ourselves to be in the pressures and messiness of life.

Let us make our own today the prayer of that peerless witness to the rule of law, St. Thomas More. "The things, Good Lord, we pray for, give us the Grace to labor for".

345

September 11, '06

Monsignor Sheridan - Pepperdine University

The handwriting on these pages is John's.

36. Ecumenical Thanksgiving & Inter-Faith Dialogue -- Everyday

J ohn was far ahead of the Catholic curve in terms of inter-faith or inter-religious dialogue and relations. Until 9/11, many Catholics in the parishes had not given serious attention to promoting dialogue and interaction across religious boundaries. Of course, after 9/11, the desire for such conversation would always be conducted in the shadow of these attacks. Such conversations certainly are good, but they are often perceived as utilitarian – that is, simply conducted only in the emergency of the moment as a way for diffusing the worst forms of hatred or clash of civilization.

While we cannot escape the reality of the tragic attack that took the lives of thousands of every faith and nationality, we can follow John's example of constancy – that is, honoring and expressing genuine interest in the faith life of others as a matter of course. Waiting until an Islamic center

347

to promote better understanding creates its own misunderstanding when it seeks to be located near Ground Zero is not the ideal opportunity for understanding or reasoned and respectful dialogue.

Today, there are important scholars and offices in the Church devoted to promoting inter-religious understanding and there is a fine Secretariat for Ecumenical and Interreligious Affairs at the US Conference of Catholic Bishops. Unfortunately, these formal, official agencies operate at a level and distance that makes it impossible for parishioners to access their thoughtful writing and conference materials. What is more helpful is the embrace of brothers and sisters of different faiths in an everyday voice, one that, in its honesty, can share unexpected loss as easily as rejoicing over good fortune. These conversations cannot be forced or conducted in the shadow of military or political agendas.

As an ambassador for President Obama, I promoted the idea of inter-faith diplomacy, not as a "one-off" to settle the latest boundary dispute in the Middle East or even as a counterpoint to the distorted recruitment of al Qaeda, though both acts of diplomacy would be a positive good if possible to achieve. In order for inter-faith diplomacy to have a chance for success in times of crisis, there must be a continuing dialogue of everyday friendship shaped by the dignity due all human persons.

In addressing the congregation of the Malibu Presbyterian Church following the devastating loss of their Church to a wildfire, Monsignor illustrates his genuine compassion by revealing his childhood appreciation for the children of Zion.

Hear now as you read, his Spirit-filled voice:

Good morning, brothers and sisters and a blessed Thanksgiving morning to you all of you. As the elder among you and one of the founders of the Malibu Thanksgiving Day ecumenical celebration, I want to thank the Lord for sparing me to this day, and I salute all of you, my brothers and sisters and pledge to you, dear Reverend Hughes and your congregation, our deepest love and collaboration as you rebuild your beautiful church, school and sanctuary.

In the 1970 fire, Our Lady of Malibu Church, rectory and parish center were burned, but like yourselves - in the work and hardships that came out of it all – we experienced a unity, a love and resolve that carried us through and that has blest us all our days. So may it be every day with you.

One small bit of background about the property loss the Monsignor alludes to in these remarks – Malibu is known for its beauty, and also its devastating fires. The flames from these mountain blazes are intense and unpredictable, as the canyon winds carry them from one place to another seemingly without rhyme or reason. Hundreds of homes in 2007 are destroyed in a handful of minutes, and most recently, the Presbyterian Church burned to the ground on a Thanksgiving weekend.

Our Lady of Malibu Church had suffered substantial losses in past years itself. In 2007, a whimsical John Sheridan, relieved that Our Lady of Malibu was spared the devastation of that year's fires, in giving thanks could not help but note the possibility that perhaps "there was something of an increase in the number of Catholic boys becoming firemen . . .Praise be the Lord, they all had Sister Mary in class!"

It was the strength of John's ecumenical nature that I am certain he could squeeze out a Presbyterian smile even amidst the sadness of the ashes. (Of course, a perquisite to light-heartedness is genuine compassion and the Monsignor and the Pastor had already promised use of the parish facilities to help keep the Presbyterian community together). Laughter in the face of disaster is a true blessing of real friends.

Fire, like other natural disasters, often brings a community together for common purpose and allows us to express our love and concern in ways that the unchallenged life does not. Monsignor, however, regularly gave thanks for the opportunity to interact with the diverse religious communities that populated Malibu, and unlike the rest of us, did not need a fire lit under him to express this inter-faith harmony.

John was especially grateful for the opportunity to interact regularly with the Jewish community. Below are his remarks made at the happier moment of the dedication of a new Synagogue in Malibu:

I declare on this solemn occasion that I am blest beyond telling by my long, intimate and grace filled relationship with the Jewish people, and with the Malibu Jewish Community. Yours has been a deep and abiding influence in my personal life, an influence that hopefully makes me a better, a less unworthy servant of God and of our brothers and sisters in the human family.

Singling out the local Rabbi with the most genuine love and admiration, John continues:

The Holy One - Blest be he: he proceeds from synagogue to synagogue and from house of study to house of study, that he might give his blessings to Israel". It is in the spirit of that venerable Talmudic proclamation, in the evening of my own life, and out of the cosmic Diasporas in which we are all called to live today, that I come to rejoice, to sing our common alleluias on this holy ground.

As a child, I was moved to tears by the story of the stones chipped from the Temple walls by Zion's heartbroken children on their way into exile. The chips from those stones are enshrined in the walls and in the hearts of the people who come to worship in this majestic synagogue, this new house of prayer and study. But in a large sense, too, we are the stones, fragments of an ancient past, borne in the hands and arms of the little ones who cared, who believed, and who hoped.

The blessings we bring and share today, echo the aspirations hid deep in every human bosom. They have found their inspired proclamations on the tongues of our Jewish antecedents. They speak our heartfelt greetings to you, their children, as we stand together today in this sacred space. May all who come this way be renewed, steeped anew in the image of Adonai Shalom, peace makers, turning the minds and hearts of all whom they meet to thoughts of peace. Shalom, Shalom.

37. Separation of Church and State

Monsignor regretted the secularization of our culture. He would shake his large graying head at such modern-day atheists such as Richard Dawkins. Long before others became concerned with this now undeniable trend, John would find ways to make us appreciate the significance of the incarnation of Christ and the freedom we have to make tangible the incarnation in our daily life in community. One could therefore expect John, with Mary in tow, to join with the Malibu community in front of the community crèche to sing of the Virgin and the silent night illumined by the angels. John was also a ready and willing judge of student art and performance keeping Christ in Christmas.

Unfortunately, today, those who express concern over the secularization of society are rather quickly thought to be a branch of the Tea Party. Monsignor loved a good cup of tea, which he was convinced I was incapable of making because I never made it hot enough for the man (but he was hardly a Tea Partyier). But then again, neither was he the converse. John did not want to see the significance of Christ in our lives reduced to a trivial political cliché or talking point. Nor did he want our pursuit of an open, honest embrace of Christ in the public square to drive believers of other faiths from the community. In short, John believed it was possible and necessary to honor a Catholic understanding of Christ alive in our community, with ample room left for other faiths to inform and shape society as well.

John observed:

Christians do not expect non-Christians to accept or celebrate the mystery of the incarnation. It is supremely comforting belief that God himself entered into human history, that God is so interested in us as to take on our human nature, that God, who man rejected, became man to reunite man to himself. Such a belief involves faith; it involves more than a mere listing of historical data. No one, therefore, would dare suggest that it could or should be universally clear, or acceptable.

Of course both the modern Church hierarchy and the Supreme Court of the United States have had a great deal to say at various times on this subject. However, it is fair to say that neither started out well from John's study of the matter.

Prior to Vatican II, papal teaching promoted legal establishment of the Catholic faith as the sole acceptable path, paying far too little deference to the individual dignity of men and women. Monsignor applauded the doctrine of religious freedom which emerged from Vatican II. This freedom is premised not upon the claimant proving – as if that would even make sense in matters of religious belief – the correctness or incorrectness of one's chosen faith but upon the inherent dignity of the human person to exercise free will in the matter.

While the Church took this helpful and clarifying step under John XXIII, Monsignor Sheridan had a constitutionalist's appreciation for the tangles of American case law that more often than not were getting more formal, more exclusionary of the open expression of faith, and less clear. John saw a

Court tying itself up in intellectualisms that seemed to go in contrary directions, or worse, because of those confusions pushed in favor of those who would deny God altogether.

John opined:

*I have felt for a long time that our American juridical approach to religious freedom and religious pluralism is bleeding inexorably to the legal establishment of atheism in our public institutions. A Russian news man visiting here a few years ago remarked that [the then] Soviet Constitution proclaim[ed] not only freedom **of** religion but freedom **from** religion. It is interesting to note that a number of our own religious freedom advocates interpret the First Amendment in precisely the same language. Do they really mean to give religious expression in America the same status, or lack of status, it has in Russia? Perhaps this is what they want. But I believe it is more a matter of their having fallen into a sort of legalist trap from which they do not know how to free themselves.*

Both John Paul II and Benedict XVI would take up the concern with the secularist trend. Sagely, John pointed towards the source of error which sometimes came in the disguise of protecting religious minorities:

Some of our lawyers seem to forget that our society is being formed more and more by pressure groups. There can be such a thing as a sustained legalized tyranny by a minority that one of the major sources of our trouble is the apparent tendency of the Supreme Court to translate, not actual American religious pluralism, but the Court's own philosophical relativism into the legal absolutes that do not reflect the social and historical realities of our country.

As was so often true with John, his words and his wisdom transcended the moment and traditional party divides.

38. Faith & Politics

John's wise commentary on not using the separation of church and state to propound a secular state is complete in itself, but in light of present controversy claiming that President Obama has made war on religious freedom, more now needs to be said. Just as it is wrong for the state to suppress individual expressions of faith, it is equally error for any one church to contemplate that the general laws can invariably coincide with their favored religious perspective.

Before delving into how religion and politics have been claimed by practitioners and students of American politics to be especially connected – what scholars would call an argument from history and authority – it is useful to those of you resisting the interconnectedness suggested to try to reach this conclusion on your own.

One way to appreciate inter-connectedness is to discern how we live our lives on multiple levels at once. At one moment, we are a corporate or government executive or professional, dealing with super-important topics and can be disturbed only by like individuals also dealing with super-important topics. The next moment, we are a father or mother racing about the house looking for the baby's favorite book or toy so we can get the baby to day care or pre-school. Next, we are begging our spouse or neighbor to retrieve the baby from day care or pre-school when the project hits a snag at work, and we are awfully grateful that the same guardians we use to insulate us at work aren't also used by neighbors and spouses not to take our call. In other moments, we are a brother or sister stewing over what the other said about our appearance at the last family get-together; or perhaps the shoe is on the other foot, and we are rationalizing that honesty is always best even if it hurts a sibling's feelings. Throughout the day and evening, we are like an ensemble cast in a live theater production. Our many roles require many voices and demeanors, and we think little of how the things happening in the many aspects of our lives nominally appear very different; and yet, they are all interconnected insofar as they call upon one narrator – you – to exercise judgment.

The interconnectedness of life trumps not just the different roles we play in any given time during a single day; it also unites us with who we have been over time. I may have acquired a good deal of knowledge in my 60 years of life, but my mind still knows me from my earliest memories right to the present. My athletic or non-athletic self at age 3 is still with me; the sense of whether to be bashful among strangers or to act with the boisterous confidence of the third margarita is an ever-present dilemma for me at parties and receptions. I may be older and better able to mask disappointment or distress, but when a date with a close friend falls through or an investment sours, I am the same person who as a boy felt disappointment when there was no one home in the neighborhood with whom to play ball, or when my exam came back with an unexpectedly low grade.

Beyond this basic framework of interconnectedness in our individual lives, there is the special connection between religion and politics. America's first president, George Washington, put it this way:

> Of all the dispositions and habits which lead to political prosperity, religion and morality are indispensable supports. In vain would that man claim the tribute of patriotism who should labor to subvert these great pillars of human happiness, these firmest props of the duties of men and citizens. The mere politician, equally with the pious man, ought to respect and to cherish them. A volume could not trace all their connections with private and public felicity. Let it simply be asked: Where is the security for property, for reputation, for life, if the sense of religious obligation *desert* the oaths which are the instruments of investigation in courts of justice? And let us with caution indulge the supposition that morality can be maintained without religion. Whatever may be conceded to the influence of refined education on minds of peculiar structure, reason and experience both forbid us to expect that

363

national morality can prevail in exclusion of religious principle.[48]

Washington was not alone in his recognition of the significance of religion to the well-being of the American republic. The same was true of Alexis de Tocqueville, a French political theorist who came to America in 1831 to study the penal system, and as a result wrote a brilliant, two-part account of the American experiment with democracy entitled *De la dèmocratie en Ameriquè* [*Democracy in America*]. In the following summary and excerpt of his writings, Tocqueville grasps the essential fact that separation of church and state was not intended to lessen the civil significance of religion, but to enhance it. Tocqueville's observations give us a special insight into the attitude of the American population at large, to whom the political framers – Madison, Jefferson and the like – were responding in public action. In this, Tocqueville might be considered the equivalent of the framers' polling data, although with considerably more erudition than pollsters supply modernly.

---

[48] George Washington, Washington's Farewell Address to the People of the United States (Sept. 19, 1796).106-21 (2000), at 20, *available at* http://www.gpo.gov/fdsys/pkg/GPO-CDOC-106sdoc21/pdf/GPO-CDOC-106sdoc21.pdf.

As to the special place of religion in America, Tocqueville concludes:

1. The success of a democratic political system depends upon a proper moral formation of its people;

2. There are multiple religious sects in America, but all acknowledge a Creator God;

3. The importance of religion to American political society is not that a particular religion is divinely true [although this is certainly important to the individual], but that it supplies "habits of restraint" or general morality; religion regulates where law cannot effectively; democracy needs this moral or religious infrastructure in ways that more statist or despotic governments do not;

4. To deny faith is to deny man's inherent nature to hope;

5. Religion is strengthened by its separation from the state because it is then immune from the state's failings and partisans; religion draws directly on the universal nature of the human person;

6. Since religion is beyond the reach of the state, it can bind

365

Americans together when their leaders fail or when the people fail each other;

7. In America, unbelievers hide their disbelief recognizing the utility of religion, and believers openly rely upon their faith; religious difference does not occasion hostility, but thoughtful concern.[49]

Here are some of these points in Tocqueville's own words:

> Religion, which never intervenes directly in the government of American society, should therefore be considered as the first of their political institutions, for although it did not give them the taste for liberty, it singularly facilitates their use thereof.
>
> The inhabitants of the United States themselves consider religious beliefs from this angle. I do not know if all Americans have faith in their

---

[49] ALEXIS DE TOCQUEVILLE, DEMOCRACY IN AMERICA (George Lawrence trans., Harper & Row 1965) (1835), *reprinted in* GREAT BOOKS OF THE WESTERN WORLD 150-157 (Mortimer J. Adler ed., 2d ed. 1990).

religion – for who can read the secrets of the heart? – but I am sure that they think it necessary to the maintenance of republican institutions. That is not the view of one class or party among the citizens, but of the whole nation; it is found in all ranks.

In the United States, if a politician attacks a sect, that is no reason why the supporters of that very sect should not support him; but if he attacks all sects together, everyone shuns him, and he remains alone.

While I was in America, a witness called at assizes of the county of Chester (state of New York) declared that he did not believe in the existence of God and the immortality of the soul. The judge refused to allow him to be sworn in, on the ground that the witness had destroyed beforehand all possible confidence in his testimony Newspapers reported the fact without comment.

* * *

367

. . . Despotism may be able to do without faith, but freedom cannot . . . . How could society escape destruction if, when political ties are relaxed, moral ties are not tightened? And what can be done with a people master of itself if it is not subject to God?

* * * Eighteenth-century philosophers had a very simple explanation for the gradual weakening of beliefs. Religious zeal, they said, was bound to die down as enlightenment and freedom spread. It is tiresome that the facts do not fit this theory at all.

There are sections of the population in Europe where unbelief goes hand in hand with brutishness and ignorance, whereas in America the most free and enlightened people in the world zealously perform all the external duties of religion.

The religious atmosphere of the country was the first thing that struck me on arrival in the United States. The longer I stayed in the country, the more conscious I became of the important political consequences resulting from this novel situation.

* * *

My longing to understand the reason for this phenomenon increased daily.

. . . I found that they all agreed with each other except about details; all thought that the main reason for the quiet sway of religion over their country was the complete separation of church and state. I have no hesitation in stating that throughout my stay in America I met nobody, lay or cleric, who did not agree about that.

* * *

. . . I wondered how it could come about that by diminishing the apparent power of religion one increased its real strength, and I thought it not impossible to discover the reason.

The short space of sixty years can never shut in the whole of man's imagination; the incomplete

joys of this world will never satisfy his heart.
Alone among all created beings, man shows a
natural disgust for existence and an immense
longing to exist; he scorns life and fears
annihilation. These different instincts constantly
drive his soul toward contemplation of the next
world, and it is religion that leads him th[ere].
Religion, therefore, is only one particular form
of hope, and it is as natural to the human heart
as hope itself. It is by a sort of intellectual
aberration, and in a way, by doing moral
violence to their own nature, that men detach
themselves from religious beliefs; an invincible
inclination draws them back. Incredulity is an
accident; faith is the only permanent state of
mankind.

Considering religions from a purely human
point of view, one can then say that all religions
derive an element of strength which will never
fail from man
himself, because it is attached to one of the
constituent principles of human nature.

I know that, apart from influence proper to

itself, religion can at times rely on the artificial strength of laws and the support of the material powers that direct society. There have been religions intimately linked to earthly governments, dominating men's souls both by terror and by faith; but when a religion makes such an alliance, I am not afraid to say that it makes the same mistake as any man might; it sacrifices the future for the present, and by gaining a power to which it has no claim, it risks its legitimate authority.

When a religion seeks to found its sway only on the longing for immorality equally tormenting every human heart, it can aspire to universality; but when it comes to uniting itself with a government, it must adopt maxims which apply only to certain nations. Therefore, by allying itself with any political power, religion increases its strength over some but forfeits the hope of reigning over all.

As long as a religion relies only upon the sentiments which are the consolation of every affliction, it can draw the heart of mankind to

371

itself. When it is mingled with the bitter passions of this world, it is sometimes constrained to defend allies who are such from interest rather than from love; and it has to repulse as adversaries men who still love religion, although they are fighting against religion's allies. Hence religion cannot share the material strength of the rules without being burdened with some of the animosity roused against them.

* * *

When governments seem so strong and laws so stable, men do not see the danger that religion may run by allying itself with power.

When governments are clearly feeble and laws changeable, the danger is obvious to all, but often then there is no longer time to avoid it. One must therefore learn to perceive it from afar.

When a nation adopts a democratic social state and communities show republican inclinations, it becomes increasingly dangerous for religion to ally itself with authority. For the time is coming when power will pass from hand to hand, political theories follow one another, and men, laws, and even constitutions vanish or alter daily, and that not for a limited time but continually. Agitation and instability are natural elements in democratic republics, just as immobility and somnolence are the rule in absolute monarchies.

If the Americans, who change the head of state every four years, elect new legislators every two years and replace provincial administrators every year, and if the Americans, who have handed over the world of politics to the experiments of innovators, had not placed religion beyond their reach, what could it hold on to in the ebb and flow of human opinions? Amid the struggle of parties, where would the respect due to it be? What would become of its immorality when everything around it was perishing?

* * *

. . . The unbeliever, no longer thinking religion true, still considers it useful. Paying attention to the human side of religious beliefs, he recognizes their sway over mores and their influence over laws. He understands their power to lead men to live in peace and gently to prepare them for death. Therefore he regrets his faith after losing it, and deprived of a blessing whose value he fully appreciates, he fears to take it away from those who still have it.

Unbelievers in Europe attack Christians more as political than as religious enemies; they hate the faith as the opinion of a party much more than as a mistaken belief, and they reject the clergy less because they are the representatives of God than because they are the friends of authority.

European Christianity has allowed itself to be intimately united with the powers of this world. Now that these powers are falling, it is as if it were buried under their ruins. A living being has

374

been tied to the dead; cut the bonds holding it and it will arise.[50]

Modernly, secular voices try to disengage religion and politics, but often rather one-sidedly. Quite obviously, to the extent we can follow the admonition to "love our enemies" in our political discourse, we start to point in the direction suggested by Barack Obama and other public voices, like those of former Secretary of State Madeline Albright[51] and scholars Dennis Hoover and Douglas Johnston,[52] to end the politics of division, especially divisions based upon faith.

To love one's enemies, however, is so contrary to the world as we know it; where Israelis and Palestinians, for example, have been at odds as far as the living memory allows. Each of us must anchor this general teaching in our freely chosen faith tradition, or it is remains without usefulness by reason of vagueness.

---

[50] *Id.* at 153-157.

[51] Madeline Albright, The Mighty & the Almighty – Reflections on America, God, and World Affairs (Harper 2006).

[52] Dennis R. Hoover and Douglas M. Johnston, Religion and Foreign Affairs – Essential Readings (Baylor University Press 2012).

In that spirit, this book connects the admonition to love our enemies with the Catholic injunction so well interpreted by Monsignor Sheridan that men and women "lift up their hearts to the Lord." Reflecting upon that instruction, I had occasion to speak to the topic of secularism for the Institute for Advanced Catholic Studies at the University of Southern California. In that lecture, I noted how the former executive editor of the *New York Times*, Bill Keller, in a recent column likened a presidential candidate who relies upon faith in public matters to a candidate who might believe that "space aliens dwell among us."[53] The column was cleverly, if irreverently, written, with Keller opining that such a belief "might not disqualify the candidate out of hand . . . . But I would certainly want to ask a few questions. Like . . . Does he talk to the aliens? Do they have an economic plan?"[54]

In his column, Keller argued that we should not be "squeamish" about asking faith questions when a

---

[53] Bill Keller, *Asking Candidates Tougher Questions About Faith*, N.Y. TIMES, Aug. 25, 2011, http://www.nytimes.com/2011/08/28/magazine/asking-candidates-tougher-questions-about-faith.html?_r=1&scp=1&sq=%22space+aliens%22&st=nyt.
[54] *Id.*

candidate has relied upon faith to win public approval.[55] This is a fairer proposition than that faced by the late John F. Kennedy, who – at a time when Catholicism made one suspect in the American political milieu – went about declaring that he would not rely on his faith to make public decisions, and that he would not expect church officials to tell him what to do.[56]

Mr. Keller has a number of questions for so-called "believer candidates" (such as Mr. Gingrich), the most essential of which was whether they elevate "the Bible, the Book of Mormon (the text, not the Broadway musical) or some other authority higher

---

[55] *Id.*

[56] In a famous speech to the Greater Houston Ministerial Association in 1960, while campaigning for president, John F. Kennedy. stated: "I believe in an America where the separation of church and state is absolute--where no Catholic prelate would tell the President (should he be Catholic) how to act, and no Protestant minister would tell his parishioners for whom to vote--where no church or church school is granted any public funds or political preference--and where no man is denied public office merely because his religion differs from the President who might appoint him or the people who might elect him." Senator John F. Kennedy, Address to the Greater Houston Ministerial Association (Sept. 12, 1960) (transcript available at http://www.jfklibrary.org/Research/Ready-Reference/JFK-Speeches/Address-of-Senator-John-F-Kennedy-to-the-Greater-Houston-Ministerial-Association.aspx) (last visited Oct. 13, 2011).

than the Constitution and laws of this country."[57] Keller explains that it would matter to him "whether a president respects serious science and verifiable history [and that he also cares] if religious doctrine becomes an excuse to exclude my fellow citizens from the rights and protections our country promises."[58]

Article VI of the United States Constitution provides that "no religious Test shall ever be required as a Qualification to any Office or public Trust under the United States."[59] It is not a violation of this Clause to make reasonable inquiry of personal belief. The Clause is aimed at precluding a religious Test instituted in law to qualify for office; it does not preclude informed inquiry by voters.

So what specifically might Mr. Keller wish to ask a candidate?

---

[57] Keller, *supra* note 12.

[58] *Id.*

[59] U.S. CONST. art. VI.

The key question, from the text of his column, would seem to be: If there is a conflict between the candidate's faith and the Constitution, how would the candidate resolve it? Presumably the right answer here, to Keller, is to give preference to the Constitution as the "Supreme Law." Yet, Catholics and other people of faith in Europe and the United States nourish the idea of "conscientious exception," remembering the good example of Thomas More and the tragic consequences of the Holocaust in disregard of limits of positive law to discharge our duty to fellow man. Curiously, before Governor Perry dropped out of the race, Mr. Keller wanted to know from him (though presumably he would have the same question of Rick Santorum) whether they think that the United States is a Judeo-Christian nation (and if so, what that would mean in practice?); and whether a candidate would have any hesitation about appointing Muslims or atheists to public office.[60]

---

[60] Keller, *supra* note 12.

The last question is particularly interesting because, in the context of the *New York Times* article, Mr. Keller's implication is that open-mindedness would not exclude the appointment of a Muslim citizen to public office. Intuitively, a believer in religious pluralism and inter-faith dialogue, such as myself, would tend to concur, but closer examination beyond the scope of this book may be needed. In particular, this more particular examination will need to come to grips with the fact that the European Court of Human Rights (ECHR), a respected, effective and on occasion progressive court, has reached the conclusion that Shari'a (Islamic law) is essentially incompatible with "the fundamental principles of democracy"?[61] As the ECHR saw it in its 2001 decision of *Refah Partisi v. Turkey*, the inconsistency stems from the fact that Shari'a, when faithfully applied, reflects the rules of the past embedded in a particular religious

---

[61] Refah Partisi v. Turkey, App. No. 41340/98, 35 Eur.H.R.Rep. 56, 87 (2001). The 2001 judgment, handed down by a Chamber of the Third Section of the ECHR, affirmed the constitutionality of the dissolution of the Refah Partisi political party in Turkey. The decision was later referred to the Grand Chamber of the ECHR, which affirmed the Third Section's judgment. *See* Refah Partisi v. Turkey, App. No. 41340/98, 37 Eur. H. R. Rep. 3 (2003).

tradition that is "invariable."[62] By contrast, the court reasoned, democratic systems thrive on pluralism and the constant evolution of public freedoms and their redefinition or expansion.[63] Beyond that, the ECHR also found that Shari'a diverges from values of the European Convention on Human Rights with respect to criminal law and procedure, the legal status of women, and the regular interventions of Shari'a into all spheres of private life on the basis of religious precept.[64] While it can be argued that the ECHR decision – a case affirming the ordered dissolution of the Islamist political party, Refah, in Turkey – might be valid only in the context of the sensitive and specific situation as it exists in Turkey,[65] the Court's considerations have been repeated elsewhere, especially insofar as Shari'a would seem to contest

---

[62] Refah Partisi v. Turkey, App. No. 41340/98, 35 Eur.H.R.Rep. 56, 87 (2001).

[63] *Id.*

[64] *Id.*

[65] The Turkish government has pursued implementation of particularly "exclusionary . . . policies toward religion" which have been argued to be "products of dominant assertive secularist ideology." AHMET T. KURU, SECULARISM AND STATE POLICIES TOWARD RELIGION: THE UNITED STATES, TURKEY, AND FRANCE 163 (2009).

the essential equality of men and women that is at the core of European Convention jurisprudence.[66]

Let us draw this chapter to a close by returning our focus to religion and politics in America. It might be thought a relief to do so since it seemingly is free of the difficult questions posed by how a democracy can coexist with a highly demanding fundamentalist tradition that argues, like Shari'a, for its application in a given society to believer and

---

[66] According to the European Court of Human Rights, "Gender equality [is] recognised by the European Court as one of the key principles of underlying the [European] Convention [on Human Rights] and a goal to be achieved by Member States of the Council of Europe . . . ."). Sahin v. Turkey, App. No. 44774/98, 41 Eur. H. R. Rep. 109, 133 (2005).Many authors, however, have commented on Shari'as seeming incompatibility with democratic ideals, including the notion of gender equality. *See, e.g.,* ELIE KEDOURIE, DEMOCRACY AND ARAB POLITICAL CULTURE 5-6 (1994) ("[T]he idea of representation, of elections, of popular suffrage, of political institutions being regulated by laws laid down by a parliamentary assembly, of these laws being guarded and upheld by an independent judiciary, the ideas of the secularity of the state, of society being composed of a multitude of self-activating, autonomous group, and associations – all these are profoundly alien to the Muslim political tradition."); Ziba Mir-Hosseini, *Muslim Women's Quest for Equality: Between Islamic Law and Feminism*, 32 CRITICAL INQUIRY 629, 629 (2006), *available at* http://www.smi.uib.no/seminars/Mir-Hosseini/Questforequality.pdf ("Muslim jurists claim, and all Muslims believe, that justice and equality are intrinsic values and cardinal principles in Islam and the sharia. If this is the case, in a state that claims to be guided by the sharia, why are justice and equality not reflected in the laws that regulate gender relations and the rights of men and women? Why do Islamic jurisprudential texts – which define the terms of the sharia – treat women as second-class citizens and place them under men's domination?").

nonbeliever alike. Is this problem foreign to America?

Unfortunately, no. It is difficult to both conduct an accountable democracy and accommodate every aspect of religious belief. As was noted, Alexis de Tocqueville, the revered 19th century observer of early America, urged great reliance upon faith to guide us in our one-on-one personal behavior; but he warned religions against indulging the temptation to make alliance with particular political parties. Faith transcends politics, and if it gets too closely associated with one side or another, when that side becomes unfashionable or unpopular so too will the faith associated with it.

Consider President Obama's declining to grant as sweeping an exemption to Catholic employers for the provision of birth control coverage to employees, not because he discounts the genuineness of Catholic theology, but because the more exceptions to generally applicable laws there are, the greater the erosion of the general provision of health care to the larger community. If more and more people claim exception from the general laws, soon there will be no rule of law at all.

It can happen, of course, that applying general laws to religious bodies could result in substantially burdening belief or practice – effectively requiring religious believers to choose between faith and public job or benefit. Insensitivity to this level of burden could be perceived as an attack on religious freedom, and the Catholic bishops are claiming this now. But care is warranted. While it would have been my preference for the good work of the bishops to have been given a more sensible and wider exemption, several facts ought to be noticed: (1) according to the most conservative and Catholic justice on the Supreme Court, who achieved a majority for his view, the Constitution should not be thought to presumptively require exemption and it is best for the democracy and accountability if the Church requests exemption from the legislature; (2) the Church is not being denied a benefit on pain of forfeiting its belief; and (3) certainly no individual Catholic is coerced to use birth control just because it is now insurable.

Is there a way to handle conflicts between the
general law and specific religious practice more
fairly? Maybe, and were I still an advisor to the
Obama administration or campaign or were my
bishops to ask my thoughts, I would urge all sides
to keep certain principles in mind. First, not
everything needs to be a law – or at least not
immediately. There are some issues that could, and
arguably should, be kept out of public decision
making. Whenever it is clear that an attempt to
legislate upon a particular issue would deepen
religious divisions in society, arguably a discussion
waiting period should be triggered, deferring the
public process of decision-making. These issues
would be placed off-limits to public decision-making
for a responsible period to explore the possibility of
greater consensus; and if consensus is impossible,
to then carefully calibrate the accommodation of
religious diversity. In fairness to President Obama,
this was apparently his thinking in promulgating a
very narrow Catholic exemption with a one year
delay. The immediate uproar from the Catholic
hierarchy did not allow this leisurely pace and the
President modified the rule so that no Catholic

385

charity, school, hospital, etc., would be obligated to directly foot the bill for birth control; instead, insurers would agree to provide this benefit "for free."

Persons outside the Catholic faith sometime express skepticism about our belief that the consecrated host and wine are the real presence of the body and blood of our Lord, so permit this Catholic to express openly the belief that wherever the funding for contraceptives will come from, it will not be "free." In any event, putting aside the requirement of suspending the laws of economics, the President's efforts to be responsive to the ethical clash is commendable.

And while the waiting period didn't help him in this instance, that may have been more a function of the failure to convey the regulation as remaining under active consideration for revision when it was announced.

Second, in advocating for freedom and democracy, such advocacy must always be tempered by the insight of John Paul II that a democracy unattached from moral truth is a "thinly disguised totalitarianism."[67] Part of that truth can only be revealed by the recognition that, in a religiously pluralistic world, there is a duty to search for common ground. That search may lead to a claim of conscience warranting exemption from the laws applying to all others, but those claims ought not be made or granted casually, lest they undermine the democratic aspiration altogether.

President Obama has a great sensitivity to the importance of faith in America and internationally. His Cairo speech calling for "mutual understanding and mutual respect" is premised upon a simple prayer he once told me and others that he said for America every day.

The prayer? That, despite our profound disagreements, "we can live with one another in a way that reconciles the beliefs of each with the good of all." This is a prayer that the Monsignor much

---

[67] Pope John Paul II, Encyclical Letter, Veritatis Splendor, para. 101 (Aug. 6, 1993), *available at* http://www.vatican.va/holy_father/john_paul_ii/encyclicals/documents/hf_jp-ii_enc_06081993_veritatis-splendor_en.html [hereinafter Veritatis Splendor].

admired. Indeed, President Obama would have received helpful guidance on how to advance the ideal of "reconciling the beliefs of each with the good of all" had he sat with the Monsignor. That was my privilege to do, exploring with tea and toast where it was appropriate for faith to determine the law that would be binding on all of us (the common good or common principles) and where it is more appropriate for the law to be silent, so that people of many different faiths can live together in peace. The law should not be said to prevent a person of any faith (or no faith) to live their life seeking the good as their mind allows them to discern it.

39. Authentic Truth or Narrative Spin?

One of the essential purposes of the separation of church and state is to permit the freedom of the church to define herself in association with the truth of the Gospel message. Freedom of speech, of course, does not prevent others from attempting to wrongly redefine or even caricature the Church. In some societies, as at the time of America's founding when blasphemy prosecutions were frequent and punishments severe, citizens are given less freedom of expression.

As advocates of both freedoms, John reminds us of our individual obligation to inform ourselves and our children about the faith so as not to be misled by the glitzy or superficial manipulations of those who have reason to see the Church fail in her mission or simply don't like the fact that the Church is present to stand up for human dignity against the abuses of power. The Church, of course, abhors relativism – the notion that anything is compatible with our good. This non-judgmental posture may allow us to go through life unnoticed, but it also leaves our life and those of others at risk. War is sold as peace-making; great, disproportionate accumulations of wealth are "reframed" as the means to jobs and prosperity for the unemployed; unborn life is seen as the enemy of gender equality. John writes:

"We must pursue religious belief in an authentic sense." Unhappily, there is some evidence that we are easily snookered by popular media. Indeed, there are books, followed closely by political strategists that argue it doesn't matter whether something is true or false; what counts is whether an invented narrative is popular or attractive to the present whim or fashionable perspective. A survey by the London Tablet has indicated that Daniel Brown's Da Vinci Code despite its historically groundless theses is accepted as history by a majority of its millions of readers. They now assume that Jesus was married and that the Catholic Church destroyed as much as it was able of the documents contemporary with those of the New Testament in order to conceal Jesus' marriage and

to keep women subject to men.

It is of course tragic that a historical fraud can be swallowed wholesale and be advertised with visual sound bites such as "Learn the truth about Jesus, and the Church" or similar legends carried by the local buses.

The narratives in the Holy Scriptures are part of the New Testament as written and attested by Faithful members of our infant church, the church, the community founded by Jesus the Christ. The vocal proclamation of the Good News was its normal outlet. "Go and proclaim, preach the Good News": that was Jesus' command as quoted so often by the Evangelists. He did not say, "Go and write a book". The well-known Gnostic and other documents like the recently unearthed Gospel of Judas are not part of "the Canon," the books of the New Testament as defined by the church, itself, should define which books constitute its canon Clearly only the church, the community founded by Jesus, could or should decide what best reflects [her teaching], which, among the many devotional - some sensationally written books written in the first couple of centuries -

carried authentically his message, and made known who Jesus the Christ was and is.

The age old plea Sentire Cum Ecclesia, ("to think, to feel with the church") was never more important.

In the end, it is truth that sets us free. Untruth, whether given the appellation of lie or the fancier one of "narrative" ends up enslaving us to whatever self-serving objective the narrative teller may have in mind.

40. Gender equality

John was a progressive on gender. This one was easy for him – all the other positions were simply regressively dumb. Perhaps too, Sister Mary would have given him more than a little Irish silent treatment had he any difficulties here. Nevertheless, this is a topic that troubles the Church in the 21st century.

Theologians argue over whether John Paul II's instruction that women not be ordained is an expression of infallible faith. Wisely, the Church has not answered this definitively, though it would be refreshing for the Church to be as candid as John in challenging the gender stereotypes that persist. Such stereotypes are based on the writings of Church fathers, who, to say the least, were even in their own time patriarchal, justifying male privilege.

John speaks without equivocation:

The Gospels are clear on the equality of men and women before God, and make no distinction between the importance of the vocation to the single and that to the married state. On this point the New Testament is dramatically different from the Old. Yes, the vocational position of women, especially of single women, not only in our Western civilization but in our Christian theologies, was affected by pre-Christian and non-Christian influences almost as much as by the Gospels.

John did not fall into the trap that recognition of gender equality either denies the significance of celibacy in religious life or the sacramental character of marriage. He compliments St. Paul:

It is true that St. Paul's concern with rectitude . . . made celibacy the way easy for religious communities of women, while his theology on the supernatural character of matrimony pointed the way to matrimony as a divine vocation. But though St. Paul clearly rejected the inferior status accorded to women in his time, many of the theologians who came after him, [troublingly did not].

John admitted that the writing of some of the Saints, notably St. Jerome and St. Augustine, were notably limited in their conception of women. *They thought of women as the mere generating force whereas man was conceived of as the spirit.*

Moreover, John's bookshelves revealed a mind not narrowly focused and far too intellectually honest to accept a theology based on forgotten or revisionist history.

John comments:

Those of us, including some theologians, who insist that women's place is traditionally in the home, forget, or perhaps do not know, that both men's and women's place had to be in the home when practically all production and creative work, when everything in fact, with the exception of agriculture, was done in the home. Before the Industrial Revolution, women were not only mothers and wives, they were producers. 72 of the 85 guilds operating in medieval England were open to women. Then came mechanical industrialization which rob women of one of her essential functions in society and with bitter sense of self-fulfillment, thus developing the idea that she must get a husband as soon as possible and give her full life to her family or risk the possibility of being a spinster, a career woman or just working wife or mother, all of which she vaguely suspects is a betrayal of her womanhood.

41. Sex

Another cultural factor working against male-female relationships befitting of a Theology of Kindness is the crude and explicit use of sex in every conceivable form of media. Sexually provocative images pervade everything. The effect on the relationship of men and women on the dating behavior of young people, on levels of violent crime and on marriage are all negative. Yet, as one comedian recently opined: "I know my rights; I'm entitled to internet porn."

John and I talked of this issue from time to time, but both of us found it embarrassing. Contrary to Freud, I would argue – as John does in the passage below – that one genuine problem with everything being explicit is the elimination of mystery. With mystery set aside, there is soon either disinterest in healthy sexual relations or a desire for the depraved fueled by the basest sources on the internet. John was candid in conversation about this, so much so that he, more than any prelate I knew, would single out the ease of access to the most vile images as the provocation of the great sin of pedophilia, which

John prayed would not cost the Church its moral authority. Of course, for many disgusted by this profound breach of trust, it did just that.

John's comments here run to the influence of sexual license more generally:

It is generally conceded that our age is unusually preoccupied with sexual matters. How do we explain this?

It is the first time in history the sexual instinct has been isolated not only from its family setting, and from Christian behavior patterns, but from the severe restrictions with which even the pagans surrounded it. We forget how our families were once a resilient support of our better behavior – sometimes even when we didn't want them to be. In my youth, our family would gather every evening after dinner to say the rosary. One day my brother, Joe, asked us if we could say the rosary before dinner as he was going to a dance that evening. The family agreed. As we got to the end of the rosary, one of the older brothers -- for sheer devilment -- piped up and said:

398

And now let's say an extra decade[68] of the rosary for the preservation of Joe's chastity. At which point, Joe got up and left in a huff saying: "You can damn well pray for yourselves"!

There are many other explanations for today's sexual license, of course: the relatively high living standards, extensive use of contraceptives, the emancipation of women from the restrictive customs and attitudes that had hitherto dominated them, and their own, as well as their male partners drive for pleasure.

Then there is modern man's uninhibited, almost morbid, determination to explore every secret in every mystery. His complete repudiation of the sacred character of human generation and his deliberate exploitation, through various media, of everything connected with the sexual instinct without any attempt to sublimate or direct its energies into full human channels. Modern man has found a way,

---

[68] Tommy Sheridan, via his wife Teresa, reports that these extra prayers -- patre nave – were a regular feature of the Sheridan household, with the young mischievously changing the Latin into "Patrick Anthonys."

or thinks he has found a way, to enjoy unlimited sexual indulgence with none of the responsibilities of marriage. The separation of the sexual instinct from its responsibilities is wreaking moral and mental havoc in our society, and, naturally, it is much more difficult to maintain Christian standards in these circumstances.

These observations pre-date the disclosure of the complicity of hundreds of church men in sexual indulgences with the most vulnerable of victims, the children of the Church ministry – altar servers, both male and female.

John was more shaken by these disclosures than any other evil we discussed. This was the direct work of the Devil. It had to be fought head-on without equivocation.

Part VII

The Future of the Church

42. Audacious vocational hopes?

If statistics told the entire story of religious vocations, it would be a sad one. Consider the following overview[69] tracking the drop in religious vocations and, to some extent, active practice in the United States:

☐ **Priests.** After skyrocketing from about 27,000 in1930 to 58,000 in 1965, the number of priests in the United States dropped to 45,000 in 2002. By 2020, there will be about 31,000 priests - and only 15,000 will be under the age of 70. In 2002 there were more priests aged 80 to 84 than there are aged 30 to 34.

☐ **Ordinations (in U.S.).** In 1965 there were 1,575 ordinations to the priesthood. In 2002 there were

---

[69] All of the following statistics were taken from KENNETH C. JONES, INDEX OF LEADING CATHOLIC INDICATORS: THE CHURCH SINCE VATICAN II (2003).

450, a decline of 350 percent. Taking into account ordinations, deaths, and departures, in 1965 there was a net gain of 725 priests. In 1998, there was a net loss of 810.

☐ **Priestless parishes.** About 549, or one percent of parishes, were without a resident priest in 1965. In 2002 there were 2,928 or about 15 percent priestless parishes. By 2020, a quarter of all parishes, 4,656, will have no priest.

☐ **Seminarians.** Between 1965 and 2002, the number of seminarians dropped from 49,000 to 4,700--a 90 percent decrease. Without any students, seminaries across the country have been sold or shuttered. There were 596 U.S. seminaries in 1965 and only 200 in 2002.

☐ **Sisters.** 180,000 sisters were the backbone of the Catholic education and health systems in 1965. In 2002, there were 75,000 sisters, with an average age of 68. By 2020, the number of sisters will drop to 40,000. Of these, only 21,000 will be aged 70 or under. In 1965, 104,000 sisters were teaching, while in 2002 there were only 8,200 sister teachers.

☐ **Brothers.** The number of professed brothers decreased from about 12,000 in 1965 to 5,700 in 2002, with a further drop to 3,100 projected for 2020.

☐ **Religious Orders.** The religious orders will soon be virtually non-existent in the United States. For example, in 1965 there were 5,277 Jesuit priests and 3,559 seminarians; in 2000 there were 3,172 priests and 38 seminarians. There were 2,534 OFM Franciscan priests and 2,251 seminarians in 1965; in 2000 there were 1,492 priests and 60 seminarians. There were 2,434 Christian Brothers in 1965 and 912 seminarians; in 2000 there were 959 Brothers and 7 seminarians. There were 1,148 Redemptorist priests in 1965 and 1,128 seminarians; in 2000 there were 349 priests and 24 seminarians. Every major religious order in the United States mirrors these statistics.

☐ **High Schools.** Between 1965 and 2002 the number of diocesan high schools fell from 1,566 to 786. At the same time the number of students dropped from almost 700,000 to 386,000.

☐ **Parochial Grade Schools.** There were 10,503 parochial grade schools in 1965 and 6,623 in 2002. During this time, the number of students went from 4.5 million to 1.9 million.

☐ **Sacramental Life.** In 1965 there were 1.3 million infant baptisms. In 2002 there were 1 million. (In the same period the number of Catholics in the United States rose from 45 million to 65 million.) In 1965 there were 126,000 adult baptisms - or converts - in 2002 there were 80,000. In 1965 there were 352,000 Catholic marriages. In 2002 there were 256,000. In 1965 there were 338 annulments; in 2002 there were 50,000.

☐ **Mass attendance.** A 1958 Gallup poll reported that 74 percent of Catholics went to Sunday Mass in 1958. A 1994 University of Notre Dame study found that the attendance rate was 26.6 percent. A more recent study by Fordham University professor James Lothian concluded that 65 percent of Catholics went to Sunday Mass in 1965, while the rate dropped to 25 percent in 2000.

Yet, where exactly in the statistics appear the dedication and love of the Monsignor John Sheridan or Sister Mary Campbell? Their impact upon the individual lives of adults and children in the parishes where they served is incalculable. Their energy, their insight, and their personal interest cannot be counted like so many items of inventory. And who is to say that now in their heavenly position, Monsignor and Sister will not find ways to augment the inventory of the religious as well? For example, already the number of deacons is skyrocketing. A religious news service report found 7 deacons in the U.S. in 1971, while there are an estimated 17,000 today. Roughly 40 percent of dioceses in the U.S. have turned managerial responsibility for parishes over to deacons. The diaconate has grown 30 times faster than the priesthood since 2000 alone. At present, deacons exercise all sacramental responsibilities, save the consecration of the Eucharist, reconciliation, and the anointing of the sick, are also all male tend to be recruited from those retired from secular professions, but things change.

The comment that concludes this chapter is taken from John's acceptance speech for an award from Catholic Charities. In it, he acknowledges the declining numbers of the religious, but also highlights the expanding Catholic membership. Drawing upon his personal experience during a period of membership increase, John remains optimistic for the health of the Church. It is an optimism in the capacity of the remaining clergy to be capable and willing to undertake greater pastoral responsibility. The lives of John and Mary are obvious examples.

John would trace the growth of the Church in Los Angeles itself to the substantial influx of Hispanic families and their predominant Catholic orientation and love of family. Thus, John writes that there is much to be optimistic about in the Western United

States, and especially California. However, the greatest source of optimism is to be found by reading between the lines and beyond the statistics. This hope for the Church is anchored in John's repeated prayer of *Introibo ad altare Dei* indicating that the hope for the Church is located in exactly the same place as our own personal hope – before the altar of God where we are reminded by the affirmation that "Christ has died/ Christ has risen/ Christ will come again" that nothing is impossible in Christ. Moreover, what is possible in Christ is a matter of looking forward, and beyond what men and women can see, not just in the presently depressing statistics, but in God's plan. And so John observes:

It will be left for future generations to note the powerfully creative Grace and genius that paralleled the population explosion in this area, meeting step by step the people's physical and spiritual needs. God, we believe, chose our leaders, our chief pastor, his assistant Bishops and collaborators for these great and difficult times, and one day, their more glowing story will be told. Introibo ad altare Dei: I will go unto the altar of God. To God who gives joy to my youth.

43. Upon this Rock – John Paul II and the Transcendence of Suffering and Scandal

John's theology of Kindness was earlier compared to the encyclical writing of John Paul II. One of the reasons that John remained ever optimistic about the future of the Church was the modern influence of John Paul II. Wrote the Monsignor: *If during our most miserable hours we would think about the Pope; how deeply and totally he trusted in the Lord in all the crises of his own life and those of his people, we would find ourselves less demoralized.*

The Pope himself often referred to the way God had prepared him step by step for his life' mission. One can easily see him as Job/Jeremiah emerging from the underground, the seminary, the quarry, the world's most authentic first hand witness to the twentieth century's twin evils - Nazism and Communism. Who could be unmoved by this miraculous transformation of life and history? The fully formed, recognized priest/ scholar, philosopher, theologian, spiritual writer, orator — called to give of his best, his young life to his native Poland, to take his place among its immortals, its liberators. Then in equally fortuitous — rather Providential — circumstances chosen to lead, to pastor all of us, East and West, North and South, to lead a world, a world where slavery of every kind is still rampant.

Perhaps to refute the notion that 90-plus years might slow him down, the Monsignor raised the rhetorical question: *John Paul: A feeble old man?*

Never in human history was greatness more transparent. "I am content with weakness......for the sake of Christ. ....For, when I am powerless, it is then that I am strong," (Paul. 2 Cor.12: 10). Greatness revealed in weakness — And John Paul is today's witness.

He taps his feet to the music of a hundred cultures, bringing to life, waking to enthusiasm the youth of a tired frightened world, uttering his never ending passionate plea for the rights of the weakest of our human species. What a searing stab — or gentle knock to conscience — to the consciences of all of us. All of us humans. And how this once strikingly healthy, energetic man has responded to suffering.

411

Suffering has given his life and teaching a permanent hold on the human family and gifted us with a Christian philosophy of personalism and a theological anthropology that underpins our Catholic beliefs in the whole range of our relationships, economic, cultural, ecumenical.

As mal-distribution of wealth through various corporate forms and bonus structures threaten the American democracy and as oppressive governments everywhere are under challenge, Monsignor reminds us to contemplate the personalist nature of John Paul's teaching. John explains:

Personalism in all its forms stands for the primacy of the person over systems of thought or governments that threaten to subsume, smother the inherent dignity of the person, his sacredness, his uniqueness. A mystic, poet, playwright, philosopher, John Paul was by the circumstances of his young life forced into pondering the mystery of the person, the mystery of who we are as persons. Instinctively concerned with people, he dialogued with compassion and depth with all who came his way, his friends in the quarry, the tailor who led him in the path of John of the Cross, the great mentors in his extraordinary milieu.

The horrors and suffering of the two world wars forced a scattering of the western world's foremost thinkers into a renewed interest in personalism. And Karol Wojtyla, the future pope, mystic, poet, philosopher, the man who was himself experiencing suffering would be familiar, sympathetic with many features of the thoughts and the milieu of those Personalists. He suffered the premature deaths of his mother, his brother and his father. He saw his beloved Poland with its glorious heritage battered, broken, caught in the demonic jaws of the Hitler/Stalin scourge.

Leaving an empty cathedral where he served Mass on the morning World War II began, he watched the Nazi planes loosing their bombs through the defenseless skies of Krakow, from where in less than a month the faculty of its great medieval university in which he was student would be sent to

413

Nazi work camps.[70] He would be in one of those death camps himself if it weren't for the Polish underground through which he got his job in the quarry. But the quarry job was no guarantee that he could escape the Nazi trap.

Suffering, in harmony in the spirit of Christ has thus

---

[70] Your author had occasion to feel the decimation of the faculty of the world class Jagiellonian University in Krakow. First, as Dean of Law and St. Thomas More Professor of The Catholic University of America, it was my privilege to teach among the successors of this great university in the summer 2002. During my visit, every faculty I visited showed me a list of the scholars killed or imprisoned in the hateful, but ultimately unsuccessful, Nazi attempt to break the spirit of the Poles by eliminating its intellectual class.

Second, the village of origin of our branch of the Kmiec family was centered more or less geographically between Wadowice, the place of birth of Karol Woytija, and Oswiecim (what the Nazi's called Auschwitz and its death camp). Out of this geographic polarity of good and evil, my grandfather and his generation escaped almost certain death or imprisonment by taking leave to France or the United States. My father who would join life in the new world opportunity of Chicago would rarely reflect upon his emigrating father, Jan, except to make note in an unpublished biography that the Depression attempted to break his father's spirit with the "cruelty of no work for a man educated at University." It is my speculation that my grandfather's study and academic aspirations logically placed him in Krakow in those terrible years of loss but also permitted his escape. From time to time, these matters of ancestry would emerge in a tea and toast, and while the Kmiec history is nowhere near the match for the illustrious Sheridan clan, John would nourish our kinship in the myth and sentiment shared by Polish and Irish poets and writers. My late father would have pointed out in the disappearance of the eagle from the red and white standard of my ancestors, as in like the disappearance of mapped national boundary that the Polish contribution would always be darker than that so splendidly delivered in melodious Celtic metre. Even the darkness of the Nazi regime, however, can occasionally be an experience that can shine light on important lessons of history. *Ambassador Kmiec's Speech at the Anne Frank Exhibition*, Jan.. 27, 2011, http://www.youtube.com/watch?v=HVDoP-jbvno

an integral place in Pope John Paul's life and his theology of life. Continuing during the first years of his papacy to ski and mountaineer with his friends when his short vacations came around, he was to be followed by suffering. Shooting, serious and critical surgeries, an accidental fall and over the last years the degenerative Parkinson's Disease. But he had not been felled. Rather, accepting, affirmative, he journeyed on living the apostolic life, his priestly and pastoral vocation to its fullest. What a teacher — especially to rascals like myself that for reasons known only to God -- is escaping, and has escaped so much.[71]

On February 1984, the Feast of Our Lady of Lourdes, John Paul issued one of the most meditative documents ever written on human suffering. In Salvifici Doloris, (Redemptive Suffering) he looks directly into the depths to which suffering can take us. How "the heart must struggle against fear while the Faith provides the context in which we relate to, deal with "the intangible." "Suffering"

[71] Not entirely, dear friend. *Mea culpa, mea maxima culpa.*

he said "is an invitation to manifest the moral greatness of man, his spiritual maturity.......Proof of this, the martyrs and confessors ..."

44. Women Religious Orders and the Gift of Female Friendship

As earlier noted, John expressed concern with the betrayal of womanhood in commenting upon various forms of gender discrimination. Recently, out of the tradition of the Theology of Kindness, I believe, Sister Mary Prendergast invited me for "tea and toast." The thoughtful conversation contemplating a one year memorial service and Eucharistic adoration in memory of John and Mary yielded enjoyable, heartfelt conversation and creative thought in ways beautifully reminiscent of similar times with John and Mary. Illustrating the continuing presence of the Holy Spirit, this report of this lovely morning is included.

Mary Prendergast began appropriately enough recalling how the two Marys came to know each other only relatively recently. They knew each other from formation, of course, as Mary was two to three years ahead of Mary Prendergast. Mary Campbell guided novitiates, including Mary Prendergast, in a variety of matters right down to the choice of religious habit which women religious in America seldom wear today.

Mary Prendergast has been guiding liturgy readings and communion services at OLM because now, in the absence of Monsignor, the demands upon the pastor, Father Bill Kerze, are too great for a singular priest to accomplish them. As one might imagine, therefore, lay conversation from time to time asks whether the issue of female ordination remains open. Understanding John Paul II to have opined against the possibility out of his prayerful conclusion that even as Jesus included women in his ministry in distinctly counter-cultural ways, he refrained from including them as apostles. The Pontiff concluded that this all-male priesthood was intended by Christ.

Somewhat surprisingly, I don't recall John and I taking this issue up in a tea and toast. What might the Monsignor have said?

One observation that I believe John might make is that conversation with a holy, yet fully approachable and caring, servant of the Lord of the opposite gender is near impossible in the present culture. We are much the poorer for its absence. In this respect, John might well point out, the disappearance of female religious orders has been chronicled, but not fully appreciated. The religious sisters were, of course, understood to be the backbone of Catholic parochial school education.

Devoted to Christ, these women worked for next to nothing in compensation, 24/7, to ensure the moral formation of our children. As vocations to the sisterhood have plummeted in North America, today the only educational curriculum that comes anywhere close to matching that previously supplied by the orders of religious sisters is that of expensive independent private schools.

The disappearance of women religious from Catholic schools by virtue of the overall decline in women religious vocation has been highly negative. In a front page story, the *New York Times* recently recorded these rather dramatic numbers: "Even as the country's Roman Catholic population surged by nearly 50 percent over the last half-century, the number of nuns dropped precipitously, to 56,000

today from 180,000 in 1965, according to the
Center for Applied Research in the Apostolate at
Georgetown University. In 2009, 91 percent of all
nuns were at least 60 years old." [72]

The *Times* purpose in writing was to trace the
impact of the loss of these communities of
dedicated women to access to health care, a
sizeable component of which is run under Catholic
auspices. The hospitals run by the Sisters are
portrayed as profitable and efficient – more so than
competing so-called private health "profit centers" --
but the essential difference discerned by the *Times*
was the ethic of genuine care, compassion toward
patients. Here again is the Theology of Kindness,
so very important to healing and the dignity of the
human person; yet, also so easily overlooked on a
balance sheet.

Now let me press the envelope, though in doing so, I
want it to be clear that these are my thoughts, not
to be ascribed to Mary Prendergast, who in this

---

[72] Kevin Sack, "Nuns, a dying breed,"
http://www.nytimes.com/2011/08/21/us/21nuns.html?_r=1&pagewanted=print

anniversary tea and toast of sorts was merely Good Samaritan of my sadness, and properly should not be held account for my "musings," as I think she calls them. But it is the fact of the conversation Mary Prendergast and I had, the very ease of it, indeed the thoughtful beauty of this male-female conversation, that I wish to highlight. This is an aspect that not even the *Times'* thoughtful assessment of the disappearing nun captures.

What has gone more unstudied and unremarked upon is the consequence of the absence of female religious orders from the social conversation of culture. Think about it: where today can males find the charitable and service-oriented perspectives of women like Mary Prendergast and Sister Mary? Where can females find the witty, incisive wisdom of a male like John Sheridan who by virtue of his own vows could participate in such conversations and relationships without some sneered calumny?

Of course, one hopes that men and women experience some aspect of conversational friendship within marriage. Yet, marriage is a qualitatively different estate than friendship. Because of the sexual intimacy of marriage, because of the joint responsibility for raising children, because of the social expectation that women who are married will also be actively participating in the marketplace, the types of conversations that husbands and wives have with each other tend to reflect these limits. In truth, the dialogue between husband and wife is not what John Sheridan and Mary Campbell had in their non-sexually intimate, but quite spiritually intimate, opportunity for reinforcing or challenging one another from a different, gender-based point of view.

Men and women rarely come across a person of the opposite gender with whom they can confide, without giving scandal (even when there is no scandal remotely present) or raising the risk of infidelity by virtue of their own mutual weakness or at least weakness more likely to be manifested outside the discipline of a religious order. The workplace, including the military, is intended to allow these cross-gender discussions, but the fidelity failure and improper fraternization rates are not encouraging. The fact that a minimum of conversational dignity is required to be protected by anti-harassment laws and training exercises in every workplace reveals how difficult it is for the world to order itself to readily occasion relationships akin to those enjoyed by John and Mary.

Men and women in the marketplace are also competitors. Even within the same business firm, the male and female firm members are likely to be competing for some distinction in terms of title, scope of responsibility or compensation recognizing superiority at their craft, and this competitive feature, while not at all unhealthy necessarily in terms of economic productivity, is de-stabilizing in terms of friendship of the unique type being described. To say that what John and Mary had in friendship may soon not exist at all is not overstatement, and it is a loss arguably as great as the loss of the dedicated women of female religious orders to the education of our children.

In the context of our conversation, Mary Prendergast revealed how she had come upon the accident shortly after it happened, but did not recognize my rented vehicle or see who was in the car other than to realize from the paramedic activity that the accident was very serious. Slowing, she could tell that the Highway Patrol did not want anyone other than emergency personnel at the scene, and so she did what she had been taught to do all her life in response to the sound of an ambulance or at the site where someone may have suffered an injury – namely, pray.

Mary Prendergast did say an earnest prayer for the healing, if it was God's will, of those in the car and the comfort of their families if they were not to be healed. Of course, it turned out that Mary Prendergast's prayer was for a family she shared with Sister Mary, the Sisters of St. Louis. Mary Prendergast drove the few remaining miles to the convent and the school where word of the accident had already been received. The report of Mary's death and the serious injury to Monsignor and myself and the need to rush us both to the UCLA trauma unit by helicopter, she said, at first anchored her feet with paralyzing weight to the ground, but the faith sustained in her community of sisters allowed her in short order to carry on.

Over tea, Mary Prendergast said in a soft voice, with a tear now running alongside her cheek, that she did not need to be told of the consequences of what she had just driven past. The Holy Spirit had disclosed the news to her.

45. Freedom to be tempted

Freedom is often extolled by political figures as an unqualified good. In many ways, of course, this is true. Freedom from unjust detention, from slavery, from the drudgery of inhuman work conditions, freedom to select one's political leaders, these are all very valuable. John, however, was careful to remind us, through the use of Biblical reference, how freedom also opens the door to choice and how choice can be the clever means of deception by which evil enters our lives. Yes, we are free to make many choices – including some like adultery, drugs, abortion -- that most assuredly will harm us, and often harm others who have come to rely upon us. Ironically, the harm that comes to us is a form of addiction or slavery such that the consequence of being free to make all choices includes the freedom to make a choice against freedom itself. Here John cautions us against the use of freedom to make these unnatural or immoral choices that pry open the door to the evil that can destroy us and all that we

426

hold dear.

President Coolidge, we all know, was a man of few words. When asked by his wife on his return from church: What did the preacher talk about. SIN, he replied. What did he say about it? She asked. He was against it, he said.

Biblically, the first sin is traced to Adam and Eve. In their case, they were given everything they needed and more, but they were human. Whether by way of evolution or otherwise, God had breathed into them the gift of self-awareness, of wonderment, of freedom. It was quite natural for them to try out their freedom, to pry into, and taste this thing, this fruit God had forbidden them. Indeed—the forbidden fruit, how alluring it can be.

Any of us who have really lived, will have known how tempting some forbidden thing can be — from another person's spouse to a martini on the rocks, or a plain chocolate bar or an ice cream or a cold beer on a hot day at the beach.

The Tempter knew even more about these kinds of

things than poor Eve or Adam who were only waking up to this whole business of freedom. We should be more awake than the first couple because there are more than a few voices in our society ready for us to forfeit freedom with the argument: "For heaven's sake. Aren't you free people? Didn't He create you free? Free to do whatever you can do? Free to clone, to create monsters, to rape in certain circumstances —to make war?

46. Freedom to resist temptation: Reforming ourselves

I f this book has inspired you to seek the way of kindness, then John and Mary remain living examples, even in death. If you miss these gentle souls, as I do, we cannot let ourselves down in our efforts to transform our own lives in the image of Christ. John's writing reminds us that there is no reason to wait and every reason to begin now.

The Christian way requires an effort to distance ourselves from past hatreds; from the mindless pursuit of material things that bring only transient happiness; from sexual practices that mock the warmth and beauty and embrace of authentic sexual intimacy in marriage; from the entertainments and activities, like hours on the Internet, that separate us from family and neighbor. Below Monsignor reminds us of the example of St. Paul and how his dramatic conversion to

Christianity, even after years of persecuting and stirring up hatred for their observance of the very commandment of love he would come to understand as the only way for him, too.

When I returned to Malta following the accident, I had occasion to have the benefit of the sacrament of reconciliation. Not surprisingly, I wanted to discuss how painful being separated from John and Mary was, especially given the circumstance that I was driving. Father Hilary, who founded the Millennium Center and Chapel that operates a social service center in one of the more popular entertainment districts where people young and old attempt to solve their difficulties with liquor or drugs, lifted his eyes toward mine and said something I have not forgotten: when you engage in sin; when you submit to temptation; when you let anger or pride overtake you; think of your friends as becoming more distant and less accessible to you for you will then be the one pushing them away. Yes, the accident was a horrible and tragic one. If it could have been avoided that would've been wonderful. But you believe, as do I, that it was wholly accidental. What is not accidental are the choices you make now. It will be your choice whether you allow these good friends to continue to walk with you or not. Sin separates you from all that is good, and John and Mary clearly were that. You really don't want to walk away from them, do you?

Here's John:

Paul assures us that in the power of the Holy Spirit, we can within an instant, change course; to be converted and hear Christ calling us. We can begin again the mission of caring, for the other, for the "insignificant" other, the other whom up to now we didn't love, didn't know, didn't accept.

This whole Theology is the whole lived reality of God; of listening to God and caring for the world, for people who will come after us, for the environment, for all God's creatures; for the people we associate with comes directly out of the Gospels, out of the heart of Jesus. It cannot be enforced on people. It may sound ethereal; it does not seem easy to

431

practice but it is the way, the Way of Christ. And it can and will be our way if we open our hearts to the Holy Spirit and let him, let God take over.

I have over the years tried to listen, think through, feel, imagine a deepening realization of God's call, God's love; a deepening love for people, for the people with whom I have come in contact, including people who didn't like me or agree with what I said, or with whom I didn't agree or for whom I did not feel a natural empathy.

More often than not I broke the covenant, but I can affirm before God's Holy Altar, it is the way to go, the way of surpassing peace. So, as the Twelve Step people say: I'll turn it over. Let the Holy Spirit show us once again what it means to love God and neighbor.

47. The Narrow Door to Salvation

The focus on kindness and God's infinite mercy should not mislead us into thinking that the way to salvation is necessarily an easy one. As the Gospel reminds us, and as Monsignor does as well in this reflection, the way to salvation is through a narrow door; it is an uphill struggle, especially since as suggested in the previous chapters our imperfect natures are inclined to misuse freedom and to be attracted to the allure of that which destroys us –an excess of power, wealth, drink, or sexual indulgence.

The Monsignor expresses some discomfort here with the concept of "being saved." In this, it reminds me of a periodic conversation, an occasional question really from my friend Monsignor John, as to whether or not, as a Catholic, I felt welcomed within the Christian, but non-Catholic, community of the faculty of the Pepperdine University. The answer was, and is, "unquestionably yes"! The practices of the Catholic

Church and Church of Christ tradition do differ.
We put far more emphasis upon liturgy and the
sacraments, for example. But I think what
bothered the Monsignor most or concerned him
mostly from interactions outside of Pepperdine was
not the differences in our practice, but the
implication that if one called himself or herself
"saved," one was in some type of exclusive club,
sometimes even with the very unfortunate
connotation that others could not be.

We do not have any real sense of eternal life
beyond the faith belief that it is unsurpassed in
beauty and harmony. Unlike the present life, beset
by constant pressure for advancement, the
necessity of meeting economic need, and the
various physical ailments that can strike at any
age but certainly challenge us as our age advances,
life in the presence of God would be free of all of
these concerns and much more. What the
Monsignor advised us to be wary of, however, was
a type of complacency born of the supposition that
our association with the right religious grouping
would, without attention to the weaknesses in our

personality, ensure our proper end or destination. Unfortunately, our imperfect personalities, when coupled with the sweep of freedom given to us by our Creator, necessitate more work than that for our salvation. In particular, we ourselves must be constantly seeking to place a greater trust in God while at the same time creating an atmosphere within our families and circle of friends to invite them to do the same. Unlike John's experience on the "old red car," confronted by an implied accusation in the question "are you saved?",(See below) my own life associations in the larger Christian milieu, especially that at Pepperdine, is exactly of the type that the Monsignor would have hoped for – namely, one where colleagues of many faiths were genuinely concerned with my eternal well-being and determined to assist a "brother" or "sister" toward the end of what God had hoped for the person, and all human kind, before the fall.

Here, then, is the Monsignor himself on this topic:

The subject that hits one in the face from the Gospel is the question posed by "someone" to Jesus as he was teaching, and making his way to Jerusalem, and to his own tortured death: "Lord, will only a few be saved?" The questioner may or may not have had our idea of an afterlife, but the context shows Jesus was being asked how the majority of people fare in terms of an afterlife, in terms of the Kingdom he Jesus was proclaiming. Personally, I have had all my life a problem with the word "Save" in relation to our Christian Faith, of our going to Heaven.

Years ago as a seminarian working Downtown during the vacations, I reported weekly to Fr. James Morris, the then Pastor of Holy Family in South Pasadena. One Monday morning on the way back to town in the old Red Car, a young well-dressed man sat down beside me, and after a minute or so, he asked me in a whisper, "Brother, are you saved?" I muttered something; he said he would be back and then behind me in the back seat, he was posing the question to an elderly hard of hearing lady: "Sister, are you saved?" "Am I what, Saved? Saved from what? Young man I don't know what you mean."

Maybe because of my failure to feel the power of biblical idiomatic thinking, or my disagreement with

436

*the evangelizing methods of some, or my own
sinfulness, the word "save," not of course the idea
behind it, just the word as applied to the next life
has always bothered me. What it clearly implies
throughout the New Testament is, indeed, Jesus'
saving us from ourselves, by redeeming us, sharing
with us His love and preparing us for the new and
heavenly life for which through him, we all are
destined. God is love, as St. John assures us, and it
is not just by reason of some vague theological
universalism, but in our simple, instinctive Christian
hope that we look forward to the refreshment, light
and peace of the Kingdom of Heaven in the spirit of
the great English Mystic Julian of Norwich: God is
Love and All will be well.*

*St. Luke in the Gospel draws together into a single
narrative and discourse the words of Jesus that are
diffused through Matthew's Gospel, and he places
them in the context of Jesus' final journey, to
challenge our too easy assumptions: How many are
to be saved is not really our business, but we must
realize that it is a struggle like going through a
narrow door. Heaven comes to us as one
commentator puts it, not through the practice of*

some vague formulae, but through charity, through conformity in the context of our own times and our ways of life, conformity with Christ, in our own self-giving, our own authentic love. For myself, "Settled" in Malibu, I have to remind myself continuously not only of the good things I enjoy but of the many people in need whom I encounter daily and to whom I try or hope to be of service.

Jesus is telling us that question of numbers or statistics of the saved should not bother us. That Stalin the mass murderer and poor Mother Teresa who with all her love, all her giving suffered doubts to the end of her life are very different candidates for salvation seems so clear even in our ways of justice, but we leave all of this to the Lord while we utter with increasing fervor our own Kyrie's, and pray for each other on the way. Amen.

48. An Understanding Heart

An understanding heart is what King Solomon asked of God. It pleased God greatly that the King did not ask for greater power or wealth or the countless substitutes for kindness and discernment that are marketed to us today. Solomon was blessed for generations thereafter. John reminded us to compare the rich young man in Matthew's gospel. The young man claimed to follow the commandments, but when Jesus asked him to separate himself from wealth, he was unable to do it. Do we worry more about debt ceilings and bond ratings and 500 point drops in the market, rather than prudently using our resources to help others?

Monsignor teaches us that:

Solomon, when asked by God what he wanted most, he replied: a warm, giving, understanding heart. When Jesus asks the young man to go, sell what he has, and give it to the poor — and to follow him, he was inviting him in to a richer way of looking at life and what life is about. That is Christ's standing invitation to all of us, too.

He was not belittling, diminishing in any way our fundamental right to acquire private property in the modern sense, nor was he in any way vanquishing human initiative, he was in fact enhancing beyond all human measure these gifts — they are all equally God's gifts.

Yesterday morning, I had breakfast with a friend who reached the top of the corporate ladder when, through the Grace of God, he became aware of the folly, the futility of striving for excessive wealth. My corporate friend changed his whole way of operating. He studied the Catholic Theology of Social Justice and he is now handling his resources in the spirit of King Solomon; showing us how it is possible to take up the challenge the rich young man did not.

49. Thinking across the generations

The wonderful thing about people like Monsignor and Sister Mary, who spend their lives as teachers or around young people as pastor, is that they recognize that our differences across generations is far less than the fashions in clothing or music or books often reveal. In my youth, the Beatles invaded America, seemingly leaving my father and Ed Sullivan equally perplexed. Off to college in the 1970s, we were packing some pretty silly looking clothing – bellbottoms, turtlenecks and the like. The only thing stranger than 70s clothing was the un-kept facial hair, which made all of us look like we just returned from a camp out.

These were cosmetic things, but they could interfere with family communications or be the source of jealousies, and it was good to see John and Mary cut through these artificialities to draw on the common yearnings of young people. What are those? Often it is no more complicated than to be understood than to understand. Understood by

441

parents in the sense of what it's like to live within a dynamic culture where there's always peer pressure to undertake practices that annoy parents – like excessively loud music or far too many idle hours at the shopping center. To have a prelate in the community able to discern those relatively innocent things from the more serious threats of drugs, excessive drinking and sexual license is an unusually happy and useful asset. John and Mary had that sense about them – knowing when to raise "red flags" as opposed to merely cautionary yellow.

Young people also want to understand their place in life. What John and Mary were able to convey is that this is a lifelong quandary best discovered by coming to terms with one's created reality as opposed to warring against it. At all times, finding ourselves or where we fit is advanced by a decent amount of sleep, a good diet, exercise, avoiding excessive amounts of time before personal computers or televisions and active thinking among themselves. Watching John address young people during or after Mass was watching someone fill in these blanks – not didactically or inflexibly -- but honestly and always with a sense of humor.

Jesus spoke to his apostles in parables when he perceives their inability to grasp all they needed to know to make their way to the Father. John, too, uses a form of parable, the Irish character story to help young men and women understand more about themselves and a life of purpose. John and Mary were not thrown off or put off by spiked hair or spiked heels or even other spiky things coming out of body parts. Those were passing fads for the most part.   John reflects:

Do today's young people get together just to reminisce? Do they talk, laugh about, mimic the people the "characters" they remember from the school, parish or community in which they grew up? Of course they do.

Some of us older ones may assume that cell phones, radio, television, the web are filling our lives, preempting our time, nights and days to the extent that we can no longer relax, laugh, talk, gossip, mimic, take off the few individuals who stood out, differed from us, us the proletarians, the ones who formed or thought we formed the back bone of the "tribe" of which we were all at one time an integral part.

50. The Real Presence

F ollowing Vatican II, a number of traditions in the Church seemed to be given less attention. Vatican II's Constitution on the Sacred Liturgy emphasized the different modes of Christ's presence and "the realness," as the Monsignor would put it, of Christ's presence in the community, both in His Word and in the Eucharist.

Catholics are often teased by their Protestant brethren of having only a passing familiarity with the Bible and Scripture. There is some obvious truth in this as prior to Vatican II greater emphasis was found in ritual or sacrament, rather than the Word. The modern return to attention to Scripture was not intended, however, to subtract from the Catholic liturgical experience other times of spiritual richness which sustain the Theology of Kindness. In particular, the Monsignor regretted that in some places, devotions such as the exposition of the Blessed Sacrament gave way or were forgotten.

John welcomed the changes of Vatican II, since it re-awakened Catholics for whom faith had become rote recital. But the nuanced writing of the Monsignor also clarified that change was not to be misconstrued as displacing the need for a cultivated reverence and full understanding of the meaning of the Eucharist.

It was entirely fitting therefore that a year following the accident, parishioners chose to honor John and Mary with both memorial Masses and a 24 hour devotional, in which prayer, song, anecdote and reading recalled the physical presence of these great teachers, and rejoiced in their continuing spiritual presence "today, now, and always."

Those present when the Monsignor said Mass will remember his intense gaze upon the Eucharist and the chalice as the body and blood of Our Lord were again sacrificed – not symbolically as others outside our tradition may hold -- but actually.

Here is John's instruction on this important Catholic difference:

We should be clear that our Blessed Lord in the Blessed Sacrament is present dynamically. . . .There are opportunities for days of exposition, gathering the community around after the Holy Mass, or in preparation for Holy Mass. This should involve the proclamation of Scripture, hymns, and so on. The Holy Hour still is one of the richest devotions in which we can become involved.

But what I would like to stress here is the reality of Christ's special presence and the reverence or recollection that we should try to develop in the context of that presence. . . .[There are] different forms of reverence, including shared prayer, silence, a sense of awe, hymn singing, all of those are compatible with reverence. But the Church and the Tabernacle are not matters of positive absolute indifference, treating the Church as if it were not a church,... No one need confine their visits with Christ to Sundays alone. Other times, other even brief occasional visits present opportunities for disciplined attempts at experiencing God and Christ in our life. We must not miss these for out of these moments comes a sense of charity, of managing time for what is important. Parents are called vocationally to

447

transmit this same devotional spirit to children, and this can be frequently done is gesture: The Sign of the Cross, the use of Holy Water, the bow, the genuflection. There is nothing old fashioned in this; only something timeless and irreplaceable.

Part VIII

Faith's Ultimate Questions

51. Giving Faith's Needed Answers

John had great admiration for Pepperdine, where I am presently privileged to teach, but he was careful never to be drawn into the faith/works dispute that has unnecessarily troubled Catholic-Protestant relations. John and Mary did not deny the significance or importance of a proper understanding of the faith-works relationship. It is just that too often, those in this discussion feel more obliged to defend their upbringing than to listen to the underlying closeness of Christian hearts. The Monsignor and Sister thus gave straightforward response to the Reformation, as they did in reference to the Church's modern difficulties: specifically, that we are saved – as is written in Ephesians 2:8 – by grace.

Luther made his point against the corruptions of the Church of his time and its misuse of indulgence. We must do the same for the victims of priestly scandal; for it is the faith of not only the grievously wronged victims that is put in jeopardy, but of all. So, too – as calls are made for additional reform to address discriminations argued to be more attributable to man's invention or rationalization than to God's loving direction – we in the Catholic fold need to be guided by the core understanding of the Magisterium that has for thousands of years affirmed caritas (or love) as that to which we are committed.

To make this more definite and therefore more workable, Monsignor John reminds us of three essential questions, recorded in Matthew 25: 31-46, detailing our essential obligations in this exile.

1. Did we feed the hungry?
2. Did we clothe the naked?
3. Did we give drink to the thirsty?

Did we, in the irreducible teaching of the New Testament, love God and love our neighbor as ourselves? It was never enough for John and Mary to just pronounce their love for us. In every encounter and every meeting, that love was manifested through their grace-filled kindness.

John himself, of course, did not claim a level of perfection; but he aspired to it in every moment of his priesthood and in every moment of his life. On the 25th anniversary of his priesthood, John distanced himself even from his own television and radio persona for which he had some considerable renown. For example, he had been handpicked to give the homily for the nationally-televised Mass on the day President Kennedy was assassinated. Stepping down from such high, intoxicating pedestals has been noticeably difficult for many, but Monsignor did it and also engaged in a public examination of his shortcomings.

It has been my hope, in addition to providing the reader with a fulsome acquaintance with Monsignor John's Theology of Kindness, to illustrate in these last parts of the book how that kindness greatly influenced my role as Obama's Ambassador and now the life that remains. Like John, I am a writer, and often insist upon keeping at the writing table no matter what. *But if I am to be honest with myself* wrote John, *if I am to convey in some way what I*

453

really feel, I must begin [by noting] that most of the time I was so busy, so selfishly busy, so routinely busy, I didn't have time enough, or discipline myself enough, to be the priest I would instinctively want to be or should be. I didn't spend as much time as I ought in prayer; I mean in conscious communing with God. I didn't spend as much time as I ought with the simple ones who thirsted in silence for a priest to talk with them, who thirsted for a priest to direct them, to comfort them, to visit them in hospitals, to answer their questions or even frame their deepest questions for them.

Reading that self-assessment, it seems far too harsh, but it reflects John's humility and how the transformation of all of our lives is eminently possible in Christ. I cannot know why it was upon my watch that John and Mary were dispatched to their eternal reward, but it has clearly transformed my life in ways that call upon me to manifest the unequivocal love of our Creator – a love that cannot be coerced, but will be Just in every respect.

52. The Special Legacy of the Theology of Kindness

L ife and death in all of its mystery continues to baffle us. Perhaps more than he knew, John's theology of kindness was shaping my life in classroom or faraway embassy.

The special legacy of the Theology of Kindness had been worked out in John's mind in the early years of his priesthood. As John explained it in a note to me, *the experience of being diagnosed with a fatal disease at 19 combined with an instinctive love for people at every intellectual level made my first 25 years in the priesthood a blessed and full life in itself. For a long time,* John wrote, *I was certain that I would die at a very young age but – it is God who disposes.*

As it would turn out, John was right. God took him at a young age. John was 94 and as young and fresh in mind as someone half that age, who

455

nevertheless had all 90-plus years of accumulated experience and grace. Grace. Yes, ultimately the Theology of Kindness depends upon an acceptance of the grace of enduring faith supplied lovingly by the birth, death and resurrection of Christ Jesus, and perfected by our works of kindness. In John's words:

If I were to search the Gospels for some consolation or warrant [for my salvation,] I would, I believe, find it only in this: I was always, or mostly always, kind. Kind to the point where others might consider me lax, but nevertheless kind, especially to those who were in serious trouble. The motives of my kindness could not always stand the test of the Gospels. Much of my kindness came not from the kind of struggle great Christian men make with themselves to be Christ like, but from temperament and heredity, from a consciousness of my own weaknesses, and the deep, almost reckless, confidence in God's unlimited kindness and an indigenous indisposition to be legalist or humanly logical in my spiritual life and counseling.

It is on my kindness, then, I will depend for an easy judgment. Not on selfless seal, not on an active, many sided apostolate, not on the intellectual satisfactions I may have given to those who came to me for argument, dialogue or discussion, not, alas, on flawless example. On kindness, and my efforts to be kind, do I hope for salvation. I've done my share of backbiting, exaggeration and arguing. I have fallen by the wayside in too many other ways to write with much enthusiasm about my past. I lost my temper too often to say that I have been always even kind. But generally I have by instinct, and, I hope by God's grace, been kind. In this I hope. For this I am grateful to God.

If we manifest Monsignor John's faith – the living faith – when our unexpected moment comes, whether by tragedy or in the gentleness of sleep, we will have no difficulty making positive answer to Matthew's questions. by this means we will unite in the heavens with the two so dear that we miss so much.

As John relates, Christians following the path of

457

Christ are never alone:

Once we can keep our eyes fixed on Jesus (Heb. 12: 2) and allow his personal care and comfort to be felt by us, then a key point of his teaching and way of life becomes clearer (a part of us); we go forward together, not alone and by ourselves. We turn to one another to share our strength and to unite our hopes with others. That is the Christian way.

53. Kindness and the Friendly Sons

There is no single quality that contributed more to John's charisma than his native Irish soul – curious, fun-loving, intelligent and warm-hearted. John, himself, believed a strong root for the Theology of Kindness was traceable to his Irish ancestry – including, especially, the poetry and spirituality of the "ol' sod."

The Friendly Sons of Saint Patrick are the keepers of this tradition in America, and maybe a few others as well. Modernly, it turns out, it is increasingly likely to discover that some of the "sons" are named Caruso, Kowalski, Gomez, or Rondeau. There is no criticism in this – far from it. Indeed, it is a compliment to the founding members more likely named O'Hara, Harrigan, or Keenan that the river of kindness originally flowing through Longford or Kiltimagh now overflows into the hearts of people everywhere.

So who are these Irish, and these dear "friends" of the Irish?

Ever since John F. Kennedy's picture went up in virtually every Catholic living room in America, the Irish have been known to be a people of special political gifts and significance in America.

While serving as a Kennedy campaign captain of the Regular Democratic Organization of Cook County for Kennedy's bid for the presidency in 1960, my late father was delighted by his constituent's choice of wall decoration. Dad would often allow me to sit in on his meetings in ward and precinct offices, and even briefly to see the late President as he came to the Chicago Stadium to campaign. Perhaps I was of some small help to Dad in the JFK campaign by walking house to house with him in the City's urban districts (school hours aside) sporting a button saying: "If I were 21, I would vote for Kennedy." As I was little more than 8 or 9 years old at the time, Dad obviously was hoping for a "cuteness factor" to help him get the word out for what, on election night November 1960, proved to be an extraordinarily close vote. Nationally,

Kennedy won by a plurality of 112, 877 votes of over 68 million cast. It was the thinnest of margins among American recorded votes.[73]

---

[73] In percentage terms among all recorded votes (numbering 68,832,482), Kennedy got a 49.72% vote plurality of .17% over Nixon's 49.55%. A reversal of just 9 votes to Nixon from each 10,000 cast would have erased the Kennedy edge and given Nixon a slight plurality. Voter turnout was at 63.1 percent of citizens -- the high point in all modern presidential elections to date.

Formally under the U.S. Constitution, the popular vote of the people informs the election of men and women to the Electoral College, and it is the vote of that College which determines the outcome. The Electoral College is a much debated institution today, when Internet voting seems at least technically possible. Nevertheless, the Electoral College emerged from a founding that could not resolve either to have the legislature choose the executive in parliamentary fashion or have the people do it directly by popular vote. Except for a few renegade electors, the Electoral College has not been independently minded. Instead, it almost always faithfully records a state in the column of whoever wins the popular plurality in that state.

The 1960 election was so close that claims that the election was stolen for Kennedy are sometimes to this day claimed by the Nixon Republicans. Nixon never filed a challenge, however.

Chicagoans sometimes wear, and perhaps rebut, these accusations with a perverse or mocking indifference. For example, thereafter it became commonplace for the Kennedy men in Chicago to smile about getting the cemetery vote out or to urge each other "to vote early and often." It is certainly true that my late father along with his friend and patron, the elder Mayor Daley, took special pride in the fact that there was a huge 319,000 vote Kennedy plurality in our home county, Cook County and Chicago. Our dinner table was blessed with stories of meetings with John and Robert

In the heady days following the election of the first Catholic President of the United States, John Kennedy – young, vibrant, and well-spoken – seemed to incorporate everything good and noble about the U.S.A.. This included, especially, the welcoming thought that America's door could stay reasonably open to new citizens from many lands, and that this great mixing of "friendly sons" would be of great new benefit and initiative to a great land.

The ships that brought the Irish in the early 1800s became the harbingers of the Germans in mid-century, and the Poles and Italians just a decade or

Kennedy (RFK was his brother's national campaign chair) at the old Sherman House Hotel in the Loop where the electoral strategy was hashed out in the proverbial smoke-filled room. The vote for Kennedy came out well (but the counting of the vote on Chicago's old lever machines which had to be mechanically unsealed in front of witnesses was longer and more tedious than newer equipment in other places. The delay naturally stirred suspicion, since it meant that the Cook County total would be one of the last in the nation to report. The final tabulation of the vote in Cook County for Kennedy was indeed greatly delayed. I wasn't permitted in those days to stay up late, but Dad worked through the night. In the end, the vote from the areas under Dad's direction in Chicago and Cook County overwhelmed what would have otherwise been Richard Nixon's victory over the State of Illinois. Had Nixon received Illinois' 27 Electoral College votes that would have very likely given him the presidency. Instead, Kennedy won Illinois by 8,858 popular votes out of more than 4,746,000 cast.

so later. The story of immigration to America, the caricature by extremists notwithstanding, is very often one of men and women whose intelligence is only exceeded by their work ethic.

Grandfather Jan Kmiec was born in Luszowice, Poland near John Paul II's native village. Jan was university-educated and emigrated to the U.S. in the late 1800s. Passport entries indicate that Jan travelled several times back to Krakow and the home village in the early 20th century in the hope of pursuing a career as an historian. Soon, however, the Kmiec family in America would prosper, and Jan and wife Marianna would have six children (including my father, who was born on July 30, 1922 in Chicago).

The onset of the Depression of the 1930s, however, ended Jan's successful, but greatly leveraged, real property business and led as well to the foreclosure of the Kmiec family home. Evicted onto the street, Jan would make an exploratory journey back to Poland possibly with the thought of resuming his love of history at the university.

By then, however, the ominous shadow of Nazi terror had already darkened Poland's door. Jan was outspoken against the Nazi hatreds and his friends warned him to be careful. It was a well given caution. After Jan had returned for good to the U.S., the Nazi's rounded up 144 of Poland's top scholars at the Jagiellonian University and sent many to die at the camps. In 1942, the survivors of the Nazi purge of learning ("Sonderaktion Krakow") formed an underground university, where Karol Wojtyla (later Pope John Paul II) would begin his own university study. The Jagiellonian University, one of the finest universities in Europe, would refuse to succumb. While it took a significant while for these towering intellects to be replaced, the university, standing adjacent to the great Walwel Castle, is still greatly respected.

The name Kmiec that Jan brought with him to America was sometimes said to have roots in nobility, stemming from the term for an educated "travelling companion" for the Barony from the 10th to 13th centuries.[74]

One of the greatest and most delightful privileges of my friendship with John was being asked by him to be his "travelling companion" to the Friendly Sons of St. Patrick annual banquet. The event of course takes place on the feast day, March 17.

The Feast of Saint Patrick is a doubly special one in my life, since in 1968 I met Carol Colleen Keenan, whose ancestors – the Keenans and the Conleys, from Mayo and Cork – came to the U.S. in the 19th century. Growing up only a short distance from the Kmiec family, Carol and her eight brothers and sisters were under the wise and gentle tutelage of Papa Joseph Timothy Keenan, who directed the bookstore at the DePaul University in downtown

---

[74] As the royals disappeared so did the elevated status of the appellation "Kmiec." Initially, thereafter a "kmiec" was described a landed villager normally in possession of a landed area in excess of 41 acres. In some places, however, the term also had the pejorative connotation of an unfree laborer or peasant farmer or servant without freedom. One prominent scholar traces "kmiec" to the Common Slavic word "*kbmetb" meaning "the head of an extended family." This latter usage is said to be credible since in court records from 1386, the Old-Polish-Latin *Cmeto –onis,* was identified as the root for the up and down history of the meaning of the word "kmiec."

Chicago. He was himself a fine historian of Irish, European, and American history. Joe never met Monsignor John and Sister Mary, but they would have been fast friends.

As suggested by this brief genealogy, a great variety of nationalities and points of origin reflect the inherent conviviality – and, yes, genuine friendship – of an organization like the Friendly Sons. In practical ways the Friendly Sons nourish the kindness and good humor needed to sustain our Catholic faith against an increasingly raw and crude culture that increasingly thinks itself to be too sophisticated for faith. Perhaps there is need of a reminder of our humble, yet pious and loving roots.

In Chicago, my own father would attend old Saint Patrick Church, where he held 4th degree membership in the Knights of Columbus. Dad was well-liked, endearing himself to his constituents with humor and a helping hand, and never mentioning the nobility reference in the etymology of our family name. With ready smile, Dad would declare to be "Mr. Nobody," the grandson of a village farmer in Poland who sought freedom in America but joined up with the Democrats instead. Especially later in life, when eye-sight failed and Mother had already "gone home," he would be filled with inventive – if not always credible – ideas, songs and poetry. By emptying himself of all pretension, he regularly gave witness of how to do good without seeking any special credit.[75] He would have especially enjoyed the LA Friendly Sons description of themselves on the web. They're a great bunch.

A quick visit to the website of the Friendly Sons reveals that it's an organization traceable to prerevolutionary days. But its good, light-hearted spirit is much less formal and stuffy than the historical references so far may suggest.

The Irish do have a fine talent for expression and even the "Friendly Sons" Internet listing beguiles as it puts forward a long list of things that the organization is not: among other things, the organization while claiming many members who

---

[75] *See* Douglas W. Kmiec, *My Father's Dreams*, AM. MAG., June 21, 2010, http://americamagazine.org/content/article.cfm?article_id=12359.

engage in charitable, professional, civic, and community service activities describes itself as not officially any of those. This of course leads to the question (and I quote directly): "So why the hell are we here, and just what the hell are we, anyway?"

Here is the answer given:

"We are a collective group of charitable, professional, civic minded, community spirited individuals who band together under the banner of the Friendly Sons of St. Patrick for no other reason than to celebrate the fact that this group of Americans of Irish descent are a pretty damn good bunch of companions to swap tall tales, legends and downright lies with!"

The Friendly Sons of Los Angeles is a highly sought after venue by public figures who are either in office or seeking it; it is also a fine place for heads of major corporations, universities and community programs to be heard. The Monsignor and I attended together in March 2008. That year was a presidential election year which when you're in the venue of the friendly Sons conjures up images of

John Kennedy and brothers Robert and Ted, God rest them.

Of course, in November 2008, history would be made when Irishman McCain would fall to another Irishman – O'bama of Moneygal. At the banquet itself, the chairman of the Securities and Exchange Commission for then-President George W. Bush had been expected to give the address, but had to beg off when, during the same time period, Lehman Brothers went belly up. That gave the nation its first inkling that others besides the Friendly Sons knew how to spin a really tall tale.

More than once John was asked to speak to the Friendly Sons, either in invocation, benediction, or as the main speaker. What follows are some of John's notes from his 2003 appearance. The notes are thoughtful and beautifully written, and give an insight into the mystically beautiful and often spiritual sensitivities of the Irish personality. The notes are far more serious than their actual delivery was. John knew how to take advantage of the moment; he could recall and insert a humorous story that would perfectly fit a context – even an unexpected one.

Which reminds me: the year I accompanied John, we sat at the head table, which prompted several hundred people to come up to John with a variant of "Why John Sheridan, I thought you were dead!" To which the Monsignor would reply with equal twinkle: "Ah Sean, you're not looking good yourself."

Here is John's diary note of his own first invitation to the Friendly Sons; when I escorted him more than sixty years later, his warmth of friendship for these many sons of Ireland and of everywhere else was undimmed:

The 1944 Friendly Sons' banquet was my first introduction to how we Irish, Irish Americans, and all peoples, for that matter, on such occasions, echo with emotive grandeur the voices of our people at the great and tragic moments of their many sided history.

I remember, from the moment the guest speaker, a business man, opened his mouth, we were

470

literally ensnared by the prophetic timbre of his voice, the sound and spell of his words, the humor, the solemnity, the sheer range and power with which he propelled us in and through the mists and myths, the passions and prayers, the saints and scoundrels of our storied past.

Storied past, indeed! John Sheridan and Mary Campbell are part of that storied past, but in loving memory and the words here written, their wisdom and friendship extends into the still unfolding present and future.

56. John's final blessing

John had received scores of accolades during his life, including the Cardinal's award, but he was always self-deprecating in the most genuine way in order to cast the credit or the glory onto someone else. This was never false praise, but it did frequently remind us that many who are not held out for awards and praise in our lives are most deserving of it. Perhaps the easiest aspect of the Theology of Kindness to be taken up in our lives would be to simply find the many who have carried us in one fashion or another, and express to them our gratitude and our love. In receiving the Cardinal's award from His Eminence Roger Mahony, John quipped: *Monsignor Kennedy, my old friend and golf partner phoned me recently: "John, you are getting an award?" "Yes." "What for?" he asked. "I don't know" I said, "I am waiting for the Cardinal to tell me." I am truly grateful to you, dear Cardinal Roger, and to your able selection committee for your delicate balance of compassion and discernment. You would have made brilliant Jesuits.*

It was John's way to be especially "complimentary" of the Jesuit order and their respected erudition by speaking of them in the converse terms, as those *wretched Jesuits.* Monsignor Toby English (who served with John at Our Lady of Malibu) observed that, while these were terms of endearment from John, they were also instructive and often delivered by the Monsignor in a series.

Reports Monsignor English: "This is how I learned humility. The first year I was called a "saint." The second-year "a saintly creature." The third year that "wretched Toby." And the fourth year "that son of Satan." You didn't have to be a Jesuit to have these appellations come your way from John. You only had to be within the category of folks that John knew enjoyed a good ribbing, or – I can see John winking a bit now in my mind's eye – who deserved it. So more than once I was the

With the gift of Monsignor Sheridan's continued presence among us, we are given a task: to be kind as he was kind, to welcome others as he welcomed them, to be jovial as he was jovial. He saw the mystery of God's love at work in "the wondrous universe," and in every person he met. In ready response, he prayed: **What can I give?** And he gave so much. With his intercession, with the help of God and one another let us go and do likewise.

-Paul Contino, in eulogy

24 September 2010

wretched Doug. Of course, John viewed these all as expressions of friendship – at least I think he did.

Monsignor John had a way therefore of moving the spotlight from himself to others. But before we close this chronicle of friendship, let this surviving friend recount how Monsignor Toby English summarized John's accomplishments upon his "retirement" as pastor:

"How does one recapture the priestly life of Monsignor John who has served dutifully and faithfully four archbishops in Los Angeles? How does one recapture one who has so eloquently graced the platforms and the pulpits of the churches, synagogues, campuses and conventions in Southern California for a half-century? How does one recapture one who articulately authored books, magazine articles, newspapers and pamphlets? How does one evaluate a man whose name is a household word in rectories, convents, schools and institutions, in homes – Protestant, Catholic and Jewish? How does one tell you the people of this parish about your beloved pastor? Each of you

474

whose lives he has touched has his or her own image of Monsignor to remember and to cherish."

Indeed, how does one give adequate thanks for a life so very well lived? Monsignor English's listing, of course, could not anticipate the enormous good that John was still to do in the remaining 20 years of his life following his retirement. Even were we to supplement the list, it would remain incomplete as it cannot possibly anticipate the good Monsignor is accomplishing now in our own lives and those of others.

John, of course, at his 90th birthday would deprive us of any elaborate show of gratitude with his own disclaimer:

My old parish priest in Ireland had a set statement he invariably made when the Bishop came around: "If due to old age or other infirmities I should say something, even a word, out of harmony with the teaching of the holy church, I hereby renew my

475

obedience to His Holiness the Pope, and to His Lordship, the Bishop of Adagh and Clonmacnois." He was free then to ramble on. It is with a heart full of gratitude, a heart resonating to an endless montage of blessed memories, that I must pay my life's tribute to this dear old church of ours, this Holy Communion which we form, in which you and I and all of us have been nourished. This church battered and bruised, but true to its mission, was never more resplendent than in our own day, as countless millions like ourselves join hands and hearts in love and prayer, caring, as Christ cared, for the sick, the suffering, the lonely.

How can we give thanks for Monsignor Sheridan?

Take, read and apply his Theology of Kindness. In doing so, we will be asking ourselves the very question that John put to himself every single day of his 67 years of his priesthood:

What can I give?

*What can I give in return to the Lord for all he has
given me, Quid retribuam Domino pro omnibus quae
retribuit mihi? Calicem salutaris accipiam et nomen
Domini invocabo. The life saving cup I will accept
and I will call on the name of the Lord.*

This brief couplet from Psalm 116 had been
imprinted on the remembrance card of John's
ordination to the priesthood. It was not something
the Monsignor put in the drawer and forgot.
Throughout his priesthood, in addition to reciting
the Psalm in his Latin breviary, he recalled it as he
leaned forward over the consecrated chalice and
before lifting it up paused reflectively to whisper
Quid retribuam Domino, pro omnibus. ("What can I
give the Lord for all he has given me!")?

In practicing the Theology of Kindness in the
memory and the way of John Sheridan and Mary
Campbell, we will be giving good answer, even as
the extraordinary faith and grace-filled witness of
their lives will remind us that nothing we can give
will be the equal of that we have received.

As we journey on, we are strengthened by these final words of blessing from the Monsignor:

The Lord bless you and keep you. The Lord let his face shine upon you, and be gracious to you. The Lord look upon you kindly and give you peace. Amen

Part IX

Personally Living the Life that Remains

54. Summing up: Of Suffering and Staying Awake

This retelling of this very special chronicle of friendship now draws to a close.

Before it does, I need to come to terms with the relationship between suffering and a strengthened faith.

It was out of love of "enemy"—or better put, the less familiar -- that I first endorsed Barack Obama.

And in loving him, or more properly the ideas for which he stood, I discovered he was hardly an enemy.

While in the legacies of recorded "firsts" it is noteworthy that he is the first man of his race to serve in the presidential office, it is more honorable to note he did not campaign on the basis of his race. His intelligence and sincerity only further affirm the irrelevancy at all times of relying upon race as a criterion of any relevance.

His commitment to using government as a source for promoting wage and economic fairness for the middle class is a genuine force for democratic good, building as it does upon the ancient teaching of Aristotle that addressing the needs of the middle will ensure democratic participation and accountability.

His willingness to address the special needs of the poor, especially the need for access to health care, is a highly commendable achievement. It brings America closer to its own ideal of a society where no person is left behind; it is also an affirmation of the sacredness of human life.

His understanding and respect for the importance of faith in our lives, including his special interest in promoting a constructive dialogue between Islam and Christianity at home and abroad, made him a responsible force in international relationships.

His willingness to stop the hemorrhaging of our resources and our spirit in wars of ill-defined or fabricated objective makes him a President capable of exercising independent judgment.

481

All of the above made Barack Obama a candidate worthy of support in 2008. While the 2012 presidential campaign is yet to be conducted, and independently minded voters such as myself deserve time to consider all, the need to complete the work in each of the above areas merits renewal in 2012.

What prompts my inclination to re-endorse Obama? It is neither campaign rhetoric nor advertisement, but the stark realization that the social justice aspects of my Catholic faith have, between John Kennedy and Barack Obama, simply been ignored or ineffectively addressed.

I am certain I would not have arrived at this position of sensitivity or empathy for the needs of others without John and Mary's tea and toast admonition to "lift up my heart to the Lord" by means of an attitude or theology of kindness.

Even then, the significance of the grief and suffering associated with the accident cannot be understated. Prior to the accident, I was able to live in my imagined world seeing myself as loving husband; reliably experienced and wise father; loyal, caring and empathetic friend; keeper of promises; advocate of democratic choice bounded by truth; a teacher able to inspire in the moment and a man faithful to God, though hardly free of sin.

I rationalized my sinfulness by the excuse of the surrounding culture ("everybody's doing it"). I had assumed that prayers, recited but not immediately lived; or worship undertaken in overt and frequent, but not necessarily, prayerful ways, would be sufficient.

In the absence of the gift of suffering, and in the absence of the shock of killing my friends, I suspect that I would have indefinitely floated upon the surface of the moment.

It is only through this understanding of suffering as a means of strengthening my relationship with God that I have come to terms with the accident of August 25, 2010.

Factors in mitigation may salve the conscience –

and yes, there is, thanks to investigating friends and medical personnel, a long list of factors that mitigate.[76] But these factors in causal mitigation neither remove my accountability, nor explain for what purpose God permits the tragedy and suffering in the first place. There are thus multiple ways for me to rationalize what happened as being beyond my direct control, but I am convinced that that is not the message God is sending. He knows how much I loved John and Mary and would never have consciously taken up a risk that would lead to their harm, let alone death.

So what is the lesson to be discovered out of suffering? Just this: I was not to be complacent in

---

[76] The possible additional contributing causes were mentioned in the Foreword and I won't repeat them here, except to not yet another medical surprise. I noted how hospital personnel during my recovery from the accident discerned that one of my medications can cause short or spontaneous blackouts in patients with a low or irregular heart rhythm. A year after the accident, while I was taking part in a UCLA Parkinson's experiment, a hole was detected in my heart said to be capable of yielding such irregularity. Is there anything else, God? Just asking.

the love of God.

Yes, I did have faith in God, but I had made it a costless faith. It demanded little of me, and I had convinced myself that it was enough to talk of faith; and for anything bordering on serious sin, God would provide a way for me to discretely confess my sins (to Him, personally) without any embarrassing admissions to the priest in the confessional or my friends—on Facebook or otherwise. Such, of course, was wishful thinking; but I needed to see the link between suffering and salvation in Jesus' life more clearly.

That said, I don't feel like a total dunce in this department, since the connection between suffering and salvation baffled even Jesus. Having taken on the weakness of our humanity, Jesus prayed the day before His death in the Garden, asking if there was any other manner in which the will of His father could be accomplished.

There wasn't. And despite my "girding" over God's interesting nonresponses to Job, and despite the plethora of intervening causes for the accident God

485

has brought forth through the concern of others to comfort me, there isn't for me either.

> And he went forward a little, and fell on the ground, and prayed that, if it were possible, the hour might pass from him. (Mark 14:35) And he said, Abba, Father, all things are possible unto thee; take away this cup from me. (Mark 14:36)

We find it easier to be excused from suffering than to follow Jesus' final words of prayer:

> Nevertheless not what I will, but what *you* will.

That is our task – HIS will. Here Our Lady is the best witness even before her son, since while conceived without sin, Mary was human, not divine, and yet, out of the strength of the grace of her immaculate conception, Mary proclaimed to Gabriel "let it be done unto me," and meant it.

It is your task and mine, to mean it – really mean it. For let me put this most directly now: the Holy Spirit, offers us such gifts of wisdom and counsel, but we should not think there will be an infinite chance to take advantage of these, for in 4 seconds one can slide down the drainpipe of eternity.

The seven gifts of the Holy Spirit are enumerated in Isaiah 11:2-3. They are present in their fullness in Jesus Christ, but are found in all Christians who are in a state of grace. We receive them when we are infused with sanctifying grace, the life of God within us, at baptism or at any time when we receive a sacrament worthily. As the current Catechism of the Catholic Church notes, "[These gifts] complete and perfect the virtues of those who receive them." Infused with His gifts, we respond to the promptings of the Holy Spirit as if by instinct, the way Christ Himself would. The gifts are seven in number:

Wisdom

Wisdom is the first and highest gift of the Holy Spirit, because it is the perfection of faith. Through wisdom, we come to value properly those essential things which we must believe through faith.

Understanding

Understanding is the second gift of the Holy Spirit; wisdom gives us the impetus to learn of God's ways; understanding allows us at least a limited grasp of them.

Counsel

The gift of counsel is akin to prudence but helps us act almost intuitively; in essence, discerning in conscience the right course consistent with faith.

Fortitude

Fortitude is a level of courage that empowers us to act for the faith, even in the face of great adversity – even death.

Knowledge

Knowledge gives a glimpse of our life as God sees it – that is with all our rationalizations and excuses washed away.

Piety

Piety allows us to undertake religious duty, no longer as duty, but as an act of love.

Fear of the Lord

The final gift of the Holy Spirit is the fear of the Lord. This gift gives us the desire not to offend God, and the grace to keep from offending him. Especially in the latter respect, it is said to be the genuine basis for hope.

This brief discussion is enough to reveal how practicing John Sheridan's Theology of Kindness is the welcome mat to our enjoyment of the gifts of the Holy Spirit

Yes, lift up your heart. But mean it. Yes, marry and take a spouse, but mean it. Yes, sacrifice the golf, the vacation getaway, the flat screen for the infant crying in the night, but at the earliest moment teach the child that it is love of others and not his own needs that must be met.

The Theology of Kindness pleads for the reckless extension of love to our most indefatigable enemy;

a love so reckless that we are willing to risk our lamp burning out in favor of those who come late to the wedding, and need our lamp oil to find their way and to be admitted. In the Bible, those who brought sufficient oil are commended for their preparation and send the others away. Better to bring oil enough for both and to be commended for preparation and generosity.

Do not find yourselves asleep when your moment comes to do God's will. For in that ill-timed nap of rest can be an eternity of anxious, sleepless nights.

Until August 25, 2010, that was my fate, for my faith grown complacent had lulled me to sleep.

The oil in my lamp had run out.

I was not able to see any longer how an ugly Satan had spun a prideful lie over my life; Satan was weakening my resolve to defend life – not in the trivial political sense squawked about endlessly on the blogs,[77] but in the sense of underappreciating the necessity for God's continued love and presence in everything we do.

Do not find yourself thrust among the apostles who could not watch for even an hour.

"Lift Up Your Heart," for in offering all, you will be given abundance in return.

Now to this moment, I have been using language familiar to Church teaching and scriptural narrative like that between Mary and the Angel Gabriel at the annunciation. But some reading of these words will pronounce this terminology including the gifts of the Holy Spirit to be so much

---

[77] I would still maintain that candidate Obama's plan to reduce the occasion for abortion to be chosen by addressing a poor woman's health and care needs is superior to an attempt to change votes on the Supreme Court and return the issue of abortion to the States. The issue to be decided well deserves to be settled not in the U.S. Supreme Court and not in the States, but in the hearts of all men and women given the opportunity to choose life. Economic assistance may promote that choice for life incrementally more than a hoped-for judicial tolerance for legal limits on the practice if the Court is reformed; but that avenue remains less likely to bear fruit and is more indirect. The answer is both should be done if the people can be democratically brought to understand how government is one means to meet the needs of the poor or to sanction irresponsibly offensive behavior, but the real change remains on the same order as the correction of my complacency. It will happen through the sanctifying grace that opens us to the gifts of the Holy Spirit or it will not happen.

hooey – begging the question: if there is a God who is love, how or why is there anything but love in our universe and daily lives?

Answer has already been given, in part, because we have already discussed how sin separated us from God, and how God could not wholly insulate us from sin because doing so would have also denied our most God-like quality: free will, or freedom. With freedom, we can chose good or bad, and the more bad choices made collectively the greater the opportunity for bad things to happen even for those who made no bad choices. There are innocent bystanders.

You may still find this discussion of abstract freedom insufficient to answer your own anger with God for a bad turn.

How to defuse this most corrosive and faith-denying anger?

I don't have a complete prescription beyond remembering that we do not always know the whole story or see the complete picture, and God does. But even if your anger is bordering on an atheistic denial of God, you might first consider what psychology brings to the discussion in terms of anger and blame.

The easiest way for me to portray the underlying psychological considerations is to make reference to an infant. Since it takes little excuse, let me tell you about my grandson Oliver. He is only six months old and really cute, but he doesn't yet have language ability, so he cries when he is hungry or has soiled a diaper.

When Oliver cries, he is attended to by his mother or my wife Carol, his grandmother, both of whom love him very much. When Carol meets Oliver's needs, he cannot say thanks since he is pre-verbal, but he does stop crying. Psychologists record that they believe the pre-verbal child imagines that this care is pure love. This imagery of someone meeting our basic needs and desires selflessly stays with us all our lives. (Maybe, this is where the President got the idea for those free contraceptives? I digress.) Thus, it is from our mothers (and grandmothers) that we experience the most wonderful sense of someone putting our needs ahead of theirs.

But is that every caregiver's motivation? No, unfortunately; in the case of a hurried, burdened hired caregiver, it might well not be. Instead, she may be meeting Oliver's needs for her interests: a quiet house so she can take care of the two other children she may be watching, or even so that she might hear her favorite soap opera.

Actually, the number of people and occasions where one person acts totally selflessly for another is regrettably small; but we imagine it, or romanticize it, to make it seem more frequent and more like mother or grandmother's care of Oliver in the crib. We tend to think of romantic love as self-less, at least in the greeting card, but in truth it is the rare couple that still appreciates how intimacy is an expression of total gift. Modern sexual talk is all about achieving the perfect orgasm for me. Pornography on the Internet or interwoven into every mainstream series never even attempts to capture intimacy. Indeed, commercial entertainment rarely has portrayed the ideal of marriage whereby husband and wife subordinate their interests to the marital unity – not because it is always the road to individual happiness; it might not be, but because there is something more ennobling in giving freely and abundantly to the other, be it spouse or children.

Again, this romantic ideal of marriage is premised upon the same imagined understanding Oliver has when his mother or grandma brings him milk. Mom and Grandma love Oliver and nothing more need be said.

By comparison, when my somewhat challenging 2-year-old grandson came for the holidays, I put off-limits a special Christmas ornament to which I took a special fancy. I was unwilling to share the ornament with a grandson still in the de-construction phase of being a two-year-old. Had he seen where I hid the ornament for safekeeping, there would have been a clash between his imagined world where everyone does everything out of love for him, and the real world where grandpa is holding onto the special ornament for himself. And understand as well, my actions would not necessarily be selfless even if Jackson saw the ornament and cried when he couldn't have it. If I relented to stop Jackson's crying, that was love for me, not him.

Now don't be judgmental, because all of you parents out there have done something similar. Indeed, a pacifier which has no food value is almost by definition being used by parents to manipulate an infant into thinking his needs are being met, when it is actually theirs that are.

So what does this all have to do with being angry at God for the evil that we or others chose to bring into the world out of our own desires? Just this: Oliver has a high expectation of care, and it is likely that Jackson does too. When they are thirsty, they have grown to expect mother or grandmother to promptly deliver up some milk. But wait; milk delivery may be impossible if the milk truck breaks down and mother and grandmother have no means to get to a store. Both Oliver and Jackson will likely cry, and both will be angry; the difference is that Jackson being verbal even at the young age of 2 can learn through verbal conversation that there is no point crying for a product that reality has independently made unavailable. The tragedy of the accident is like this too; there is no point in going to war against reality. No amount of imagining or anger will change it. With pre-verbal Oliver matters are not that simple. The independent reality will not be understood; all that will be perceived is an unrequited need contrary to all the self-less love he had grown accustomed to associate with mother and grandmother.

Thankfully, a good deal of reality is quite stable, or – to stay with our milk metaphor – the milk truck almost never breaks down. Leave your reading glasses next to the bed and they will be there in the morning. We count on at least this level of stability, but we tend to undercount the possibility of serious disruptions like, for example, a major storm, a car accident, an unfavorable health diagnosis. These throw us off so much that, like Oliver confronting a sudden lack of care because of delivery truck breakdown, he (and we) will cry (or the equivalent) until exhausted. Oliver will fall back on his happier imagined world where every need met; we will blame God. Earlier you will remember I spoke of becoming complacent in faith; that was merely the religious expression of psychological overconfidence in an unchanging reality.

Because of this complacency or failure to appreciate the risk of change, we should blame ourselves for being ill prepared. But we don't, of course; we blame God. Oliver, God love him, we assume does not do this because of the lack of vocabulary, but his brother Jackson, even at the young age of 2 is blaming Mom, and maybe even Grandma, for his thirsty unhappiness.

You'll remember Adam did this to Eve, and to God. The woman gave me the apple, and you, God, gave me the woman! We blame God for a reality that we have collectively damaged by importing bad choices into an otherwise perfect world. It's little wonder God doesn't just shut us down for all this finger pointing at Him and others, but He is nothing if not patient.

This account of reality is sometimes thought to be

mistaken because it leaves no room for God's plan or providence. In fairness, however, the account of reality given above does not deny God having a plan, it merely reminds us that there is no reason to see God's planning as static with no active role for us. To the contrary, it is here where through prayer and good works we are given the freedom and the grace to obtain the gifts of the Holy Spirit, and in putting them to work, make decisions that do not hide in an imagined world, but take full account of the real one.

Instead of anger with God for our own misperception, faith invites us right at this juncture to place full faith and credit in Our Lord. It is hard to do; remember again Jesus looking to have the cup of suffering (of reality) pass from Him.

In accepting reality, Jesus was accepting the reality of the cross—a symbol of the ingratitude and misuses of freedom by those God gave the gift of life. When Jesus did fully accept the cross, He linked suffering with – paradoxically – salvation and our hoped-for victory over death.

499

What is our reality? Because of defiance, because
of sin, we are broken; our perfect life at one with
the sole and ultimate source of goodness is
shattered. We can either come to terms with that
reality, or we can try —unsuccessfully – to run from
it by conjuring imagined defenses or placing blame
on God. Christ accepted reality of suffering to offer
us the chance to be unbroken; to be healed; to be
saved. As Saint John of the Cross prayed:

> O Lord, my God, You are no stranger to those who do
> not estrange themselves from You. How can anyone say
> that it is You who absent Yourself?
>
> —St. John of the Cross
> *The Sayings of Light and Love*, 50

When Jesus cried out: "My God, My God why have
you forsaken me, he was referencing not defeat,"
but the victory over sin and death, for that initial
question uttered in pain upon the cross is
completed in Psalm 22:

> the generation to come will be told of
>   the Lord,
> that they may proclaim to a people yet
>   unborn

the deliverance you have brought.

—Psalm 22:32

55. The Final Chapter – The Devil Can't Make Us Do It

It is most gratifying to learn from the readers of this book during pre-publication how they found the work to poignantly convey Monsignor John's pursuit of the theology of kindness and now inspired their own. I hope the reader finds this to be true in his or her own life. When people relate their experience: of loving more unconditionally – both others and themselves; of letting their planning dictate less of their lives so they can focus on the moment and the person in front of them, they are carrying forward the meaning of Monsignor John's encouragement to entrust ourselves fully to the Lord.

When these book-inspired conversations are privileged to continue, I tend to probe a bit further with a goal of ascertaining whether the book has succeeded in revealing how our lives are inseparable from the person least to our liking. Seeing past what annoys us in that person and setting it aside is the truest affirmation of kindness. If we are, in fact, able to love our enemy, we are

502

sharing in the experience of God's own incarnation where Divine perfection and human shortcoming interact. When we move from our uncaring, anonymous, suspicious human heart toward an understanding one, we are perfecting ourselves in God's likeness.

Naturally, readers wish to know about me. Am I Lifting up my heart to the Lord?

Initially, my honest response had a catch in my voice. "I think so," I would say, still wondering whether God might not have been wiser to ensure our safety and well-being with a protective shield – not to deny our individual freedom to love Him and our neighbor, but enough for us to feel that God will keep disproportionate evil in check by pushing back very serious evil that might be stalking us at any given moment. After all, going back to God's problematic wager in the Book of Job, no doubt Job, too, had these weaknesses or the Devil would not have pestered God to make the wager. I certainly have mine: pride – look at me, Mr. Ambassador; envy – look at whomever the President picks to carry out the balance of my term;

inattentiveness to family – being consumed by work or internet discussions thereby deafening me to the discussions and needs of those close at hand; lust – avoiding the pretense of just bumping into sexually explicit sites or music videos (and no, that doesn't mean frequenting these sites directly); injustice – not thinking through class materials in a sufficiently comprehensive fashion to render just service to my students. Each of these failings is a source of shame and shame is fuel in the devil's engine.

Within John's writing about faith and kindness in light of that faith is his encouragement to remember that ours is the faith of the Cross.   Prior to the accident, this was only rhetoric to me. It no longer is – having witnessed Monsignor John's death; having been the beneficiary of so much good will and prayer in Malibu and Malta, and thus having been permitted to sample the mercy of the Lord, and to grasp in a fuller sense the kindness of the Lord's death on the Cross. The witness of John's suffering as a young man and then again after the accident, I now appreciate the selflessness of Jesus on the cross. Such sacrifices baffle us as a nation,

504

and as individuals, and yet, it is in their seeming illogic that we find the most extraordinary acts of kindness and love. We honor the day of the Cross, and in a similar way, we admire the soldier who rescues his fellow soldier from hostile fire repeatedly putting his own life at risk. There seem to be a number of ways in which self-less action is possible.

Of course, from ambassadorial witness, I know that there are many needs in the larger world that we only dimly perceive and really don't understand, like those of faith traditions we have not taken a moment to study or social practices – like homosexual practice – that contradict Old Testament passage especially, but hardly lie beyond the Sheridan embrace of people of different faiths than ourselves. It is an embrace that doesn't wait to find out if some democratic process or judicial interpretation is to sanction same-sex marriage.

My inquisitors want to know how this story ends.

Frankly, so do I.

505

Some want "closure," which is a succinct, modern way of delivering the advice: move on. I agree, of course, to the extent the mind allows, all of us with vivid memories of John Sheridan or Mary Campbell must now continue without them. Clearly, a significant purpose of this book is to facilitate all of us taking the dark moment in the canyon ravine and washing it with the light of Christ. That this is possible is scriptural: nothing is impossible with Christ. Only that light has the capacity to free this soul weary of loss.

As a lawyer, I have known the general inability of the law to give adequate answer or remedy. To be sure, the law does the best it can to help us avoid tragedies like that which befell me, but without grasping the opportunity to give more greatly of oneself to God. As this compilation of the aspects of the Theology of Kindness informs, the law's pronouncement that the facts do not warrant prosecution or criminal penalty says little to calm the soul.

Some comfort is drawn from the pragmatic thinking that the accident eliminated one of Monsignor

506

John's greatest fears: namely, being the saddened survivor. I admit this, but if you'll permit a bit of whimsy that argument always conjures up in my mind the opening of a shuttle company called Kevorkian's: shuttle and departure service – 2-for-1 value – and we do mean *departure*.

Of course, the accident can be seen to have one other pragmatic result: this book, as well as a biographical movie production of the life of John and Mary. To put it bluntly, without a U.S. Ambassador home on vacation running reasonably well-known church figures off a canyon road, a silent, less notorious end akin to Tennyson's beautiful description of death as "God's finger touch[ing] them, and they slept" might not have provoked the need for their legacy to be compiled and kept alive. Of course, John and Mary would have been remembered fondly, as my late father is remembered fondly. Dad died a few weeks before the accident, but those who knew him are content with some version of the following conversation: "So sorry to hear about the passing of your father. Had he been sick long? No, that's a blessing. How old was he? Hmm, 87. Eighty-seven, that really was a good long life, wasn't it?"

This is a well-meaning colloquy, but it usually does not result in a constant reflection upon the meaning of his life.   Dad died of cancer on May 20, 2010, a few weeks shy of his 88th birthday. His discomfort at the end was well treated with the expert assistance of hospice workers, and with my brother and myself at his side trying not to drop him as we carried him back and forth from the bed to the easy chair in his final days. I miss my Dad. Yes, he had a great deal to say about a good many things – no, actually *every*thing[78] – and sometimes I have to catch myself before I dial his number. On Sundays when most of the country watches NFL football, I had pretty much devoted those hours to Dad-talk. I miss those talks (no , I miss him and a somewhat smaller amount of talk), but his was a life well-lived and ended, and no further memorial – save the very informal one I have in our family room that is always at risk of removal because of its dust-

---

[78] *See* Douglas W. Kmiec, *My Father's Dreams*, supra.

catching capacity – is needed aside from his distinguished flying medals, a certificate from the President, and a portrait both of him and his WWII B17 "flying fortress." At my death or even when out-of-town on business, I suspect these mementoes will disappear and eventually be misplaced by other hands.

By contrast, the suddenness of John's loss, and the tragic circumstance, impels the community that knew them to hold out as gift the witness of their lives to others who were not as fortunate. *Moreover, a year after their death, the relevance of their lives of kindness to those who counted themselves as dear friends and those who knew them not at all is nothing short of remarkable.* Those who never met John or Mary at all have been moved to take up entirely new patterns and activities in their lives; to forgive what they previously viewed as unforgiveable; to be, in short, open to the Holy Spirit who has come now more prominently into view. In short, as a community, we are resolving to stand so long as God gives us the light of their presence in our hearts to be the continuation of their kindness.

509

It is to be expected, of course, that the intensity of our collective efforts may not last forever. Few things do. Indeed, I reasonably expect that in a relatively brief time, the exposition of this book will be superseded by other admonitions of kindness. The memory of John and Mary, like the memories of each of us, will pass. There is only one caveat:

I will not forget.

My love for John and Mary was great during life; it is a covenant until death. I view what happened as the equivalent of the military draft. My number in the low 200s as I finished college at Northwestern wasn't reached for enlistment in Vietnam; my number came up on August 25, 2010.

I have come to recognize only after the Monsignor's passing that, for whatever reason, God has specified my small bodily claim on the universe as one of the battlefields upon which God and the Devil have decided to redo Job, double or nothing.

Earlier in the book, I was very uncomfortable almost demanding that God explain Himself. I even had the temerity to suggest that Our Father had not been responsive to Job's questions. I now know better. My problem is not lack of faith in God; it is under-appreciation of the sinister temptations of the Devil. To keep my guard up, henceforth, I intend to call the Devil by a variety of names – to "trash talk" him as the kid's say. A breach of kindness? No; actually, a recognition that there is nothing kind in the Devil.

Mr. Pusillanimous-pitch-fork-carrier, you do not have the spiritual wherewithal to knock off our Creator. We disappear without our Creator and, for the sake of symmetry and a good final reel, God, the first cause of first causes, will in all likelihood vaporize you. John's eyes, the day before he died, were searching mine for continued faith in Our Father; and believe me, it's there. John, rest assured that if ever my previous self-important-self thought I could make the crossing all on my own without God's help – or even stay on a canyon highway in a Hyundai -- *a Hyundai!* – I now fully grasp my total dependence.

Those of you who want a piece of this action, come aboard. In the cataclysm being fought with Satan

511

for me, I'm betting on God, and I intend to war with the Devil with everything I've got. Mr. The-Apple-Won't-Hurt-You-Snake-in-the-Grass, get ready for the Moshe Dayan of Christians. And don't even think about a two-state solution.

Yes, I know this battle for my soul has been going on for a good long time; but Señor Hot Stuff, the Mohammed Ali of kindness is back in the ring. I will dance like a Sister Mary butterfly, and sting you with the bees of abundant kindness.

You are wrong, you Corrupting Enemy of Truth, to mistake objectivity and fair-mindedness for wishy-washy soft-headedness. John and Mary knew the difference and what it meant to defend the "one true, little "c" catholic and apostolic faith." That's right, Devil-May-Care-Faux-Academic, who John Courtney Murray rightly called out as the barbarian at the gate,; your number is up. You see, Father of Darkness, the Monsignor and Sister were not just kind; they were intelligent defenders of the faith. They were the keepers of the Gospel of Life; the holders of the Splendor of Truth. They knew that work was made for man not man for work. Go ahead, try to suppress the truth of the human person, unborn or born; we shall prevail.

Stalin once derisively asked "how many divisions does the Pope command?" Answer: you can't begin to count them. Our God knows our names before we are born; He has even numbered the hairs on our heads. God knows how he finds the time.

You see, the Catholic faith is kind and intelligent, and its members are bright enough to know that God does not make junk – not even you. It likely galls you that God is so gracious in his mercy that, for now at least, he is prepared to welcome you and all who stray from him, misled by your secularisms, materialisms, and every other ism or scheme you invent to distract from the things that really matter.

And Mr. hate-filled, Luciferious Libeler, you may have thought it amusing to get bishops and priests entangled in politics threatening; or denying communion in partisan fashion; or that saddling me with the tragic loss of two sainted friends would render me uncertain of my own faith and of my own very nature. Wise up, dastardly-defamer; not even the inexcusable ugliness of pedophilia netted your desired result. People of faith know the difference between the sin and the sinner. Stop wasting your time reading blogs or putting your useless, conniving face on face book. Get a good book – no, get *the* Good Book and read it. You will discover what leadership really means; it's not about tearing families apart or stoking international conflict, but about building up the human character in God's image of love.

May I suggest, Son of Perdition, that you seek shelter as fast as you can in God's forgiveness, because our drone missiles of love have an unerring trajectory to explode all of your divisive ideas using race, gender, faith or any other criterion of hate. So, Pointy Tail, you thought you had me when you stole our loved ones. You thought you had me when we resolved to back a candidate not fully on board with the truth of human life. Hah! We laugh in your face.

Yes, we persuaded Catholic friends to help a man of a different color lead us. We hoped, in his opposition to war and his concern for those who

have little, that he is a leader like Solomon; asking
not for power for its own sake, but for power to
follow an understanding heart. It's not clear we got
what we voted for, but Mr. Hit-Below-the-Belt, this
isn't politics. When you get mixed up in something,
politics *is* bean bag. Love extended is all that
matters; it is irrelevant if the means is by private
source or public office. Smart Republicans and
Democrats will anchor their policies in love of
neighbor to manifest their love of nation, and those
who persist in the politics of hate will scald their
destructive lips on the kettle they bring to boil.
Kindness will allow our people to see under your
false veneers of power and wealth and fame. You
probe for our weaknesses and then extort us
through shame and silence to do your bidding. No
more.

Don't sneer at me, Satan! Your mockery only
brings renewed strength to this wounded heart
whenever the presence of John and Mary is dearly
missed, as it is. You know I pine for them with
every breath. You know many are just as saddened
as I by their absence, but you never learn. When
you falsely accused Thomas More and had his life

taken for your lies, he bettered you in every way.
He even put the mind of his own executioner at rest
"for the man sends him to God." Well, you may have
been able to manipulate my pride and stupidity so
that I would be unable, for whatever reason, to
prevent a tire on a light-weight inexpensive car from
losing its traction. Too bad. You caused us all pain
taking John and Mary earlier than their Creator
would have lovingly allowed; but Prince of
Darkness, did you notice they were together?   And
since this ever faithful pair of religious servants on
earth could manifest so well the heavens, and all
the power, majesty, and might of the God head even
on earth where it cannot be directly sampled, do
you honestly think their capabilities are dimmed
by their enjoyment of them? Nice work, Satan; your
diabolically-imposed loss ended up situating the
chief strategists of love and kindness in heaven and
they are now positioned for our defense.

Of course when you saw you had zero chance with
John and Mary, you cowardly little snivel of a sinful
snake, you worked on me. You loaded intense grief
upon a cooked-up fabrication so I would be publicly
embarrassed, not only in my native land, but

shamed in the country that I had come to love and respect. You deceiver of ancient mariners, now that I think on it, you probably had a hand in the shipwreck of St. Paul in 60 A.D. Good work. Malta showed Paul, the shipwrecked saint, "uncommon kindness," and how many Churches is it on a small island? 365. That's right, you can read it, it's right there in the Acts of the Apostles

So go ahead, Satan, make my day and have me rebuked for promoting interfaith harmony, especially at a time when governments are influx and the Islamic religion – at least when it's not in your thrall –is a religion of peace. I bet you thought you had me a couple of times. First, separating me from my family. Multiple surgeries. Then, making it impossible for me to sleep, stoking my anxiety and limiting my effectiveness. When I tricked you and didn't just hold onto power for power's sake, you flashed your evil purpose back at me, again increasing my initial confusion and disappointment, when the White House somehow managed to keep the President from saying even a single word for following up on his promised effort at religious understanding. You just don't get it: the cause of freedom of religion, allowing people everywhere to know God as their mind is open to them; and, so long as equal right is extended to other believers, it is far greater in purpose than a single ambassador or president. Did you actually think I would forego my attachment to that greater value simply because you had the very bureaucrats who made the good work of the Embassy in support of inter-faith dialogue push me out the very door of the new embassy compound, constructed on my watch?

You are the antithesis of kindness and your promotion of greed; grief, doubt, hatreds, and ignorance of all type *is* going to fail. I don't know if God himself, or John via the heavenly Skype in my heart, is lifting me up right now; but Beelzebub, the way you have wagered with God over me is lower than (what Thomas More called Cromwell) a "dockside bully." You lost the bet over Job; you lost your bet over Martin Luther King, Jr.; you lost your bet over Cardinal Bernardin; you lost your bet over the Kennedy brothers. You, sir, are the "Satan of squat," and you're a sore loser for it. Consider my grief and sleeplessness at end.

For a while – for too long a while – you actually had me so badly misdirected that I was contemplating coming after John and Mary by my own means, as if I could lay out that map and follow it to any place but darkness. I don't like to be in the dark, so I am not going anywhere until the light of God's reason points the way. That may be a few minutes from now, an hour, tomorrow, or ten or twenty years hence. It doesn't matter; I am happy now. I know you haven't got a prayer. Hey, that's funny, fire boy, you haven't got a prayer.

But you won't give up easy; you'll continue to sadden and to disorient. You've done it to me, and somehow you've even confused and made skeptical my Carol. Listen up, fire lizard; don't lay a single ashen claw on that good woman. Yes, you've given her doubt, but I am restored and I intend to love her with such abundance she won't have time for your misdirection.

These are tough times for a great many families, for single moms, for children in poverty. That's all your work, lousy Lucifer, just like accidents, mistakes, misjudgments, and even things much

519

worse: the taking of life in abortion or the destruction of adolescent life in war, or the elimination of irreplaceable animal and plant life. You're busy with your agenda of selfishness, hate and waste; but God knows the truth of it all, as Tolstoy wrote, and he waits. He doesn't rush to judgment like you, you who just run over people to get your way or crush them in cars. God has infinite mercy, even for you who has none and never manifests anything except a false front to make your evil seem right – forcing a religious charity to support abortions or contraceptive practice, or making it impossible to locate group homes for juveniles and others with alcohol or drug addictions. You dress up and sell some things like drugs or illicit sex to liberal progressives, while you convince conservatives that our natural rights include guns.

Listen well, chameleon corrupter, God is putting up with this for now. He's pleased to have John's support and our little book here spreading the Theology of Kindness far and wide. But we know that we cannot defeat you without Him. That being so you should not count on the kindness that we are extending to all, including you double-crosser, to last forever. Eventually, God will tire of you, and He will rescue those of us who then remain. If you want to make short work of this world – and yourself – just keep on creating conditions inviting the spread of weapons of mass destruction. Remember, friend – and that is an offer, not a statement of fact – when all things pass away, you, and all who are part of you, will go Poof. Zeroed out. Game over. Those of us on the side of the light shall live forever in the light. All have this chance, so take my advice: stop testing God's patience, because on the final day of judgment, I suspect He will arrange for John and Mary to be strolling safely and kindly with Saints Francis, Dominic, John Bosco, Mother Theresa, and San Gorg Preca; and, Lord willing, Carol and myself and all in His family saved by love. In other words, God is permitting us – for a limited time only – to convert your heart with love; with kindness.

Trust us, you do not want to miss this deal. Because, Devil, you really don't want to trigger the final wrath of God and the Apocalypse. Now I know that sounds a tad vengeful, and were you to have joined John and me or others for tea and toast, John might be skeptical of the ugly death and destruction forecast there for the end time. Devil, you should not take very much comfort in John's imagined happy ending, given what you have been up to in this world.

The mass killings of the innocent in Yemen, Syria, and Libya; the prolonged dispute in the Middle East; the millions of unborn dissected; the millions more dying of disease and famine that you aid and abet. The prospect of nuclear proliferation with Israel or Iran or both wiped from the map. These are sins of such magnitude that, when put together with uncaring materialism or short-sided unilateral withdrawal from the world to remain in affluent ignorance, a just God cannot by definition allow freedom to go this way indefinitely.

I know what you're saying, "not God; not dependable ol' Yahweh; not Rocky Stallone of the ages." Well, those nicknames are clever, Dark Deceiver, but don't get too smart. Yes, I have been indulging in the practice, and I know even as against you, John would not have succumbed to the temptation of even this small unkindness directed at evil itself. And John would remind you that the God who made all is still your God, not just our God.

I don't like to disagree with the Monsignor, so I'll lighten up a bit. As you know, Devil, earlier in the book I took the risk of suggesting – again I hope constructively – that God be a bit more active in making our yoke as light as he promised it would be. Will He? Not sure. It's a free will matter. What's that? Does anyone in the front office ever answer my letters? Very funny. Anyway, I'm on record calling for God to get a bit more pro-active. He knows why I make that recommendation, but it's His choice.

The bottom line for you, Beelzebub, is to be careful of thinking God's mercy will remain always available. That is not the script. You're on notice.

And one last thing, Devil: you should never align yourself with the kind of forgiveness open to a John Sheridan or Mary Campbell. John and Mary were souls of the first-rank; they had temptations, perhaps, but nothing higher than a venial sin. Now, it is possible, out there in County Longford in the mists of time, that there was some wild-eyed cow-tipping that John got himself mixed up in. Or maybe Mary on a busy day inadvertently took home a number 2 pencil. Yes, it's true; once, during the Sheridan family evening rosary (as John told the story), his brother Farrell wanted to move the rosary up an hour or two so he could go on a date. All was well until one of the Sheridan siblings let loose with a special prayer for Farrell's chastity that evening. This did not amuse Farrell and he stormed out without doing the last decade. Satan, were your sins no more than that the world would have suffered no disease, war, or crushing greed and envy.

Sure, go ahead if you want, rifle through John's papers. Maybe he repeated an off-color joke, or ran short of Irish whisky and drank an inferior grade of some other nationality. Why, John, being a Californian by adoption, may have even rooted for the heathens of Troy at USC over Our Lady's lads out there at Notre Dame Univeristy in South Bend, Indiana singing their well-armored hearts away about dear Mother being "proudly in the heavens 'neath thy Gold and Blue". And, of course, also ""neath" about 100 inches of snow and ice in any given year right through May, and such is likely ample penance for those with the good sense to revere "Notre Dame, Our Mother, tender, strong, and true."

No, you helmeted-horned-heathen, I don't want to bet on upcoming SC-Notre Dame games. Haven't you and your legions in the BCS done enough to unhinge the game? Look, even if John did succumb on occasion – out of respect for the judges and lawyers he knew down at the Catholic Center, or due to the allure and precision of the USC marching band – to prefer the Trojans over the lads living out the studiously pious life and legacy of Knute Rockne and the Four Horseman, it would be at most a shame, a trivial shame.

The Gipper? I thought you would throw him up at me. It cannot be denied that the Gipper caroused all night, caught pneumonia on the steps of Washington Hall when he missed curfew and died at St. Joe Hospital in a scene that was actually cut from the movie "Knute Rockne All American."

You couldn't even keep your carouser in an old black and white movie.[79] Phooey.

What's that, you don't see the point? It's really quite basic: a few historical accounts may claim it was a copyright dispute that kept the near 40 year-old-Ronald Reagan's portrayal of 20-something George Gipp on the cutting room floor. But then, you are too self-possessed to assess not just George Gipp's inappropriate habits with women and drink, but the fact that – in his last chance at redemption on his death bed – the Gipp tells them to win not one for Our Lady or for her Son, but for him, George Gipp. Ludicrous!

But let this be yet another lesson, you coacher of evil: you can today stroll all over the meticulously kept and splendid campus of Notre Dame, and

---

[79] A copyright dispute resulted in the scene being frequently excised. The result is near cinematic incoherence where Reagan, as Gipp, complains of a sore throat and the next moment his lifeless self appears in a hospital bed to the accompaniment of something akin to a chord from the death march.

you'll scarcely see George Gipp mentioned. Why, you're more likely to see a statue of Rudy or Regis Philbin. Both of them gave of themselves to the school. And in the legions of great players, Gipp had talent; but like all who fall in with you, it was wasted. In any event, you don't find Grantland Rice breaking out in poetry claiming to see the Gipper "outlined against a blue-gray October sky."

Well, gentle reader and friend of John and Mary, I admit it's getting late. What's that, you say? Yes, we need rest to resist temptation, because snake eyes over there comes around at all hours. So let's wrap it up with this moral, shall we: Steer clear of the old deceiver, and it's best if you think about the other guy. Be a little thoughtful about his needs; why it would even be okay to be, as those wretched Jesuits say, "a man for others." In this life, if you can't be John Sheridan or Mary Campbell, be Gandhi and Mother Theresa.

If you follow the corrupter of all things good, you're likely heading to the wrong end zone. Keep going the wrong way year after year, and before you know it, your coach will be named Faust (and you know that won't work out and NBC will be reduced to showing golf reruns). Indeed, if Father Jenkins and the board aren't careful, the devil is just crafty enough to have Notre Dame on the Discovery Channel or in the news for Nobels, Pulitzers, and stuff you have to dust. A fate worse than death itself.

It is commonplace around the parish to hear friends say that John is with us. "Monsignor John now, along with Mary, is looking after us with special care," it is frequently said. In the past, I might have doubted these claims. I don't anymore. John and Mary are present in every kindness extended; a kindness so imbued with the Spirit that even the devil himself should not think himself immune from the power of love shown to us by "God's gracious gift" – a man named John, and Mary (who upon entering religious life, in the habit of the time, assumed the name Monica, the ever patient and hope-filled mother of Augustine). Later, Sister Monica reverted to Mary, the name given her by her large and loving family in County Mayo. Like the Blessed Virgin herself, Sister Mary Campbell took all that she witnessed at the foot of the cross and held it in her heart.

Let us do likewise and lift our, now strengthened and joyous, hearts to the Lord!

That's right, be off with ya, Beelzebub.

Oh, happy, happy day.

Figure 10. One of the last truly wonderful evenings in Malta before taking up the cross of tragedy; presiding over the commencement of De La Salle College to the obvious delight of all. How wonderful to be among people of faith!

529

Acknowledgements

I have been sustained in the writing by the love of my spouse, Carol, and my children (Keenan, Kate, Kiley, Kolleen and Kloe) and the high energy packages known as neputi or grandchildren (Jackson and Oliver). The generous understanding of the families of those who perished in my care, John Sheridan and Mary Campbell, SSL, remains as unceasing as it is undeserved. Of special note are Judge Bridget Reilly and Aine Sheridan and her thoughtful husband Adrian; Teresa Sheridan; Louise Reilly; Jenny Reilly (all kin by blood or matrimony of the Monsignor) and (for Sister Mary, siblings James Campbell, Angela Campbell, and Peggy Campbell Rowley – and her husband, Gerry, who very generously put his keen eye to the text for improvement and lent his fine voice in Irish tune for enjoyment), John's rectory mate, Father Bill Kerze, and every one of the Sisters of Saint Louis, (especially Brid Long, Mary Prendergast) near and far.

There have been an extraordinary number of prayers said in my behalf by the members of our local parish, (Our Lady of Malibu in California) and by virtue of my time abroad as U.S. Ambassador, the people, the bishops, clergy and governmental leadership of the Republic of Malta. Sister Rose Oliveri, a Silesian Sister of Monsignor's age and with the same zest, observes the 24th of each month as a day of special significance. It is an anniversary of their patron Saint John Bosco as well as the day of my own birth, the 24th of September, and Monsignor's funeral.

In Malta, my spirit was bolstered greatly by the prayerful assistance of many, including those priests who permitted me to regularly be included in their congregations: Father Michael at Divine Mercy; Father Hilary at the Millennium Chapel; Father George at the San Anton Chapel where I was blessed to learn greater Maltese to keep even with his homiletic instruction and doubly blessed to worship next to Mrs. Abela Sr. who also helped with my Maltese as she kept track of her son, George, the president of Malta and his lovely first lady, Margaret.

I don't know how many diplomats are permitted to say this, but as I am already retired, I am uninhibited in declaring that I shall be forever grateful for the association with President Abela, whom I will count as a good friend well beyond my years of service in his native land. In this respect, President Abela introduced me to Richard and Myriam England whose faith is powerfully influential in architecture and with respect to Marian worship. A special thanks to my language instructor, Ambassador George Doublesin and his wife, Gabi, both accomplished scholars.

My colleagues in the Embassy and in the diplomatic corps of the embassies of other nations are held dear in my memory. If the nations of the world could interact with the friendship we shared, there would be no conflict incapable of resolution. No one ever acts alone in such large matters, so the compliment of the President of Malta for "the sterling work" during my tenure carried out with "grace and dignity" leading to the "further strengthening of the diplomatic relationship" between the United States and Malta is here properly shared with the dedicated and highly

talented men and women – from America and Malta
– with whom it was my privilege to serve. Lenese
Walls gets special mention for relocating to be my
Office Manager and whose work was the very
definition of outstanding.

Of course, having committed to visiting all 365
Catholic Churches in Malta, let me also mention
with fondness Jimmy Vella and Anthony "Taylor"
who got me there as well as the priests and
parishioners at the Church in Balzan; the pastor
and sisters of Good Shepherd; and my "walk-to"
Churches, St. Mary's in Attard and a bit farther
away, Saint Aloysius and all the "wretched Jesuits"
(you'll have to read the book to understand this to
be a compliment) at the College chapel.   My friend
and fellow diplomat, Tommaso Caputo, the papal
nuncio more than once cheered me with special
early morning Mass in the splendid chapel where
His Holiness Benedict XVI worshipped during his
visit to Malta in April 2010. Faith life is also greatly
enriched in Malta by procession and band club, and
I owe a special note of gratitude to the L'Isle Adam
Band Club and its club leadership under the
direction of Massimo Azzopardi who offered to pick

up my spirits while I was hospitalized, as well as Saviour Mercio and George Branch whose escorted tours through San Gorg in Qormi were incomparable faith experiences. Joseph, Robert, Nathalie, and Joanne whose dedication to the smooth running to the ambassador's residence in Malta made our family part of theirs from the first day.

The priests, sisters and most caring administrators and nurses who guided me during many visits to assisted living centers, group homes for the highly disabled or for those suffering addictions of one sort or another. As is so often the case, those who we seek to cheer up, seem to encourage us even more. The all-star in this category for me is Henry Miller, 103, in the Holy Family Home whose voice has now been given advance residence in heaven, but whose large personality still fills the room. Special gratitude to Nurse Betty Lee, Joseph and Joyce, who until quite recently were all at Holy Family Home in Naxxar as well as the Little Sisters of the Poor, and the Reverend Doug McRoberts of the Scottish Presbyterian Church for stepping up to help care for some of those we rescued from Tripoli

and whose current mission focuses on the needs of
detained refugees. Of course, Father Mintoff's John
XXIII Peace Lab will have a warm spot in my heart
for allowing me to extend the Embassy's outreach
(and when possible assistance with resettlement) to
irregular migrants who traversed Malta in search
for the human dignity to which God's love entitles
all. Relatedly, thanks to Martin Sheen and Emilio
Estevez for helping with some timely fundraising
dollars from the premier of "The Way" in Malta.
Finally, it was in the nature of Monsignor John and
Sister Mary that from the moment of introduction to
them, each of us could claim them as the dearest of
friends.

John always feigned not to remember names, and while he might not have biblically numbered all our hairs, more often than not he knew and could recall so much about us that his holding back of the name only provided the excuse to linger longer in his presence. I am grateful to Monsignor and Mary's many friends, far too numerous to mention, for the abundance of stories retold about them in my presence. These stories all overflow with love. The Monsignor was a great friend of the Davis family and very much enjoyed Rich and Jane Davis' "power dinners," which in terms of intensity of inquiry into matters theological rivaled in quality of guest and insight the best of an Oxford seminar. I was also grateful to receive the

Asked what he would like to have said at his funeral, he answered :- "Three words - THANKS FOR COMING". I'm afraid I have disobeyed him. But as he wrote himself: "The Irish are devils with the pen, they don't know when to take it up and they don't know when to put it down."
Bridget Reilly, niece

536

delightful reminiscences of the Sheridan and
Campbell families in Ireland and the carefully
drawn perspectives of the Drs. Birthistle in
Hancock Park to tales from Captain O'Malley' who,
like myself, reveled in having occasion to take
Monsignor to Peter's barbershop in Santa Monica.

Peter is a genuine barber -- no fancy shop with
young women all called Tiffany giving shampoos
and cutting your hair differently each time. Peter's
philosophical gifts are also in the old-time barber
tradition, and whenever I head over (no pun
intended) to Santa Monica, it brings John to life in
our conversation.

Dr. Birute Anne Vileisis from Loyola provided her
notes from meetings with Monsignor just a day or
so prior to the accident. Bill and Jane Baldau
maintain the Legion of Mary, and have shared their
unique insight into Monsignor's long history in
southern California. Other wonderful anecdotes
and memories were shared by: Joe and Anne
DeMeri; Danny Shea and his bride (they think they
are still on their honeymoon), Joan Slimocosky,
Bryan Garofalo, Carl Bindenagel, Gunnar

Gunderson, Fr. Juan Romero, Jack Corrodi, Jim
Cuggino, Dr. Bill Lamers, Margaruite McDonald,
Grant and Judy Nelson, Bob and Trish Pushaw,
Tom and Ginny Vandergon, Brian and Kathy
Oppenheimer, Maureen and Mike Jannini, Carolyn
Craft, Kim McCarthy, Rick Wallace Peggy and Tom
Thomas, Tom Beutell, Vivian Beutell, as well as
some additional "usual suspects" from the 8:00
a.m. Mass, including Tom Cosentino, Carol Dillon
and the daughters Dillon, Sister Brigid, Carl
Karcher, Joe and Loretta Barrera, Lawrence Kaldor
and his Teresa, Marie, Rita, Estella, Faith and Ken,
Tisha, and the fantastic Gallagher family who never
travel without several generations in tow. The
encouragement of my adult religion class,
especially: Louise Greene, Betty and Bob Odello,
Bill, Paul and Loretta, David, Mary Lou McGee. Zev
Yaroslovsky, whose public service to southern
California seems almost as timeless and welcoming
as Monsignor's own longevity sent a thoughtful
tribute as well.

I am especially grateful to those in the writing,
publishing, and acting business who took time not
only to do an advance review commentary of the

book, but often sent along needed prayers to truly "lift up" my spirits when the weight of the loss of John and Mary would leave me too distressed to write or do much else.

For Jim Wallis of Sojourners, Martin Sheen and Joe Cosgrove whose friendship and sound counsel is ever welcome, Michael Sean Winters, Father Jim Heft, and Senator Lugar, who in the midst of a primary battle, did his best to find out what the White House was thinking when it launched me into inter-faith diplomacy only to then allow the forces of darkness to side-track or impede the efforts. This executive mischief or mystery remains inscrutable, but there is no hard feelings on my part, especially since the failure of the State Department to implement the President's Cairo vision has been superseded by the positive steps being taken outside of government by Dr. Juanito Camilleri, the Rector of the University of Malta, Dr. Tim Pownall of the Pacis project at Pepperdine as well as a host of university leaders at USC and Loyola who have all been working with this former ambaxxatur to evaluate and fashion a graduate study program in the Abrahamic religions

539

(Judaism, Christianity and Islam) together with diplomatic capability to both avoid and resolve disputes with religious root. Father Jim Heft delivered the first Sheridan-Campbell lecture on Islamic and Christian understanding at the University of Malta in late May 2011 which was a tremendous success and as it occurred shortly before my departure from Malta as Ambassador, left both inspiration and a salving example of what might have been had the State Department actually wanted to follow the President's original inter-faith direction and brush up on the law of the American Constitution so that erroneous "walls of separation" aren't invented or read into unrelated departmental rules in a manner that limits America's ability to serve as a useful, and peace-enhancing, resource for the nations of north Africa.

The support for the research and writing at Pepperdine University could not be better: much gratitude to President Andrew Benton, Provost Daryl Tippens, Dean (Judge) Deanell Tacha, my executive assistant, Candace Warren and two up and coming, poised and intelligent Master degree graduates of our School of Public Policy, Jillian

Kissee and Kathleen McAfee. Research librarians Alyssa Thurston, Jodi Kruger, and Don Buffaloe read the manuscript for clarity and usage, for which assistance I am most grateful. My brother having reached retirement age (65 – how did that happen?) left his medical registrar post at the University of Wisconsin and in keeping with his abundantly generous heart has signed up for the Peace Corps and will soon be assisting many in sub-Saharan Africa, but while he was waiting on his assignment, he very thoughtfully "volunteered" to read the manuscript a second time, along with my cousin Mary Gordon for typos and the like.

And the most special note of acknowledgement of all is reserved għall-patrun tar-Repubblika ta 'Malta, San Pawl, u for our patroness: Our Lady of Malibu.

DWK

The Feast of Saint Katharine Drexel,[80] 2012.

---

[80] Katharine Drexel was the second American-born citizen canonized as a Saint. Born into wealth, she donated her family's entire $20 million dollar fortune to establishing a religious order that gave special emphasis to the needs of the African migrant to America or Native American tribes. The founder of Xavier University (La.), Sister Katherine's religious order had established over 63 schools and had brought 500 religious sisters into teaching at the time of her death in 1955. While Sister Mary was not of Saint Katherine's order, her love and devotion to the individual educational achievement of her students, who she remembered by name years after having taught them in the classroom, would have been deservedly admired by St. Katharine, whose wisdom is an apt way for me to close these acknowledgements of some of the many people who have prayed for me throughout the challenges of the past years described here. Wrote Saint Katharine:

> It is a lesson we all need – to let alone the things that do not concern us. He has other ways for others to follow Him; all do not go by the same path. It is for each of us to learn the path by which He requires us to follow, and then do so.

Appendix – John's Favorite Irish Poets beyond Yeats.

In listening to the Monsignor recite or annotate the poetry of his native Ireland, one was coming very close to the mystical source that added brilliance to his light of faith. In what follows those who knew John's voice will find it saturating every line. The breadth of poetical expression here taps but a portion of his literary interests – he was, for example and especially in my company, an admirer of Czeslaw Milosz, the highly respected poet of Poland. Milosz's expressed guilt as a Holocaust survivor resonates strongly now in my life, and I cannot help thinking that John pointed it out to me prophetically, realizing that I would bear a similar cross. John would want me to know that I was not alone in this burden. Certainly what follows reveals John's scholarly side, which he – out of humility – would attempt to keep hidden in the cabinet like the Jameson's 18 or the Tullamore Dew (with about as little success).

More than once, John, with a surge of energy would proclaim:

The fact is, we are poets, story tellers, we love words. In their point and punch, in their meter and melody, in the Word, the Word made flesh, we discover who we are.

John found special enjoyment in Brendan Kennelly, one of Ireland's premier poets, story tellers, philosophers. Below, John notes how Kennelly regaled us with how his ninety year old auntie responded to her husband when he asked her on their 68th wedding anniversary a few weeks ago. *"Do ye love me as much as ever, Anne"? What is it, Mike?" I'm saying, don't ye love me as much, or more than ever? "Ah, sure now Mike, Don't you think that's asking a bit much!!"*

Kennelly also captured the spontaneity John hoped for in each new day. In particular, John saw this as Brendan's philosophy:

I would like all things to be free of me/

Never to murder the days with presupposition./

Never to feel they suffer the imposition/

Of having to be this or that. How easy/

544

It is to maim the moment/

With expectation, to force it to define/ Itself.

Beyond all that I am, the sun/

scatters its light as though by Accident./

Proof is what I do not need. Yes, the sun scatters its light.

I am uncertain whether, in a whisky and crackers afternoon (as distinguished from a tea and toast morning,) John had introduced into our reading the Kennelly poem above; but re-reading it now, it wonderfully captures John's ability to see all things new in each new day. This may be a by-product of "retirement," but within the parameter of even active employment, there are free hours that ought not be "maimed" with imposed presupposition.

Pass the crackers, dear Monsignor, and please continue.

Seamus Heaney, the Nobel Laureate, told his UCLA

audience in last year's lecture that his universally prized translation of Beowulf owed more to the sounds and syntax of the speech patterns of his home and neighbors than to his vast formal schooling. I think looking back, we can all identify with Heaney. The Irish schools, modeled on the English system, made the study and memorization of poetry and drama an imperative. But their Irish students, after all the famines, wars, tyrannies, had the Gaelic culture to which you and I are heirs, deep in their psyches; it can spring so easily to the surface in our Friendly Sons' and similar gatherings. I often think of this when reciting the 137th Psalm, one of the most moving poems in the Hebrew psalter:

By the rivers of Babylon/

there we sat and wept/

remembering Zion;/

On the poplars that grew there/

we hung up our harps./

For it was there that they asked us,/ our captors, for songs/

our oppressors for joy./

"Sing to us", they said,/

"one of Zion's songs."/

O how could we sing/ the song of the Lord/

on alien soil?/

If I forget you, Jerusalem,/

Let my right hand wither!/..

O, let my tongue/ Cleave to my mouth/

If I remember you not./

As among the Jews and all peoples, our traditional lyrics, epics, elegies, laments come alive in moments

547

of celebration with something of the magic, the gaiety and pathos of our first awakening. Like Thomas Moore's "Oft in the stilly night ere slumbers' chain has bound me/

Sad mem'ry brings the light of other days around me"/

Today's Irish poets fluent in Gaelic as well as in other languages have easy access to the depth and subtlety of their cultural heritage and, indeed, to the libraries and museums of Europe where much of that ancient literature is on tap. Poets like Heaney, Hewitt, Boland, Deane, Durkan, Kinsella and their numberless compatriots echo:

"The sounds of Ireland/

that restless whispering/

you never get away/

from, seeping out of/

low bushes and grass,/

heather bells and fern,/

wrinkling bog pools,/

scraping tree branches/

light hunting cloud,/

sound hounding sight,/

a hand ceaselessly/ combing and stroking/

the landscape, till,/ the valley gleams/

like the pile upon/ a mountain pony's coat.

The above passage is from John Montague's "The Windharp."

Having grown up in the Irish mid-lands, Monsignor John held tightly a love of nature, mountains, lakes, trees, streams, the sacredness of life, of space, of all that is human, all that is loved and redeemed in the God of Christ. To John, this is *the stuff of our Celtic poetry.*

John loved to browse among the books and he had a special fondness for anthologies. He delighted in finding what he called *a host of literary gems written or copied between the fifth and thirteenth century by bards and scribes from the different Celtic schools, especially the monasteries in whose quiet little scriptoria the monks recorded unabashedly epic, legend and story, featuring saint and sinner, the chaste and the erotic alike.*

Here is a rhyme that John fancied from Sedulius Scottus dating to the ninth century:

I read or write, I teach or wonder what is truth,/

I call upon my God by night and day./

I eat and freely drink, I make my rhymes,/ and snoring sleep, or vigil keep, and pray./

And very 'ware of all my shames I am;/ O, Mary, Christ have mercy on your man./

John, like the Holy Father, had no tolerance for the violence of war. He turned to a poet like Tom Kettle, a patriot, scholar, and man of Faith, to express his insistence upon peace in light of the senseless costs of war. Kettle died in 1916 in France, an officer fighting in World War I. Kettle writes the following words to his infant daughter a

few days before his death, telling why he also
abandoning his child, his wife, his home which he
loved with all his heart, why he too felt called "to
dice with death in the stinking trenches of France:

*So here (here) while the mad guns curse over
head/*

And tired men sigh for couch and floor/

Know that we fools, now with the foolish dead/

Died not for flag, nor King/

nor Emperor/

But for a dream, born in a herdman's shed,/

And for the secret Scripture of the poor".

Man's heart yearns for peace, said the Monsignor,
and nowhere better expressed than by Yeats when
he wrote in The Lake Isle of Innis free:

*And I shall have some peace there, for peace
comes dropping slow/*

551

*Dropping from the veils of the morning to where
the cricket sings.*

Our hope in the impossible is in Christ, said
the Monsignor, a hope averted to by Caelius
Sedulius in the 5th century poem: *"Christ quiets
the Tempest;"*

"The Lord arising, bade the Winds, be still,/

The swelling waves subsided at his word/

Not even Ocean when its deeps are stirred./

With fellest rage resists; nor yet the course/

Of storms careering all in furious force./

The happy sea to Christ in homage brings/

Its lofty billows down, the tempest springs/

In joy away on softly wafting wings./"

Given Monsignor's love of poetry, it was not surprising that in representing the family in giving eulogy for her uncle, Judge Bridget Reilly concluded her splendid remembrance with one of the Monsignor's favorites from Yeats. After a clever Monsignor-like salutation of "Your Eminence, My Lord Bishops, Reverend Fathers, Sisters, Your Excellency, Ambassador, Friends, Wretches, Rustics and Saintly souls," and a bit of the family tree, Judge Reilly continued:

> Most of you know that John came to California in the late 1930s to complete his studies after serious illness in Ireland. He embraced Los Angeles and then Malibu and all the people along the way. This is where he made a life he loved and where he wanted to be. I suspect he never changed a light bulb or cooked an edible meal, and he was the worst driver in the northern hemisphere. He drove with great intent and focus on the route but seemed to have a blind spot for road signs. The red line through a U-turn and "do not" signs appeared to be a source of

encouragement to do the opposite usually with acceleration and some great gusto.

But what this gloriously technically incompetent man did have was a gift – that was almost genius – an extraordinary capacity to connect and empathize with people of all makes and shapes, creeds and ages. He was intellectually curious and had a high level of what we now call emotional intelligence.

Even as small children six thousand miles away he could make each one of us feel special. He never failed to reply to our letters. From 1958 in boarding school my correspondence with him flourished, always eliciting a prompt reply which included a cheque for the dollar equivalent of £1 sterling. I was very moral then and did eventually question whether my part in engaging so enthusiastically in this series of letters was utterly pure and without any mercenary taint. The correspondence continued over 50

years. The upshot was that a strong and close
relationship grew between us, as it did with
my siblings and younger cousins in Aine's
family and now theirs and our children. To
our astonishment he mastered email and
Skype, with a screen the size of a football
pitch, and he continued to connect and relate
closely to the younger generation including
Louise, young Patricia in New York, and
Noelle's little girls in Ireland. He knew all
their names and they reciprocated, writing
and visiting. My sister Mary's daughters, Jill
and Barbara, visited him just weeks ago and
my daughter Louise flew from Switzerland for
a week to be at his bedside in UCLA.

It is appropriate to mention that Aine is his
special niece in Tommy's family. She moved
to New York in 1985 and he was lucky to
have her constant contact, care and visits.
With her customary generosity she says she
used to sneak off to Malibu when times got
hectic in New York City and returned
refreshed and re-invigorated. She enjoyed

every minute with Uncle John - that he gave much more than she ever gave him. She encapsulates all our views. He was lucky, we were lucky. He was proud of his family (even the family skeletons) and we were proud of him.

The patterns of relationships with close family extended to a wider circle of relatives and were replicated with so very many people who became friends: Just like a parent whose well of affection grows with each child. My sister Kathy has written about "that unique John V. Sheridan brand of affirmation - a blend of unconditional love, respect, mischief, humor, and perpetual wonder at the infinite, stupefying variety of God's creatures - (which) remains a marvel and a headline to all his 'families' on both sides of the Atlantic. Uncle John never let you down (unless you sat on his coat and lit the famous 'short fuse', though even then the storm was short lived).

But above all he was a priest. He used his

powerful gift in the service of his, a loving, God. It was always totally obvious that he was utterly committed and happy in his vocation. And he bore witness in so many ways. We saw him pursuing his daily devotional obligations wherever he was. By his priesthood he reassured us. At every mass, every service, his words were spoken as if for the first time. It was often humorous, personal, but was always deeply holy. (Gail Boska, and many others similarly, I am sure, long since forgave him for referring to her groom Mark as "Jim" right through the marriage ceremony).

We his Irish family of origin are so grateful to you his next and daily family in California for the life you enabled him to lead; the unusual and extraordinary loyalty and generosity of your care, love and time. From the days of Bishop Ward's family, his Musketeer friends the Monsignors Redahan and Kennedy now gone, The families Fitzgerald, Guhos, Collins, Birthistle and others down through the decades, to parishioners and others in Malibu who became his Malibu family. You fed his body and vitally nourished his soul. He had intellectual stimulation of the highest level, companionship and care. We've met many of you - individuals and families, the Sisters of St. Louis, and not forgetting Sister Mary who was particularly important in his later years. At the end he was enveloped in world class excellence and care in the Ronald Reagan wing in UCLA. I would like to do a roll call, but the credits in this movie would be rolling into the night - so forgive me. Your names are inscribed on our hearts.

Fr. Bill and Monsignor John enjoyed an excellent relationship of mutual respect, appreciation and friendship. John never wanted to live away from his home in Malibu and feared that great old age might negate his choice in that. His strong faith

and love of God persuade us that God had a

plan for him. We are so sorry for Doug that it necessitated his involvement and that he suffered as a result. Doug Kmiec was among John's most staunchly loyal, generous and much loved friends with whom he had regular intellectual jousts. We all hope that Doug with his own strong faith will soon be able to accept God's plan and be at peace with that.

We hope that many of you will visit us in Ireland as we sincerely thank you for your kind expressions of support and sympathy and very kind offers of hospitality. For so much we are grateful. Louise, my daughter, before Christmas asked Uncle John what would be like to have said at his funeral. He answered: 'Three words - THANKS FOR COMING.. I'm afraid I have disobeyed him. But as he wrote himself: 'the Irish are devils with the pen, they don't know when to take it up and they don't know when to put it down'.

.

I will finish now with words which he loved

559

and which you may recognize, published in
1899:

Aedh Wishes For The Clothes Of Heaven
(W.B. Yeats)

Had I the heavens' embroidered cloths,
Enwrought with golden and silver light,
The blue and the dim and the dark
cloths
Of night and light and the half light,
I would spread the cloths under your
feet:
But I, being poor, have only my dreams;
I have spread my dreams under your
feet;
Tread softly because you tread on my
dreams.

And the last word is fittingly in prayer;, one of
the Monsignor's most favorite prayers (attributable

to Mary Stuart):

Keep us, O God, from all pettiness.

Let us be large in thought, in word, in deed.

Let us be done with faultfinding and leave off all self-seeking.

That we put away all pretenses and meet each other face-to-face, without self-pity and without prejudice.

May we never be hasty in judgment, and always be generous.

Let us always take time for all things, and make us to grow calm, serene and gentle.

Teach us to put into action our better impulses, to be straightforward and unafraid.

Grant that we may realize that it is the little things of life that create differences, that in the big things of life, we are as one.

And, O Lord God, let us not forget to be kind!

Amen

www.ingramcontent.com/pod-product-compliance
Lightning Source LLC
Chambersburg PA
CBHW021350090426
42742CB00009B/800